WITHDRAWN

THE EINSTEIN
OF MONEY

Joe Carlen

THE EINSTEIN
OF MONEY

THE LIFE AND TIMELESS FINANCIAL WISDOM
OF BENJAMIN GRAHAM

 Prometheus Books

59 John Glenn Drive
Amherst, New York 14228–2119

Published 2012 by Prometheus Books

Cover image © iStockphoto.com/Brian Adducci
Cover design by Jacqueline Nasso Cooke

Inquiries should be addressed to
Prometheus Books
59 John Glenn Drive
Amherst, New York 14228–2119
VOICE: 716–691–0133
FAX: 716–691–0137
WWW.PROMETHEUSBOOKS.COM

16 15 14 13 12   5 4 3 2 1

Library of Congress Cataloging-in-Publication Data

Carlen, Joe.
    The Einstein of money : the life and timeless financial wisdom of Benjamin Graham
/ by Joe Carlen.
        p. cm.
    Includes bibliographical references and index.
    ISBN 978–1–61614–557–6 (cloth : alk. paper)
    ISBN 978–1–61614–558–3 (ebook)
    1. Graham, Benjamin, 1894–1976. 2. Capitalists and financiers—United States—
Biography. 3. Investment advisors—United States—Biography. 4. Investment
analysis. I. Title.

HG172.G68C37 2012
332.6092—dc23
    [B]
                                                                    2012013317

Printed in the United States of America on acid-free paper

CONTENTS

ACKNOWLEDGMENTS

First, I'd like to acknowledge my parents, Peter and Sarah, and my brother Amos. Second, I'd like to thank Steven L. Mitchell, the editor-in-chief of Prometheus Books, both for recognizing (along with others at Prometheus) the merit of a modern biography of Benjamin Graham and for his editorial assistance with *The Einstein of Money*. I would also like to thank Brian McMahon, Jill Maxick, Catherine Roberts-Abel, Melissa Shofner, Jade Zora Ballard, Lisa Michalski, and the entire staff at Prometheus Books for help with various aspects of this project. Mindy Flanagan, manager of business programs for international students at UCSD Extension, also deserves thanks for facilitating the internships of Jisun Park, Yumi Nishizawa, and Christine Xie. The aforementioned students assisted with research for this project, and Ms. Park deserves special acknowledgment for her help with some of the current investment examples. Yuki Kato, another intern from that program, assisted with promotional efforts for this project.

I'd like to thank Warren Buffett for granting me an interview in which he provided invaluable insight into "Ben"—the man who is still Buffett's primary business/investment mentor (and a dear friend for whom he still holds great admiration and affection). I would also like to extend my gratitude to Mr. Buffett's son (and the acclaimed musician) Peter Buffett for his pivotal role in connecting me with his father. I am also greatly indebted to Graham's children, Benjamin Graham Jr., MD, and the late Marjorie Graham Janis—both were most generous with their time, and Dr. Graham also provided some outstanding interview contacts and family photos. Marjorie's daughter Charlotte Reiter, as well as Charlotte's cousin Pi Heseltine (another of Graham's granddaughters), provided excellent insights and photos for which I'm very grateful.

I'd also like to extend special thanks to other personal and professional associates of Graham who shared their remembrances with me: Charles Brandes; Irving Kahn; Thomas Kahn; Dr. Robert Hamburger and his wife, Sonia; the late Dr. Bernie Sarnat and his wife, Rhoda; and the late Professor Fred Weston of the UCLA Graduate School of Business. Their interviews provided a rich layer of additional detail and anecdotes regarding Graham's towering intellect and eccentric personality. I would also like to thank the other prominent value investors and academics who were interviewed for this project. These include Mark Russo, Pat Dorsey, Professor Richard Roll, Andrew Kahn, Mitsunobo Tsuruo, Hideyuki Aoki, Robert Hagstrom, David Poulet, and Raphael Moreau. Most of those interviews were made possible by the 2011 Value Investor Conference organized by the renowned Buffett/Berkshire expert Robert Miles.

I would also like to thank my friends and colleagues: Robert Bell, Nathan Stinson, Jeremy Tiefenbrun, David Kanoa Helms, Russ Weinzimmer, Hannah Bui, Max Rizzuto, Simon Eisner, Tom Flaherty, John Friar, Ieden and Harlan Wall, Jon Davis, Elizabeth Shulman, Ron Hall, Lynn Whitmire, Cheri Hill, Mary Anne Andrews, Sergio Fernandez, Shefali Kumar, Karen Messenger, Michael Weitzman, and the late Eric Leonard. I would also like to acknowledge my Uncle Bob, Aunt Monica, Aunt Eliane, Mark and Jennifer, Al and Daphne, and other extended family members. As well, Frank Scatoni deserves thanks for encouraging me to follow through with a modern biography of Graham. Last, but certainly not least, thanks to Benjamin Graham himself for having left an extraordinary legacy that is "rich" in both financial wisdom and human insight.

INTRODUCTION

*F*orbes's 2011 ranking of the world's billionaires places Carlos Slim at number one, Bill Gates at number two, and Warren Buffett at number three.[1] The subject of this book, Benjamin Graham, is cited by Buffett (and those who study and write about the Buffett phenomenon) as the most profound influence on his investment approach and, by extension, the one to whom the most credit is owed for Buffett's success as the greatest investor in recorded history. However, given the fact that Bill Gates was seen reading Graham's *The Intelligent Investor* in 1993,[2] Graham has long been known to Gates as well. As for Mexico's Carlos Slim, the world's wealthiest individual has frequently spoken of his admiration not only for Warren Buffett but for the writings of Buffett's mentor, Benjamin Graham.[3]

In his inimitably understated manner, Buffett once said that "no one ever became poor by reading Graham." Indeed! Fortunately, despite the fact that Graham himself passed away over thirty-five years ago, the engine of wealth creation that he developed in his extensive writings has not gone unnoticed by the three men who now sit atop the *Forbes* billionaire list. The modern investor community has long taken notice of Benjamin Graham's impact on investment strategy: "Financial Genius,"[4] "Investing Legend,"[5] "Value Guru,"[6] "Path-Breaking Value Investor,"[7] "Best Financial Mind of the 20th Century,"[8] "High Priest of Value Investing,"[9] these are all terms selected by the *New York Times*, the *Wall Street Journal*, *Bloomberg*

Businessweek, *Kiplinger's*, and the *Financial Times* (UK) to describe him. Notably, these are quotes from articles written between 2005 and 2011 about a man whose Wall Street career began almost a century ago (1914) and ended over fifty-five years ago (1956).

In more tangible terms, many of the world's top fund managers, past and present, are directly linked to the "value" school of investing founded by Graham. Aside from Buffett, these include the likes of Charles Brandes and Irving Kahn (both enormously successful and still-active value-fund managers who knew Graham personally), Mario Gabelli, John Bogle, and a host of recently departed value disciples who left behind decades-long records of consistently well-above-average portfolio performance. This group is exemplified by Bill Ruane and Walter Schloss, both Graham aficionados who had considerable personal contact with their investment mentor during the latter part of Graham's life. Not coincidentally, the financial performance of their respective funds was nothing short of legendary and, like Buffett, they attributed much of this success to Benjamin Graham. As one would expect, the value-investing approach has been emulated by many other funds, not only in the United States but throughout the world.

This most formidable investment approach was originated by a man born in nineteenth-century Victorian England, who died in France some eighty-two years later, a man who came into the world as Benjamin Grossbaum, the third son in a family of Jewish kitchenware importers, and left the world as Benjamin Graham, the "Dean of Wall Street." Unlike the market speculators of his day and ours, Graham had both the boldness and the intelligence to originate a more rational and reliable basis for security selection. Through the application of a rigorous academic discipline (the same one with which he graduated second in his class at Columbia University) to the "smoke and mirrors" that is often the stock and trade of Wall Street, he formulated a sound system for investment, which, unlike almost all others, can still be productively and profitably applied seven decades after its inception. The enduring impact of this approach was most apparent at the 2011 Value Investor Conference in Omaha, Nebraska (held just a few days before Buffet's annual Berkshire Hathaway shareholders meeting).

Both the prominence and the diversity of fund managers, presenters, and attendees at the Value Investor Conference were remarkable. Some presenters specialized in global value investing while others focused on particular elements of domestic value investing. As for the attending fund managers, they hailed from all corners of the globe and ranged in age from around twenty-five to well over seventy. There was a younger generation of prominent value investors (e.g., the noted author and fund manager Pat Dorsey), those who have excelled in important applications of the field (e.g., the global value specialist Tom Russo), and value-fund managers operating from the financial centers of Asia, Europe, Latin America, and Africa. Moreover, many of them are CFA (Chartered Financial Analyst) charter holders, a designation that, like value investing itself, owes its existence to Graham! The interviews of these professional fund managers, quoted in this book, provide great insight into the ongoing application of Graham's principles and methods throughout the world.

As for the lay investor, as Warren Buffett highlighted when I interviewed him for this book, Graham's *The Intelligent Investor* (originally published in 1949 and intended primarily for the non-professional investor) consistently ranks in the top 300 (number 247 as of this writing) of the more than 7 million unique books sold on Amazon.com. In a publishing world where this week's bestseller is often all but forgotten months if not weeks later, such strong sales over several *decades* is almost unparalleled. (Mr. Buffett said that the Bible might come close!) Graham's earlier, lengthier, and more technical investment tome (cowritten with David Dodd) titled *Security Analysis* (published in 1934), is still referred to as "The Value Bible" by many professional investors and is reported to have sold over 750,000 copies to date. In fact, a later edition of this classic was featured in the 2006 Academy Award–nominated hit film *The Pursuit of Happyness*. It was the book that a struggling Chris Gardner (played by Will Smith) was required to study as part of his 1981 internship at Dean Witter (presently Morgan Stanley Dean Witter).

The phenomena highlighted above are only the most apparent expressions of Graham's formidable and enduring legacy. However, as impressive as these examples are, they compose a surprisingly incomplete reflection of the intellectual powerhouse that was Benjamin Graham. Perhaps this is best illustrated with an example supplied by Graham himself: writing in 1957, he stated that "if my name has any chance of being remembered by future generations . . . it will be as inventor of the commodity reserve currency plan."[10] This was not false modesty about his contributions to investment finance; from his perspective at that time, this seemed quite plausible. After all, how many noneconomists (Graham had no formal training in economics) in the 1930s and 1940s developed economic proposals that were seriously considered not only by the Roosevelt administration but also by economic theorists the stature of John Maynard Keynes and Friedrich Hayek? Furthermore, those words were written a number of years before Warren Buffett became the household name that it is today.

So, from the vantage point of 1965, it was not at all certain that Graham's investment philosophy would ever gain the level of attention that Buffett's record-shattering investment approach has helped bring to it. And yet, in 2012, for the vast majority of those who are aware of him at all, Graham is only known as the author of *The Intelligent Investor* and/or as Buffett's mentor. Of course, value investing *is* the most significant aspect of his professional life and legacy. However, as with Graham the economist, Graham the business ethicist, Graham the inventor (he had several innovative patents pertaining to such fields as mathematics and Morse-code systems), and even Graham the literary professional (a play that he cowrote actually made it to the Broadway stage, and his English translation of a favorite Spanish novel was considered to be of the highest caliber), Graham the investor is the expression of an intellect of almost unparalleled breadth and depth.

Those who have read many investment books would agree that

Greco-Roman philosophy, Elizabethan poetry, and frequent forays into behavioral psychology are hardly standard fare for such volumes. However, these find ample expression in investment and economics books authored by Graham, the only person ever to be offered professorships in three different departments (Mathematics, Classics, and English) upon completing his undergraduate degree at Columbia University. Moreover, his posthumously published (and only partially completed) memoirs reveal a man who thought deeply and critically (including considerable *self*-criticism) about all aspects of the human condition: psychology, friendship, romance/sexuality, philosophy, and other deeply personal and controversial aspects of life. High finance is hardly known as a breeding ground for such reflection, but Graham never felt compelled to conform to the "Wall Street Way" either in deed or in thought.

Such was the context for the value-investing paradigm that germinated from the seeds of Graham's "Renaissance Man" imagination to become the governing philosophy behind the allocation of what has now become hundreds of billions of dollars (with no small measure of pounds, euros, yen, yuan, rupees, and other currencies as well). Graham experienced the trauma of a riches-to-rags existence firsthand as a child, due in part to his mother's enormous losses in the stock market "Panic of 1907." Later, he would suffer considerable losses himself during the Great Depression after scaling the heights of the Roaring Twenties (Graham's personal income in 1928 was $600,000—the equivalent of over $7.5 million in today's currency). As such, to really internalize Graham's primary investment concepts, it is instructive to learn them in the context of his life experiences. Furthermore, the high volatility and tremendous uncertainty of today's economy have rendered this context more relevant than it has been for several decades.

That is why this book is structured semichronologically. Each chapter that describes a particular period of Graham's life is followed by a chapter dedicated to a particular investment concept that is linked in important and relevant ways to Graham's experiences highlighted in the previous chapter. In this manner, each of the primary principles will be given sufficient attention to be understood reasonably well while the chronological chapters maintain the thread of Graham's compelling life story. Certainly, his personal life did not lack for drama. Along with a certain measure of domestic tranquility and prosperity, the man bore his share of stinging blows (most notably, the tragically premature deaths of his two sons). Moreover, his somewhat unrestrained romantic appetites were a destabilizing factor in three unsuccessful marriages (the first of which was particularly stormy) and eventually led to a deeply controversial yet successful long-term romance during the final stages of his life.

As I learned from interviews with Graham's surviving children and other friends and family, his personality was a curious one in many ways: Warren Buffett, among others, was mystified and *impressed* by his unusual generosity (e.g., Graham's decision to use current stock selection examples at his finance courses, essentially giving away his trade secrets to his own financial detriment), while others close to him were mystified and *dismayed* by some aspects of his romantic conduct. Nonetheless, he was universally respected and mostly admired. After all, the enormity of his positive qualities —his legendary intelligence, discipline, generosity (both financial and otherwise), and, above all, his impeccable professional ethics— outweighed his personal shortcomings. Furthermore, it seems that he did succeed in maintaining high personal integrity in many aspects of his personal life but, unlike his professional life, there were some exceptions. Unfortunately, for him and for some of those with whom he was close, the sheer weight of his intellect and drive, among other factors, led to certain personal and interpersonal complications.

Personality quirks and all, the story of his meteoric rise from poverty to prominence, during some of the most significant events in Wall Street (and world) history, is unusually inspiring. Since Graham lived and prospered during a momentous time in American history (1894–1976), our discussion will span his involvement in two world wars, the "Jazz Age," the Great Depression, the post–World War II boom, and the tumultuous era of the 1960s and early 1970s. Indeed, Graham's life is one of those rare biographical narratives that carry both immense historical significance and dynamic personal drama. However, first and foremost, Graham was a man of *ideas*. Consequently, this book has been structured to serve the dual purpose of providing the reader with an understanding of the man himself as well as a solid grasp of his most essential ideas. As indicated in the subtitle, it is an integrated exploration of Graham's life *and* wisdom, both of which are rich with meaning and practical relevance for the modern reader.

CHAPTER 1
LOSING IT ALL

Benjamin Grossbaum was born in London, England, in 1894, toward the end of the reign of Queen Victoria. Grossbaum was his legal surname until his family "Americanized" it to Graham roughly twenty-three years later (for the sake of clarity and consistency, our subject will generally be referred to as Graham throughout the book). His father, Isaac, was born in Britain and was proud of his British upbringing (a pride that, apparently, was never diminished by the family's subsequent emigration to the United States) while his mother, Dora, originated from Poland. Isaac Grossbaum, along with his five brothers and his father, Bernard, owned and operated a business that imported china, bric-a-brac, and related merchandise from Austria and Germany to the United Kingdom. The Grossbaums were able and industrious merchants, Isaac being especially gifted in this regard. The Grossbaum family was also strictly orthodox in its practice of the Jewish faith.

Isaac was one of eleven children. Among the devoutly religious (Jewish or otherwise), such large families were (and are) not unusual. What was somewhat unusual, even in an orthodox context, was the extent of discipline that Isaac's father imposed upon his children. Because he was so fearful of any "ungodly" influence, he enforced a draconian code of conduct upon his household so severe as to prohibit such "sinful debauchery" as whistling! According to his memoirs, Graham recalls his paternal grandfather, nicknamed "Old Grossbaum," in fairly stark terms: "A man with a square, expansive, grey-black beard, a skull cap, a severe expression, and a fanatical gleam in his eyes."[1] However, considering that Benjamin grew up in a home where he was exposed to French lessons and other secular/non-Jewish activities, it seems that, while officially orthodox (at least while Isaac was still alive), the family Graham was born into was somewhat less pious than that of Bernard Grossbaum.

Moreover, despite being a young and presumably fertile couple, Isaac and Dora had quite a number of childless years between Benjamin's birth and Isaac's death. Such a gap is rare among the most pious practitioners of Orthodox Judaism. As Graham writes in his memoirs, "Out of delicacy or a lack of the inquisitive sense, I never asked mother how it came about that there were none after me."[2] Regarding Benjamin's mother, Dora, her family was also comprised of highly devout Orthodox Jews. This family was known as the Gesundheits. Graham recalls his maternal grandfather as a "stout, jovial man with a white beard,"[3] and Grandmother Gesundheit as a "stout, emotional, and domineering lady."[4]

Of course, the hilarity of the Gesundheit name did not go unnoticed, and there were many who couldn't quite hold in their laughter after verifying that the Gesundheits were not kidding and it really *was* their family name. As Graham recounted several decades later in his memoirs, Gesundheit "was a name which was the cause of much amusement for others and embarrassment to us."[5] Not surprisingly, circumstance and common sense intervened to ensure that the name would not last long in the New World. Graham's cousins, who immigrated to America, would eventually change their surname from Gesundheit to Gerard ("for the children's sake," as one of the surviving Gerards recounted to me). However, behind the amusing name was an intellectual lineage that was anything but laughable.

Graham's maternal great-grandfather was a celebrated religious scholar in nineteenth-century Poland and even served as chief rabbi of Warsaw for several years. At the time, that was among the most prestigious positions anywhere for an observant Jew. One had to be extremely learned in many different areas to become a chief rabbi of any Jewish community, let alone what was, by a significant margin, the largest Jewish community in the world at that time (comprising somewhere between 30 and 40 percent of the Polish capital's total population).[6] Indeed, from a nineteenth-century Jewish perspective, such a position was almost comparable to the papacy for Polish (and other) Catholics of that era. So it would be difficult to understate the stature of such an honored post and the level of both respect and trust that the world's largest Jewish community must have had for Graham's great-grandfather.

Not surprisingly, there is an entry for Graham's maternal grandfather, Jacob Ben Isaac Gesundheit (1815–1878) in the *Jewish Encyclopedia*. Despite the fact that he died long before Graham was born, the entry for Mr. Gesundheit reveals three remarkable parallels between the two men: Jacob was a noted scholar in his field (Jewish law and religion) and wrote a number of works that were "very highly esteemed by Talmudical scholars of eastern Europe."[7] Apparently, he was also an enthusiastic teacher, having led a *yeshiva* (a Jewish seminary) in Warsaw for forty-two years. Last, although he was a devoted religious scholar (and, one presumes, an observant Jew), as chief rabbi, he apparently held views on some religious matters that were considered to be excessively liberal by some of the more pious members of his community. This created a stir that ultimately led to his loss of that prestigious post.

Revealing another, almost eerie, similarity to his great-grandson Benjamin, whose memoirs remained both unpublished and incomplete when he died, the *Jewish Encyclopedia* entry notes that Jacob "left several works in manuscript."[8] As will be elaborated in subsequent chapters, Graham, like Jacob Gesundheit, also became known for highly esteemed scholarly written works and many years of teaching in *his* field of investment finance (thirty-seven years, to be precise). And, of course, he used both the typewriter and the classroom lectern to communicate an investment philosophy that, relative to the accepted "wisdom" of Wall Street at the time, was entirely unconventional. So it seems that thinking outside of the mainstream and being willing to espouse unorthodox views had some relatively recent precedent in the Gesundheit branch of Graham's family tree.

Rhoda Sarnat, the daughter of Maurice Gesundheit/Gerard (Rhoda Gesundheit's brother), had extensive contact with Graham throughout much of his life. I interviewed her and her late husband, Dr. Bernard Sarnat (who, prior to his retirement, was a plastic surgeon of some renown), just a few months prior to the latter's passing. Having studied the family tree in some detail, both of them expressed to me that they saw a link between the Gesundheits' intellectualism and Graham's exemplary success in a highly analytical field. In a recent biography of Dr. Sarnat, the illustrious genealogy of the doctor's wife is highlighted to a considerable extent. While the author concludes that, of the Gesundheit progeny, "the most famous of all was Benjamin Graham,"[9] he certainly is not the only great intellect in that gene pool.

In fact, Rhoda's own father (and Dora Grossbaum/Graham's brother), Maurice Gesundheit, was a respected intellectual in his own right. Curiously, after several years of rabbinical studies convinced him that he was actually an agnostic, Maurice abandoned religious studies for mathematics. In turn, he became a professor in this field at the University of Manchester. Later, upon leaving the United Kingdom for America, Maurice became, as Graham recalled in his memoirs, "quite a success as one of the earliest of the 'systematizers' or 'efficiency engineers.'"[10] To one degree or another, this intellectualism is evident in many of Maurice Gesundheit/Gerard's children, most of whom have excelled in medicine and various other academic disciplines. Perhaps the most significant among these is Ralph Waldo Gerard. A son from Maurice's first marriage (and Rhoda Sarnat's half-bother), Ralph earned his doctorate in neurophysiology, and his research won him two Nobel Prize nominations (but no awards).

During Ralph's lifetime, the late scholar wrote or cowrote over five hundred scientific papers and nine books that pertained to heady topics and carried such titles as "Biological and Cultural Evolution: Some Analogies and Explorations"[11] (a paper published in *Behavioral Science*) and "The Effect of Frequency of Simulations on the Heat Production of the Nerve"[12] (a paper published in the *Journal of Physiology*). Of the descendants of the great chief rabbi of Warsaw, Ralph Gerard was a close runner-up to his first cousin Benjamin Graham. Aside from sheer volume and complexity, Gerard's output is comparable to Graham's in its originality and its tendency to draw enlightening parallels between seemingly distinct disciplines. (Despite—or, perhaps, due to—their similarly impressive intellects, the two cousins never got along very well). Another notable Gesundheit was Rita Auerbach, Dora's first cousin and, according to the Sarnats, one of the first women elected to the British parliament. While it's unclear that this political accomplishment is an indication of great intellect, it certainly reflects a willingness to flout convention.

The extent to which heredity shapes the course of one's life lies at the heart of the "nature versus nurture" conundrum, a still-unresolved (and potentially unresolvable) controversy that is outside the scope of our discussion. However, the pronounced expression of intellectualism and original thought among numerous members of the Gesundheit family line is certainly worthy of exploration in a work highlighting Graham's intellect. Such a lineage is clearly a plausible explanatory factor behind the uncanny brilliance that has become the defining characteristic of Graham's life and legacy. As for the Grossbaums, while considerably less intellectual, the business acumen of Bernard and Isaac also found some expression in "Benny," as his parents would call him. Considering that he established the first of three successful investment enterprises of his own before turning thirty, Graham had some talent in this regard as well. Moreover, his career as a manager and comanager of these enterprises proved that Graham was able to interact both profitably and fairly with clients, employees, and partners alike.

Grossbaum & Sons, as the family's kitchenware/ornament import business was known, saw great opportunity for expansion in America.

So, only one year after the birth of Isaac and Dora's third (and final) child, Benjamin, it was decided that Isaac's family would take that fabled nautical journey from Europe to Ellis Island. However, unlike many of the European immigrants of that period (particularly Jewish immigrants, almost all of whom were emigrating from eastern and, to a lesser extent, central Europe, as opposed to the generally more tolerant and prosperous United Kingdom), it seems that the Grossbaums probably intended to return to their point of origin. After all, Isaac held both a deep affection for Britain and an almost umbilical attachment to his family in London, particularly his father, Bernard. As such, the prospect of relocating permanently in a distant (albeit English-speaking) foreign land and leaving his father and brothers behind in Britain did not appeal to him.

Little is known of Dora's feelings about leaving London. Considering that she had already relocated once before (from her native Poland) and that her family roots were elsewhere, it is probable that the move was less wrenching for her. As for their three children, the eldest, Victor, was only three years of age; Leon was two; and "little Benny" was only one. At such a young age, it is unlikely that any of them carried any strong feelings (let alone influence) regarding such a transition. So, despite Isaac's attachments, with the booming turn-of-the-century US economy making headlines across the pond, it was deemed essential for Grossbaum & Sons to establish some sort of presence in America. It is likely that the Grossbaums intended to return to London once that was in place. It is telling that, for the first four years in which Isaac governed his household (as was the norm during that era) in the United States, the Grossbaums rented part of a private home. Despite possessing ample means to rent or purchase a home of his own, it took several years of living in the United States before Isaac relented and established an independent home for his family.

In 1895, with both hope and a measure of sadness, Isaac and his family boarded a ship from London for New York City. Aside from their somewhat unusual point of origin (for that particular epoch of US immigration), the Grossbaums differed from the masses of mainly southern European and eastern European immigrants of the Ellis Island era in two other important respects: they brought a significant sum of money with them to establish the American branch of Grossbaum & Sons and, unlike the great majority of immigrants from the Ellis Island era, they already spoke English. Their relative wealth, coupled with a mastery of the native language, endowed the Grossbaums with a considerable dual advantage in adapting to American life as first-generation immigrants. To illustrate, unlike the fourth-class passengers on the ship (who, most likely, originated from points east and/or south of Britain), the Grossbaums, as second-class passengers and British-accented English speakers, were not even asked for papers by Ellis Island immigration officials! Indeed, for several years, it seemed that the Grossbaums' cultural and monetary advantages (along with Isaac's tireless work ethic) would ensure a smooth ascent up the golden ladder of the New World.

Instead of the neglected tenement slums endured by most Jewish immigrants of the Ellis Island heyday, the Grossbaums' first (rented) home in New York was just off Park Avenue! While the house was shared with their landlord, it's safe to presume that such an address carried both prestige and considerable expense. Aside from the Park Avenue home, Graham's recollections of his early childhood make reference to all manifestations of ragtime-era affluence: vacations in trendy summer resorts; trips to Hot Springs, Virginia; at least one extended stay in Europe; governesses; regular trips to fashionable boutiques and fine food stores; gold watches; the latest phonographs and recordings; cooks, maids, and even "servants' quarters."[13] Moreover, from both a personal and a familial perspective, it was an idyllic time. Graham recalls children's locomotive trains in Central Park, typical troublemaking from the growing Grossbaum boys (of which Graham, being the youngest and least mischievous, was the most reluctant participant), and what seems to have been a fairly harmonious union between Isaac and Dora.

So, while many immigrants of the era were suffering from the dangerous and unsanitary conditions observed in the 1890 classic *How the Other Half Lives*,[14] it seems that the Grossbaums were living in a parallel universe of luxury, prestige, and even glamour. Moreover, despite being Jewish at a time when open anti-Semitism was fairly common, the Grossbaums not only succeeded financially, but they even gained some exposure to American "high society." Perhaps the most notable illustration of such exposure in Graham's own life is the friendship that he, as a five-year-old, developed with a young child of the Swift family (meat-industry moguls) during his family's stay in Hot Springs. Within a year of that trip, the Grossbaums took up residence in a private brownstone house on Fifth Avenue. This move was a definitive indication that not only had Isaac made the American branch of Grossbaum & Sons a great success but also that he did not anticipate a permanent return to Britain for the foreseeable future.

Perhaps that is why Isaac, now reconciled to staying in America, took the family to England the following summer to spend the whole season with his family and those members of Dora's who lived in England as well. So, Isaac, Dora, Leon, and seven-year-old Benjamin set sail for London. (Graham's eldest brother, Victor, had become such a prankster and rebel by then that, instead of traveling to Europe, he was sent to a disciplinary summer camp in Pennsylvania!) The family enjoyed a pleasant extended vacation in London and Brighton (where Dora's parents lived). According to Graham, the British operations of Grossbaum & Sons had been suffering badly just as Isaac's American branch had been thriving. Consequently, Isaac had become the primary breadwinner for his father, his ten siblings, some of Dora's family, and, undoubtedly, a much larger contingent of nephews and nieces. So it is probable that there was a heightened element of reverence and gratitude for the family among their British hosts.

Graham's father had had several health problems in the preceding years, and it is almost certain that his constant work on behalf of Grossbaum & Sons, successful as it was, took a heavy toll on his health. Isaac had been working and traveling (developing distribution throughout the United States) so intensively that, despite being nine years old when his father died, an adult Graham wrote that "of my father I remember very little indeed."[15] Such an exhausting schedule, coupled with the mental stress of being responsible for an enormous extended family, probably left him both physically and emotionally drained. Certainly, Isaac's inhuman working schedule left him vulnerable to illness at an unusually young age. Shortly after summering in Britain, Isaac's father, with whom Graham's father was particularly close, died of pneumonia at the fairly early age (even by 1903 standards) of fifty-six. Graham would learn later that this unexpected passing was at least partly due to emotional shock. It seems that his grandfather had dealings with an assistant who not only proved to be a thief but also threatened Bernard's life at gunpoint when he was discovered.[16]

Tragically, the news of "Old Man Grossbaum's" untimely death was a severe emotional shock of its own for Isaac. Like Graham's grandfather, Graham's father proved ill-equipped to withstand a great emotional shock. Indeed, his already-fragile health left him precariously vulnerable to the effects of such a devastating and entirely unexpected loss. Prior to his father's death, Isaac had been diagnosed with a "mysterious ailment" but, soon after the emotional shock, Graham's father was diagnosed with full-blown pancreatic cancer. Graham recalls the moment that his father became aware of Bernard's passing:

> The news came suddenly in a cablegram. I remember my father reading it and straightaway bursting into a loud lament. Even clearer is the picture of him sitting in a low chair, with slippered feet on a footstool, and wearing an old suit with the sleeves willfully slashed and buttons torn off. This was part of the Orthodox custom called "sitting shiva"—an elaborate ritual of mourning for a departed parent.[17]

Shortly thereafter, Isaac's health deteriorated dramatically, and he was promptly hospitalized. Like his recently departed father, with his immunity (probably) reeling from deep emotional shock, Isaac succumbed to a disease that feeds upon a weak immune system. However, unlike Bernard Grossbaum, Graham's thirty-five-year-old father was still a relatively young man. Initiating a tragic series of events for the Grossbaum family, in February 1903, Victor, Leon, and Benjamin were summoned to the hospital, where their grievously ill father proceeded to bless his three bewildered boys. Subsequently, they were escorted quickly from his hospital bed to wait for their mother at home. Eventually, a teary-eyed Dora opened the door and, as Graham recalls,

> at the sight of our scared faces, she cried out, "My poor, poor boys. You are all orphans." I suppose we started to cry, too, for even I was not too young to understand that from that moment on everything would be different, unhappily different.[18]

With both a steadiness and a rapidity that must have been alarming, the fatherless Grossbaum family proceeded to lose, quite literally, *everything*: Graham recalls how the mounting financial challenges during this distressing period "carried us down into evermore straitened circumstances, and continuing for several more years in a struggle to keep from falling still lower."[19] Three of Isaac's brothers (all of whom had been working at Grossbaum & Sons in some capacity) endeavored but ultimately failed to sustain the business. Then, the reins were passed to Dora's brother Maurice who, despite his well-respected intellect, proved similarly ill-suited to running such a business. With characteristic perceptiveness, Graham observed that his uncle had "neither the engaging salesmanship nor the day-to-day resourcefulness that had been the foundation of Father's achievements."[20]

Tragically, in the absence of capable management, the same business that had sustained a large transatlantic extended family for nearly a decade collapsed with remarkable speed. As Graham recalled in his memoirs, "By the end of a year or so the business had lost so much money that the remaining stock (inventory) was sold for what it would bring, and the business given up completely."[21] Meanwhile, in order to keep her family afloat, Dora proceeded to sell the expensive furniture, jewelry, and other tangible assets that the family had acquired in more prosperous times. Within a few years, these assets, along with the money from their sale, had vanished. Graham described the first three years after his father's death (1903 to 1906) as "the years that formed my character."[22] However, that's not to suggest that Graham was some kind of pampered child gone astray before adversity struck his family.

In fact, despite the great success of his father's business, Graham was never "spoiled" in the usual sense. On the contrary, his parents were avid disciplinarians and, long before Isaac's passing, Graham had already proven to be an excellent student and an obedient child. However, thus far, he had only seen the world from the perch of success and plenty. Isaac's tragically premature death would introduce the stigma of failure and the pain of poverty into his family as formative life experiences, the memories of which would remain with Graham vividly and permanently. Indeed, the lessons that he drew from these experiences are evident from the conservatism that underlies Graham's celebrated investment philosophy. More immediately, the general state of need that afflicted his family was certainly a motivating factor in Graham's continued academic and, later, professional success.

Perhaps the most direct example of the impact of this adversity on the young boy's life is the fact that, within a few months of his father's death, a nine-year-old Graham was on the streets of New York selling the *Saturday Evening Post*. While Isaac was still alive, "Benny" was expected to attain academic excellence. Afterward, he was *still* expected to perform well at school (in fact, the academic pressure intensified as the scholastic success of the Grossbaum boys was seen by their mother as the family's ultimate exit route from poverty) while taking on as much part-time and seasonal work as possible. From selling magazines to tutoring his fellow students in math and working at a dairy farm, a theater, and a telephone-assembly operation, such work remained an integral element of his life from age nine all the way through high school and college. In fact, even as a young professional on Wall Street, he would often moonlight at various other jobs (e.g., tutoring children of high-ranking US military officers in various subjects) to bring in some additional income.

So, although his investment education came relatively late (as least compared to Warren Buffett, who began reading investment books at the tender age of eight), Graham certainly knew the value of a dollar from a very early age. Having earned most of his first dollars from (mostly physical and) strenuous labor, Graham became permanently averse to excessive financial risk. For many on Wall Street, money was (and is) almost an abstraction—a score-keeping system with which to see who's "on top." Graham's experience of money was much more visceral. It was the very real and tangible force that had elevated then decimated his family's position, and it was also the means of survival for which he had labored since he was a student in the fourth grade. There was another character-building activity assigned to Graham at this time, which, like working, exerted a lasting influence on his views of money and, eventually, investments.

With his family's hired help gone, the three boys were now assigned various household chores. While brothers Leon and Victor dried the dishes, made the beds, and helped with other cleaning, "Benny" was assigned most of the shopping. Reflecting on that time of poverty several decades later, Graham marvels that "somehow or other we managed to get the things we needed."[23] When trying to determine how they were able to do that with a substandard income, he reveals that "as a matter of course we bought only bargains."[24] Graham and some of his relatives and friends enjoyed playing tennis. So, as an example of this bargain hunting, he recalls purchasing "used" tennis balls from the Manhattan Tennis Club at the heavily discounted price of three for twenty-five cents. As Graham recalls, these allegedly ruined items proved to be "quite good,"[25] and they "lasted a long time."[26]

As for Graham's mother, to her credit, she adopted a more modest lifestyle than she had grown accustomed to and, although her discomfort and embarrassment were evident, she never complained about the family's reversal of fortune. Although Graham took note of her missteps during this time (e.g., secretly baking then hiding a batch of relatively expensive butter-rich cookies for her personal consumption), overall, he was greatly impressed by his mother's selflessness and determined resilience during those difficult years. When Isaac was still around, Dora enjoyed all manner of luxury. Revealingly, she once identified herself, albeit partly in jest, as "die Erbsenprinzessin,"[27] German for the fabled "Princess of the Pea," who demonstrated that she was a bona fide princess by sensing a pea that was hidden beneath her mattress (the Gesundheit family in which she was raised spoke German fairly well). Yet, when tragedy struck, Dora proved willing to put away such fanciful notions and apply herself to whatever needed to be done, including the most menial work. Her boys were astonished by the transformation:

> But after the loss of her husband she seemed overnight to develop an unsuspected toughness, resiliency, and resourcefulness. She did whatever she had to do—even to scrubbing the kitchen floor, for her the ultimate trial of Job.[28]

Perhaps her most courageous act during this time was refusing the marriage offer of a generous middle-aged man while her family was in the midst of ongoing financial turmoil. Surely such a marriage would have been the quickest route back to solvency, and she would never have had to struggle for her family again. However, after being taken to dinner and the theater and being pampered with expensive chocolates, she still could not bring herself to accept the offer because, as Graham recalls, "without love she would never remarry, regardless of the advantages."[29] (Apparently, she never did find love again for, despite multiple marriage offers, she remained single for the rest of her life.) In fact, she did all that she could to keep the family independent of *all* forms of external assistance. Nonetheless, subsequent events would prove that, despite her drive, she possessed neither the skill nor the judgment to deliver on her good intentions.

Sometime after the demise of Grossbaum & Sons, Graham's mother decided to convert their home, a smaller and more utilitarian house (they had long since moved away from their Fifth Avenue address), into a boardinghouse. After all, it seemed like a fairly straightforward business and a certain way to bring in additional income. Unfortunately, the boardinghouse failed to generate the expected revenue and, within two years, this venture was abandoned as well. When it was, the Grossbaums had lost their only source of income and had spent most of their savings trying to sustain a failing business. Consequently, they were forced to auction off their home and most of their possessions. It is clear that this loss and the manner in which it occurred was a deeply humiliating experience that Graham (and, most likely, the other three members of his family) took personally. Writing over six decades later, Graham recalls the "shame at our disgrace of our being sold out publicly under the [auctioneer's] hammer."[30]

While this may have been the Grossbaums' most embarrassing setback, it proved not to be the last. Following the boardinghouse debacle, Dora's most notable attempt at improving her family's lot proved to be a fateful one for both her and her youngest son. Desperate for some way of leveraging her few remaining resources for profit, Graham's mother opened a margin account to "invest" (or, according to the criteria Graham would later establish, speculate) in the stock market, specifically on US Steel. Her knowledge of the market was limited and her experience with it even more so. These factors coupled with the fact that she had the misfortune of investing just a couple of months prior to the Banking Panic of 1907 (which was not dissimilar to the more recent "Banking Panic" of 2008). The panic wiped out the market, including much of her investment, and her bank's subsequent closure liquidated what little remained in her account.

This incident, unfortunate as it was, marked Graham's introduction to "Mr. Market." Prior to the panic, the young, devoted son would check the financial pages of the daily paper to track the stock value of US Steel. Of course, at that point, Graham had no knowledge of securities, but he "knew enough to be glad when the price was up and sorry when it was down."[31] His mother's market misadventures were his first indication that investing "on a whim" involved great financial risk. However, beyond that, once Dora's margin account had evaporated, so did Graham's interest in the market. For a number of years still, the market would retreat to the relevance of background noise, which it had always been for Graham. That is, until circumstances would bring it to the foreground for the whole of his professional career. As Graham writes:

> Little did I or anyone else suspect that many years later the financial pages were to become an open book to me and that the dreamy, impractical, ink-stained Benny G. would become a figure on Wall Street.[32]

What *was* clear back then was that Dora Grossbaum was unable to provide for her family. So, on two occasions, despite the acute embarrassment and discomfort that it caused her, she put her pride aside and moved the family in with her brother Maurice: "Mother was happy to have her boys living with her, but she had a deep dislike of living with anyone else."[33] It seems that, for her, having to rely on her sometimes-harsh and temperamental brother for her own children's welfare was particularly irksome. Graham recalls stormy arguments between Dora and Maurice that became so heated that the two Polish-born siblings would switch from English to Polish at a certain point. That way, the children wouldn't understand the offensive words they were yelling at each other.

There were other irritants at work in the merged Gesundheit-Grossbaum household: From Dr. Sarnat's recollections of conversations with his late father-in-law, he recalled that while Maurice got along well enough with Benjamin and Leon (both fairly quiet and studious), the more mischievous Victor set off his temper fairly often. However, it seems that all the Grossbaum boys viewed Uncle Maurice as a brilliant but somewhat tyrannical figure (Maurice's relationship with Graham would take on both professional and financial dimensions in subsequent decades). Meanwhile, from his recollections of conversations with Graham, Dr. Sarnat told me that Graham never got along well with Maurice's son Fred (the same Fred Gesundheit/ Gerard who would go on to become a Nobel-nominated neurophysiologist): "Fred's personality was difficult and Ben described him as a 'spoiled brat.' I imagine that he was giving Ben a hard time."[34]

In this way and others, Graham was certainly inconvenienced by his family's misfortunes and, in some instances (such as the home auction), personally embarrassed. However, most of his discomfort resulted from the strain of increasingly dire and humiliating circumstances on his mother. For some time, Dora and her sons were living on $75 a month (less than $1,800 in today's money [i.e., an annual income of less than $22,000], well below the poverty line for a family of four) after once having lived in a large house with a full-time cook, a maid, and a governess. While he certainly did not like this dramatic reversal of fortune, it seems that Graham, fully occupied with school, work, friends, and all manner of books, was able to get along fairly well without the old luxuries. However, being very close to his mother, he was pained to see her struggling valiantly but desperately to provide for her family. This pain became the catalyst for much of Graham's future success.

The famed author, investor, and public servant John Train characterized this dynamic aptly in his 1980 classic *The Money Masters*:

> The family was greatly reduced in circumstances. His mother never adjusted to the change, and her anxieties undoubtedly contributed to Ben's subsequent preoccupation with achieving financial security.[35]

Meanwhile, Graham's mother recognized fairly early on that, due to advantages of both character and intellect, her "Benny" was her best hope for reclaiming the family's former stature. According to Graham's memoirs, his mother's hopes for his future were evident, and there can be little doubt that they made an indelible impression upon his psyche. When recalling one of his first youthful inventions (Graham would go on to produce a number of innovations that were entirely unrelated to investing), Graham indicated that he had high hopes for his improved apartment visitor bell ringer: "The impractical dreamer of the family was going to restore its fortunes, nay, raise it to new heights of affluence."[36] This he would do, albeit with an entirely different set of "inventions." (Once his ringer contraption malfunctioned, it caused all manner of mayhem for visitors and great annoyance for his mother, who forced her heartbroken son to dismantle it!)

Writing as an accomplished and financially secure retiree in his Beverly Hills home, Graham's fondness and nostalgia for this difficult period is evident from his memoirs. However, it is also clear from his writing that, so many years later, some of the harsher memories of loss and humiliation still stung. So one surmises that some of his retrospective fondness for the time was an expression of satisfaction for not only prevailing over such difficulties but, ultimately, benefiting from them. As he writes, "Adversity is bitter, but its uses may be sweet. Our loss was great, but in the end we could count great compensations."[37] The older Graham makes it unambiguously clear that the general state of need that afflicted his family after his father's death was both distressing and inspirational. The determination to restore his family's stature and make his mother proud became the primary motivation in his academic and, later, his professional success.

Even more important, at least from a value-investing perspective, Graham's riches-to-rags youth shaped his outlook on money—both earning and spending it. Being compelled to contribute to the household income from a young age and to minimize expenditures by shopping on a shoestring budget, Graham already understood (many decades before the concept was popularized in financial self-help literature) that monetary success involved playing good offense (i.e., earning money) *and* defense (i.e., spending as little as possible for good value). As he writes:

The years of poverty since Father's death had touched me only lightly. They had developed in my character a serious concern for money, a willingness to work hard for small sums, and an extreme conservatism in all my spending habits.[38]

This "extreme conservatism" would give Graham an enormous (some would say definitive) advantage when picking stocks and bonds for purchase. Ultimately, it found its expression as the quintessential tenet of his investment philosophy: a principle known as the margin of safety.

CHAPTER 2

THE MARGIN
OF SAFETY

In his million-selling classic *The Intelligent Investor*, Graham wonders what his reply would be if he were asked to distill the essence of sound investing into a single phrase. In response to this self-directed challenge, Graham writes three words all in caps: "MARGIN OF SAFETY."[1] To further underscore the supreme importance of this principle, the question introduces a chapter that he titled "'Margin of Safety' as the Central Concept of Investment."[2] Like other "Grahamisms" (such as "Mr. Market"—featured in a subsequent chapter), "Margin of Safety" is a deceptively succinct and simple term representing an enormously powerful concept. Not surprisingly, it has become *the* sacred motto of value investors. With respect to the margin of safety, Warren Buffett, writing in 1990, concluded that "forty-two years after reading that, I still think those are the three right words."[3] When I interviewed him over twenty years later, he identified the concept as one of three essential Graham principles that, "if they become part of your DNA when investing, you really can't go wrong."[4] (This book includes chapters dedicated to each of these three principles.)

INVESTMENT VERSUS SPECULATION

Before delving into the margin of safety itself, it's instructive to understand why Graham saw the need to develop and apply some form of it at least nine years prior to the 1929 stock market crash. As discussed in the previous chapter, due to the grave financial losses that his family suffered during his formative years, Graham developed an unusually conservative approach to money. Such a risk-averse outlook was especially rare during the period preceding the crash, when Graham "cut his teeth" on Wall Street. While most firms and investors were driven by the lure of large speculative gains, the ever-cautious Graham was primarily concerned about safety of principal (i.e., the initial sum of money invested) and only secondarily about additional gains. So it didn't take long for him to realize that many of the same securities (a term encompassing both stocks and bonds) promising large and quick profits were, in fact, very risky and far more likely to deliver large and permanent losses. As Graham stated in one of his mid-1940s lectures at the New York Institute of Finance regarding the merits and methods of value investing: "We all know that if we follow the speculative crowd we are going to lose money in the long run."[5]

So how did Graham define speculation? Interestingly, his was a negative definition in the sense that any "operation" (i.e., taking a position in the market) that did not meet his criteria for a genuine investment was, by default, a speculation. In his (and David Dodd's) own words, "An investment operation is one which, upon thorough analysis, promises safety of principal and a satisfactory return. Operations not meeting these requirements are speculative."[6] This might seem like common sense to the modern reader. However, as evidenced by the enormous number of absurdly priced securities in the late 1920s that supposedly professional and reputable investment firms were buying and promoting, such common sense was decidedly *un*common at the time. In the midst of a massive Wall Street bubble, safety of principal (and, according to Graham, sound investment) became an afterthought as short-term price expectations governed market behavior.

Of course, similar bubbles have recurred several times since. Recently, the late 1990s Internet bubble was characterized by utterly insane prices for stocks issued, in many instances, by companies with no earnings whatsoever! Just as his mentor would have done, no matter how high the Internet stocks soared, Buffett did not even consider *any* of them. After all, from a value investor's perspective, neither safety of principal nor satisfactory returns were likely to be the ultimate outcome of such investments. On this and so many other matters, the Oracle of Omaha's "clairvoyance" lies in his ability to arrive at conclusions based on a thorough analysis of the facts. Often his conclusions conflict with those of many others (some of whom base their expectations on emotions or sloppy thinking, and some of whom are incentivized to arrive at unfounded conclusions, etc.) but Buffett persists nonetheless. There is no question that Graham set the example in this regard. When I asked Warren Buffett about which aspects of Graham's personality were most conducive to success in investing, he remarked that, among other factors, "he was not swayed by what other people thought or how the world was feeling that day or anything of the sort."[7]

Indeed, much of what set Graham apart was his conviction that just because "the crowd" was pursuing a risky strategy, this should not suggest that such a strategy was less speculative (an adjective that, to Graham, represented grave and unnecessary risk) than the facts indicated. On the contrary, he saw the clamor of a mass of giddy investors as an ominous sign. More often than not, it was an indication that market hysteria had reached a dangerous tipping point; that is, that a financial bloodbath was imminent. However, such a view is contrary to how most people think (and, according to some behavioral scientists, even contrary to "the herd instinct" in our evolutionary wiring). That is why Graham is often referred to as a *contrarian* investor (as is Warren Buffett—who else but a contrarian would take a massive position in Goldman Sachs in the midst of the 2008 financial meltdown?). As Graham wrote in *The Intelligent Investor*:

It would be rather strange if—with all the brains at work professionally in the stock market—there could be approaches that are
both sound and relatively unpopular. Yet our own career and reputation have been based on this unlikely fact.[8]

Fortunately, Graham was sufficiently independent-minded and self-
assured to pursue his own course, even when it seemed to conflict with
the general direction of the analyst and investor community. As Graham
reinforced time and again, "you are neither right nor wrong because
the crowd disagrees with you. You are right because your data and
reasoning are right."[9] So, while speculative Wall Street fads launched
and crashed all around him, Graham dedicated much of his early career
to devising a system of security analysis that would flag such dangerous
speculations in advance while highlighting genuinely promising
investment opportunities. Indeed, the distinction between investment
and speculation lies at the heart of Graham's investment philosophy,
and it is the primary impetus behind his development and promotion of
the margin-of-safety principle. Since Graham observed that anticipating
short-term price movements was a fool's errand, as scientific and
predictable as a turn at the roulette wheel, he came to dismiss all such
"technical" or "market" approaches as outright speculation.

As such, he arrived at the conclusion that a safe and reliably
rewarding investment system could not revolve around market timing,
in the traditional sense. That is why he wrote that if an investor
"places his emphasis on timing, in the sense of forecasting,"[10] that
person will "end up as a speculator and with a speculator's financial
results."[11] Or, put another way, that "investor" would no longer be an
investor but a speculator who, to Graham's way of thinking, would
be the direct opposite of a true investor. The margin of safety is the
essence of value investing because it is the metric by which hazardous
speculations are segregated from bona fide investment opportunities. Generally, Graham focused on selecting securities representing
sound businesses; that is, companies with strong balance sheets (well-
capitalized with relatively low debt) and an extended record of strong

earnings. He found that, while such an approach provided him with a greater degree of control over outcomes (and immeasurably greater safety than the "hot stock" approach), it was hardly an exact science, and it could still involve considerable peril if the strong company were purchased at too high a price.

The problem, as he saw it, was that the market didn't always recognize and reward the selection of strong or "investment grade" securities in a manner and a time frame that one could predict. Worse yet, securities of stable companies were not always immune from highly *un*stable market pricing. As such, even when selecting sound securities, one needed some kind of buffer to protect against market fluctuations. That buffer is the margin of safety—the difference between the real or *intrinsic* value of the business underlying the security (as determined by independent analysis) and the price assigned to that security at the moment (as determined by the market). As Graham defined it, the margin of safety constitutes a "favorable difference between price on the one hand and indicated or appraised value on the other."[12] If one can purchase a sound security with a large margin between the intrinsic value and the market price, in the long run, both safety of principal and some measure of appreciation are all but assured. Stripped to its essence, as prominent value investor and Columbia finance Professor Joel Greenblatt framed the concept in a 2011 *Barron's* interview, "it's about figuring out what something is worth, and then paying a lot less for it."[13]

MARGIN OF SAFETY = INTRINSIC VALUE − CURRENT MARKET PRICE OF SECURITY

The margin of safety was a mechanism devised by Graham to shield both his principal and his future returns from the short-term unpredictability of security prices. After several years on Wall Street, Graham resigned himself to the fact that, despite the boastings of innumerable stock market–tracking "whiz kids" (referred to back then as "market analysts"—as opposed to security analysts), the data demonstrated that there is no reliable way of anticipating, let alone controlling, such short-term price movements. However, there *was* a reasonably reliable way to prosper, since eventually the market does tend to reward neglected but strong companies with a substantial increase in their security's price. The linchpin of this method, that is, the method through which one can identify such strong but temporarily underpriced securities, is the margin of safety. According to what Graham and Dodd wrote in the original (1934) edition of *Security Analysis*, it was also the primary distinction between security analysis and the market analysis (i.e., stock market charting to anticipate price movement) fads of that time (and all periods since):

> Security analysis and market analysis are alike, therefore, in the fact that they deal with data which are not conclusive as to the future. The difference, as we shall point out, is that the securities analyst can protect himself by a *margin of safety* which is denied to the market analyst.[14]

INTRINSIC VALUE

In order to calculate the margin of safety of an equity offering, one needs only two values—the market price of the security in question and the intrinsic value of the proportion of the underlying business represented by that security. For example, Coca-Cola is currently trading at almost $70 per share—that is the market price of the security in question (Coca-Cola common stock). If, upon a thorough analysis of the company's financial statements, one determines an intrinsic value of $91 per share (i.e., the analyst believes that the true or intrinsic value of Coca-Cola is $209 billion and, considering that there are approximately 2.3 billion shares, that translates to $209 billion/2.3 billion or almost $91), there is a $21 discrepancy between the market price of the security and its intrinsic value, which thereby creates a margin of safety of thirty percent ($21/$70). Conversely, if the intrinsic value is determined to be less than or equal to the current market capitalization of $160.41 billion (as represented by the current per-share market price), that means that purchasing Coca-Cola common stock today provides absolutely no margin of safety to the investor and, as such, does not constitute a sound investment opportunity.

The price of Coca-Cola common stock, like any stock or bond is, of course, an immediately known and unambiguous quantity. However, the intrinsic *value* of the underlying business that is represented by the security cannot be gleaned from a stock chart. Determining that value through a methodical analysis of the security is the central task of the Graham-inspired value investor. A defensible intrinsic value deduced from a reasoned and dispassionate assessment of the facts (i.e., devoid of market hysteria) enables one to determine the presence and size of the margin of safety. In *Security Analysis*, Graham and coauthor David Dodd wrote that the securities analyst is "concerned with the intrinsic value of the security and more particularly with discovery of discrepancies between the intrinsic value and the market price."[15] However, the authors of the 1934 classic recognized that intrinsic value is not always easy to discern, writing that "it is a great mistake to imagine that intrinsic value is as definite and as determinable as is the market price."[16]

Indeed, the mechanics for determining the intrinsic value of equities can vary according to various factors. However, for the purposes of this chapter, an outline of Graham's primary evaluation methods is appropriate: Graham believed that if the per-share figure of a *profitable* company's current assets minus all its liabilities (i.e., net current assets minus net liabilities) was more or less equivalent to the share price, that was indicative of a satisfactory intrinsic value relative to market price; that is, an acceptable margin of safety. The problem with this approach is that, as Graham wrote in *The Intelligent Investor*, "very few companies turn out to have an ultimate value less than the working capital alone, although scattered instances may be found."[17] Such "net-net" opportunities (i.e., securities priced at the per-share value of the issuing company's net current assets) are even scarcer in today's market. Moreover, as Graham observed, "A stock does not become a sound investment merely because it can be bought at close to its asset value."[18]

SIMPLIFIED STOCK VALUATION

Graham developed this relatively simple formula for arriving at a reasonable estimate at intrinsic value:

$$V = E \cdot (8.5 + 2G) \cdot 4.4/Y$$
V = Intrinsic value
E = Earnings per share (EPS)
G = The company's projected growth rate
Y = Average interest rate (or "yield") on AAA corporate bonds

Of course, the value of G is not as immediately attainable as the values of E and Y. Fortunately, one of Graham's other formulas enables one to determine the implied value of this future (and hence, by definition, undetermined) growth-rate variable:

$$G = (P/2 - 8.5)/2$$
P = Current stock price

Regarding this formula, Graham cautioned readers of *The Intelligent Investor* that he provided one "because of the inescapable necessity in security analysis to project the future growth rate for most companies studied. Let the reader not be misled into thinking that such projections have any high degree of reliability."[19] Graham's words regarding the growth-rate formula apply equally to the valuation formula presented above. However, it still has some value as a filter with which to determine whether a stock is worthy of further consideration.

DISCOUNT CASH FLOW (DCF) METHOD

A more common method for estimating intrinsic value is the discount cash flow (DCF) method, which Graham employed regularly, as does Buffett. Through this method, all future per-share earnings, discounted to their present value, are aggregated to arrive at a "net present value" that can serve as a defensible intrinsic value. In other words, the intrinsic value of the share of the business represented by the stock is equal to the proportional share of the business' future cash flows. The core DCF formula itself is not overly complex: $CF^n / (1 + r)^n$ where CF represents the expected cash flow for the period in question, r represents the "discount rate," that is, the rate at which future cash flows are discounted to determine their present value, and n represents the compounding period in question. For example, the value of a $1,000 cash flow four years hence, utilizing a discount rate of 10 percent, would be $\$1,000/(1.1)^4$, which is approximately $683.

However, estimating the correct discount rate for a given situation can be a fairly involved process. As the acclaimed young value investor and author Pat Dorsey writes in his book *The Five Rules for Successful Stock Investing*,

> Unfortunately, there is no precise way to calculate the exact discount rate that you should use in a discounted cash flow (DCF) model, and academics have filled entire journal issues with nothing but discussions about the right way to estimate discount rates.[20]

For example, the discount rate applied to a small company with a history of uneven earnings should be somewhat higher than that applied to a large company with a history of stable and fairly predictable earnings. Indeed, there are a number of steps, of varying levels of nuance and complexity, involved with calculating intrinsic value through the discount cash flow method.

Fortunately, there are now a number of free online resources (like Guru Focus's Fair Value Calculator, at http://www.gurufocus

.com/fair_value_dcf.php) that have automated this process. Such services provide a rough approximation of intrinsic value for almost any publicly listed common stock and some (like Guru Focus) calculate the margin of safety as well. For those with the time and inclination to learn how to apply this method themselves, appendix 1 provides a summarized step-by-step application of the method to Merck & Company, Ltd. This more rigorous process provides the value investor with more opportunity to understand how to calibrate the calculation (e.g., the determination of an appropriate discount rate) to the specific company in question. Even if you'd prefer to use an online resource going forward, I strongly recommend working through the DCF process at least once on your own to gain a deeper understanding of how its resulting value is computed.

Before determining whether or not a stock is worthy of further consideration, alongside a rough estimate of the margin of safety, it is also advisable to apply Graham's essential screens (summarized in chapter 4). The proper application of those screens compels the investor to ensure that, along with its margin of safety, various other aspects of a company's historical and current financial performance are satisfactory. In this manner, the investor is forced to examine the company's capital structure (i.e., debt versus equity), working capital position (i.e., current assets minus current liabilities), and other important factors that many intrinsic value calculations do not take into account.

Lastly, it is also important to highlight the fact that much of the power of the margin-of-safety concept is that it doesn't need to be calculated with 100 percent (or even 80 percent) precision and certainty. As acclaimed value investor and author Robert Hagstrom wrote in his book *The Essential Buffett*,

> Graham proposed that it was not essential to determine a company's exact intrinsic value; instead, an approximate measure or range of value was acceptable. Even an approximate value, compared against the selling price, would be sufficient to gauge the margin of safety.[21]

MARKET TIMING AND
THE MARGIN OF SAFETY

It might seem somewhat contradictory that, on the one hand, Graham dismisses predicting price movements as unsound speculation while, on the other hand, he recommends the margin of safety mechanism to identify securities that are likely to appreciate in the future. After all, when one purchases a security with an attractive margin of safety, one is betting primarily that the security will appreciate not necessarily in intrinsic value but in its *market* value (i.e., the quoted stock price will rise). So there's no question that, at some level, the value investor *is* predicting a price movement. However, the key distinction is that, unlike the professional market timer, the value investor does not presume to know when or even to what extent he or she will be rewarded for identifying a security that the market has mispriced (i.e., priced below the intrinsic value of the proportion of the issuing company represented by the security).

Graham realized that price volatility could be problematic even when one had invested in strong companies. However, he gave up on anticipating the *timing and specific measure of future price movements*. Or, to put it another way, he came to accept that market volatility is a force of nature that one cannot control. As Pat Dorsey told me, "Having a margin of safety is critical to being a disciplined investor because it acknowledges that as humans, we're flawed."[22] Indeed, much of the concept's power lies in its realism and humility. Instead of another dubious stock-charting method, Graham sidesteps that morass entirely and considers a new paradigm from which to profit from, instead of control, market volatility. Being the inventive thinker that he was, Graham set about formulating a system through which this volatility could be transformed from a threat to an enormous opportunity. In what was probably the single most influential intellectual achievement of Graham's life, he succeeded.

As he writes in *The Intelligent Investor* (regarding common stocks specifically, though the essence of the quote applies to a wider range of securities), since even high-quality stocks "are subject to recurrent and wide fluctuations in their prices, the intelligent investor should be interested in the possibilities of profiting from these pendulum swings."[23] Application of the margin of safety proved to be an effective way of *exploiting the market's inaccurate security pricing for one's own benefit*. Critically, it does so without requiring any forecasting as to when the pricing is likely to change. Instead, it identifies a gap significant enough to suggest that the pricing is likely to appreciate both substantially and eventually. In this manner, it eliminates much of the fruitless guesswork involved with many forms of nonvalue investing. As noted author and finance professor Lawrence Cunningham wrote, "Graham called the margin of safety the central concept of investment because its essential function is to render an accurate estimate of the future unnecessary."[24]

Graham noticed that, in most cases, large discrepancies between intrinsic value and market price tend to narrow as, sooner or later (and the value investor does not pretend to know which it will be in any given instance), the market recognizes its errors. As will be discussed in chapter 8, this is why, once the value investor has found the right time to purchase the security (i.e., at a time when the low market price offers a high margin of safety relative to its intrinsic value), the day-to-day gyrations in market price are not particularly important. The Graham school of investing revolves around identifying strong value through the margin-of-safety principle and then remaining confident that "purchasing a dollar for only fifty cents" will bear fruit at the opportune time. So, even when the market price falls considerably lower, the disciplined value investor does not sell in a frenzied panic. Instead, like a fisherman during bad weather, the Graham disciple waits patiently for the storm to subside, knowing that a sunnier and more plentiful time is bound, as a law of nature, to resume in due course. When it does, having purchased fifty-cent dollars, the value investor is now well positioned to sell each of these cheaply acquired dollars for $1.00 or, in a particularly "sunny" market, even $2.00 or more.

Charles Brandes, CFA, an exemplary value investor whose company Brandes Investment Partners manages over $34 billion in assets, has addressed this principle effectively in the most recent edition of his book *Value Investing Today*. Brandes, a Forbes 400 member who was tutored by Graham personally in the early 1970s, provides a useful summary of how one takes advantage of market fluctuations to maximize the initial margin of safety and the subsequent gains that such a margin enables:

> The stock price rises above and falls below the company's intrinsic value. These price fluctuations create opportunities for value investors. When the stock price of the company falls sufficiently below the intrinsic value, it creates a buying opportunity. . . . Value investors expect that over time, as others recognize the true value of the company, its share price will climb toward its intrinsic value. As this happens, the margin of safety shrinks. When the share price equals or exceeds the company's intrinsic value, the margin of safety has disappeared and the shares should be sold.[25]

Even Brandes, one of the living masters of the value investing discipline, does not claim to know *when* the "share price will climb." However, his decades of success with this method have endowed him with a large measure of confidence that it *will* climb. That is, the price of a security purchased with a substantial margin of safety will generally appreciate as the market eventually corrects the imbalance between the security's price and its underlying value. Of course, when it does, Brandes (like all effective value investors) is ready to sell at a substantial profit.

MARGIN OF SAFETY AND BOND SELECTION

With respect to most bonds, Graham determined that the margin of safety was usually readily apparent (however, considering that

Graham and Dodd devoted several hundred pages of *Security Analysis* to bond selection, there are many intricacies and exceptions that fall outside the purview of this summary). Essentially, along with the bond's price and coupon rate (the interest paid to the bondholder), it is determined by examing what Graham calls "earnings coverage"; that is, the number of times that the "fixed obligations" (i.e., all interest payments that the issuing company is obligated to pay on all its debt offerings) of the bond issuer are covered by its earnings.

However, as with stocks, it is imperative to examine the earnings record (of the company issuing the bond under consideration) over several years. Generally, Graham recommended computing an average of the past five years of earnings. In this manner, one can ensure that the current performance is in line with a reasonably long-term pattern of strong earnings that is likely to persist for the foreseeable future. As a rule of thumb, what Graham called "industrials" (i.e., bonds issued neither by railroads nor public utilities) should exhibit an earnings coverage ratio of at least 3.0—that is, an industrial company (e.g., Coca-Cola) issuing a bond should have annual earnings that are at least three times larger than all of its annual interest payments on all its bonds (and other forms of debt, if applicable). Bonds selling well under par (or "face value," which, in most instances, means less than $1,000 per bond) with strong underlying assets and earnings resemble underpriced common stocks in some respects (including the analytical framework with which they are selected).

SAFETY OF PRINCIPAL

As it is written in the value investor's bible (*Security Analysis*): "In security analysis the prime stress is laid upon protection against untoward (i.e., unfortunate) events."[26] Having experienced severe financial misfortunes in his youth and having witnessed all manner of financial folly on Wall Street, Graham grasped the danger of risking capital that one already had for the *potential* of additional capital.

While it is impossible to eliminate all investment risk, Graham's methods (particularly, but not only, the margin of safety) greatly minimize such risk by filtering out disadvantageously positioned securities from the outset. That is the primary reason why they have proven to be so successful. After all, it takes only a few large losses to decimate overall investment performance (or, at least, reduce it to a below-average market return), even if many other investments proved to be successful. As noted author and value-fund manager Robert Hagstrom wrote in *The Warren Buffett Way*,

> There are two rules of investing, said Graham. The first rule is *don't lose*. The second rule is *don't forget rule number one*." [27]

To help illustrate the importance of keeping one's principal safe while investing, it is instructive to think of the classic Aesop fable "The Tortoise and the Hare." According to the fable, due to his boastful overconfidence and poor judgment, the sprinting hare winds up losing the race to the comparatively slow but prudent and ever-steady tortoise. In Wall Street terms, the hare is the hotshot "cutting-edge" investor with his ear to the ground listening to all the latest rumors about which security is "set to pop." For example, the Wall Street "hare" made out quite well during the 1995–2000 "dot-com bubble" but then proceeded to lose almost everything when it burst. Meanwhile, investing "tortoises" like Warren Buffett were eschewing the high-flying Internet stocks for more workaday enterprises that were available at attractive prices (and wide margins of safety). Part of the reason why the "old-fashioned and boring" securities were so cheap was because they were being ignored by all the "hares" chasing securities issued by such distinguished high-technology enterprises as Furniture.com. As a former employee of the bankrupt company told CNET, "We would get an order for a $200 end table and then spend $300 to ship it. We never could figure it out."[28]

So, although the "hare" may have outperformed the traditional value investor in a year like 1999, once the bubble came and went, whose reputation and fortune fared better? Considering that many of the "revolutionary companies" behind the Internet stocks were bankrupt by 2002, is it likely that the hotshot speculative investor outperformed Buffett's annual average of 14 percent during that bubble? (For that matter, have such speculators outperformed Buffett during *any* bubble?) Following the example set by Graham, value investors are quite content with results that, in any given year, are likely to be strong but not necessarily spectacular (of course, their results are not immune to market crashes, and negative annual results certainly occur). However, over time the avoidance and minimization of large losses makes an enormous difference. This difference will be highlighted in further detail later in this book when the well-above-market-average performance of Berkshire Hathaway, the Sequoia Fund, Walter & Edwin Schloss Associates, and others will be examined. The common thread among these legendary funds is that they were and are run by Graham devotees—most of whom had the privilege of learning directly from Graham as students and/or employees.

Much of the power of the margin-of-safety concept lies in its wide applicability. It is something of an "all-purpose" risk-minimization tool with which one can proceed with a fair degree of certainty that, regardless of day-to-day price fluctuations, one's principal is likely to be secure. (After all, it is money that purchased securities representing an intrinsic value that the market had underpriced by a significant margin.) As such, it provides the desired safety without requiring elaborate (and usually inaccurate) forecasts of future price movements. In one of his acclaimed mid-1940s lectures at the New York Institute of Finance, Graham imparted the following wisdom to a class of Wall Street professionals:

> We find from experience, though, that where the past margin of safety that you demand for your security is high enough, in practically every such case future will measure up sufficiently close to the past to make your investment a sound one.[29]

Indeed, when rigorous application of the margin of safety is coupled with some measure of diversification (which smoothes out the impact of an occasional outlier that, despite carrying a strong margin of safety, fails to appreciate as expected), one is all but assured of a favorable result. That is why, as Lawrence Cunningham wrote, Graham's margin-of-safety concept is "the silver bullet of investing."[30]

With respect to safety of principal, it's important to note that the margin of safety is the value investor's primary but not exclusive protective mechanism. Depending on the situation, it cannot always be relied upon as a fail-safe indicator of safety without any additional context. In many instances, it must be assessed alongside other factors. Nonetheless, selecting securities with a significant margin of safety remains the value investor's definitive precautionary measure. As Warren Buffett told an audience at Columbia Business School in 1984 (for the fiftieth anniversary commemoration of the original publication of *Security Analysis*):

> You do not cut it close. That is what Ben Graham meant by having a margin of safety. You don't try and buy businesses worth $83 million for $80 million. You leave yourself an enormous margin. When you build a bridge, you insist it can carry 30,000 pounds, but you only drive 10,000-pound trucks across it. And that same principle works in investing.[31]

HIGH LIKELIHOOD OF SUBSTANTIAL APPRECIATION

Certainly, as its name suggests, the margin of safety's core purpose is to help protect investors from the permanent loss of capital that is the usual outcome of unsound speculation. Indeed, the practice of identifying sound investments through application of the margin-of-safety method is nothing less than a quantum leap forward in minimizing investment risk. However, contrary to the usual risk/reward relationship (i.e., the less of one, the less of the other), the wider the margin of safety, the lower the risk and the *greater* the potential for gain. For example, purchasing ABC security at a 50 percent margin of safety (i.e., the market price is only half of the calculated intrinsic value) provides both a bigger protective cushion *and* a larger profit opportunity than purchasing the same security at only a 20 percent margin of safety.

That is why Graham's margin of safety is far more than a smart concept; it is truly a paradigm shift in investment selection. It changes the traditional risk/reward dynamic permanently, as the wider the margin, the lesser the risk and the *greater* the reward. As value investor extraordinaire Howard Marks wrote in his recent book *The Most Important Thing,*

> Whereas the theorist thinks return and risk are two separate things, albeit correlated, the value investor thinks of high risk and low prospective return as nothing but two sides of the same coin, both stemming primarily from high prices. Thus, awareness of the relationship between price and value—whether for a single security or an entire market—is an essential component of dealing successfully with risk.[32]

The margin of safety has proven to be an effective method for assessing and measuring "the relationship between value and price" and how it is likely to affect the long-term performance of the investment opportunity under consideration.

In fact, it is the nucleus of the ingenious analytical framework through which Graham, like a Wall Street alchemist, transformed the speculative madness of the market into a methodical and reliable way of earning strong returns on one's capital. He determined how to leverage the market's short-term folly, so destructive of wealth for so many investors, to the longer-term investor's great advantage. He determined that the optimal way to capitalize on this short-term versus long-term price discrepancy was to recognize strong intrinsic value when the market was neglecting such value and, consequently, assigning a discounted price to the security. Then, as outlined above,

Graham would wait to sell until the almost inevitable moment when the market *did* recognize the strength of the issuing company's earnings and/or balance sheet. However, the additional dimension here is that, at the point when the market recognizes its initial mistake, the pendulum often swings too far in the opposite direction, with the market inflating the security price well *above* the intrinsic value! That creates an opportunity to sell one's position (purchased earlier at a large discount to the company's intrinsic value—i.e., a large margin of safety) at a sizable profit.

Apparently, Graham had been practicing some form of the "sound securities at reasonable prices" approach since he was twenty-five (and probably even earlier).[33] One of the more illustrative margin-of-safety transactions of his early career involved Du Pont (the prominent US chemical company). Graham recognized an enormous discrepancy between the market price and the intrinsic value of Du Pont common stock in 1923. According to his calculations, the market price was roughly equivalent to Du Pont's ownership stake in General Motors. (The company had begun purchasing shares in the promising automotive company several years earlier and former Du Pont president Pierre Du Pont served as one of GM's first chairmen.[34]) Astonishingly, the market price disregarded Du Pont's own large (chemical) business and other large non-GM assets held by the company. About the large margin of safety offered by Du Pont stock, Irving Kahn and Robert Milne wrote: "In time, this anomaly ended with the market price of Du Pont rising to reflect the value of the chemical business."[35] So, in a classic value "coup," a twenty-seven-year-old Graham identified a significant margin of safety, took a position in the underpriced security, waited patiently for the market to correct its mispricing, and then, when it did, he proceeded to sell at a tidy profit.

Over twenty years later, Graham would apply the same fundamental approach to his investment partnership's purchase of 50 percent of the then-little-known Government Employees Insurance Company, or GEICO (yes, the very same insurance company that has since grown to the point where one rarely goes through a day without seeing and/or hearing a certain British-accented reptile!). Graham paid less than $750,000 for a half-interest in a company that proceeded to make Graham, and later Buffett, an enormous fortune. With respect to Buffett, some (but certainly not all) of his most legendary transactions were true "Beethoven's Fifths" of the margin-of-safety principle. Among the most notable in this regard is his 1973 purchase of 9 percent of the Washington Post at a margin of safety in excess of 70 percent. As Howard Marks wrote, "The concept of intrinsic value is so important. If we hold a view of value that enables us to buy when everyone else is selling—and if our view turns out to be right—that's the route to the greatest rewards earned with the least risk."[36]

A 1990 *New York Times* article reveals that, as with many other successful Buffett transactions, a wildly underpriced intrinsic value (i.e., a wide margin of safety) was Buffett's primary rationale behind the $10.6 million purchase:

> By his [Buffett's] calculation, the company was worth between $400 and $500 million, but the market valued its stock at only $100 million. "The people selling it to us were institutions," Buffett notes. "They probably would have come to the same conclusion about the intrinsic value that I came to, but they wouldn't have cared because they thought the stock was going down tomorrow." At the end of 1989, Berkshire's investment was worth $486 million.[37]

That is contrarian value investing at its finest. However, particularly in later years, Warren Buffett saw fit to modify the margin of safety principle to some extent. In particular, influenced by the thinking of Phil Fisher (the celebrated investor and author of *Common Stocks and Uncommon Profits*[38]) and the advice of Buffett's friend and partner Charlie Munger, he began to look at more qualitative factors (such as management integrity, uniqueness of brand, etc.) to assess value. This, in turn, led him to loosen the traditional Graham approach of purchasing securities cheaply to, in some instances, "buying a wonderful business at a *moderate* price."[39] Of course, that approach still revolves around an implicit margin of safety and he still sees his current work as rooted in Graham's approach. When I asked Mr. Buffett about some of his modifications, he replied:

> Well, what I do now and, it still has its founding in Graham, but it does have more of a qualitative dimension to it because, for one thing, we manage such large sums of money that you can't go around and find these small margins anymore. Ben would not have denied that, but he would say that what I do requires putting in a lot more effort and time than what would be available to the average lay investor.[40]

So, for the vast majority of investors (i.e., those without Berkshire Hathaway's enormous holdings and consequent need for large capital allocations), Buffett still recommends a fairly traditional application of Graham's margin-of-safety principle.

Of course, the margin-of-safety principle works equally well when investing in foreign securities. In fact, in some ways it can be even more powerful, particularly in the developing world, as the disparity between market perception and the true dynamics of the issuing company's business can be even more pronounced. I interviewed Tom Russo, one of the leading specialists in the application of value investing to global securities, and a partner in the highly rated value fund Gardner, Russo, and Gardner. Regarding the margin of safety and the high-growth developing markets, Mr. Russo observed that

> the margin of safety comes from the market myopia as the market certainly gets depressed about international markets from time to time. And then capital is very siloed and so there's really a very finite amount of capital that's dedicated to the developing emerging markets. So, when that becomes frightened and it disappears, the buyers strike and that can lead to vast swings and, in those swings, when greed falls behind fear and fear prevails, you can buy with a very high margin of safety.[41]

As Mr. Russo stated, "When greed falls behind fear and fear prevails," margin-of-safety opportunities abound, regardless of where one chooses to invest. Conversely, when greed prevails, strong margins become scarce.

In fact, in a broader application of the principle, as the margin of safety narrows across many stocks (or particular groups of stocks— e.g., tech stocks during the late 1990s), that can be an indication that a market correction is imminent. James Montier, a Graham-inspired asset-allocation professional at GMO, a large global-investment-management firm with more than $100 billion under management, sees the sharp market drop of late 2008, and 2009 through the prism of the margin of safety. In a recent *Wall Street Journal* article, Mr. Montier stated that from 2006 to early 2008, "people were acting with no regard to a margin of safety. Everyone was reaching for return and behaving very badly."[42] Indeed, market participants were disregarding long-term fundamentals in the pursuit of quick gains and, again, just as during similar periods during Graham's lifetime, this behavior laid the groundwork for an inevitable crash. As Mr. Montier continued, "We knew it wouldn't end well—just not when."[43]

So, almost eighty years after Benjamin Graham and David Dodd coined the term (and at least *ninety* years after Graham was applying some form of the concept), the margin of safety remains eminently relevant to the investor on multiple levels and contexts. The concept was the product of an intellect of unusual breadth and depth—one with a natural facility with numbers *and* a knack for solving complex problems with often (deceptively) simple and effective solutions. As described in the next chapter, both Graham's extraordinary intelligence and his uncommon capacity for independent/unconventional thinking were immediately apparent from the moment he started school.

CHAPTER 3
TOP OF THE CLASS

Graham's academic career launched inauspiciously with a brief but enjoyable tenure at a public kindergarten: "I remember only sitting in ecstasy before a box containing sand and a large shell, with which I played to my heart's content."[1] Unfortunately, due to the inordinate difficulty that five-year-old Graham had with the buttons on his pants, the teacher needed to accompany him to the restroom. Eventually, this became too much of an inconvenience for the kindergarten and Graham would have to wait until he was six and a half before resuming his official education. Revealingly, this state of affairs was a great annoyance to Graham: "I was very impatient to start, my brothers having taken insufferable airs because they were in school and I was still a baby."[2] It seems that his drive and competitive spirit had already found expression at a fairly young age.

In September 1900, Graham entered the first grade at New York City's Public School 157 on the corner of St. Nicholas Avenue and 123rd Street. Even though the subject matter consisted of learning letters and small words from index cards, Graham stood out immediately from his classmates. With respect to both aptitude and attitude, his teachers recognized that Graham was a student of uncommon caliber. At that time, elementary school classes were divided into two half-year sections, which commenced in September and January respectively. So, in fairly short order, Graham was advanced a semester ahead from Grade 1A to Grade 1B. This pattern was repeated in September 1902 when Benjamin Grossbaum was enrolled at the "primary department" of P.S. 10 on St. Nicholas Avenue and 117th Street, where he entered Grade 3A. By February 1903, Graham had advanced to Grade 4A (his teachers advising that he skip 3B entirely). In his memoirs, Graham recounts such instances with a subtle but evident pride:

> I spent just one term or half-year in the primary department, starting in the 3A grade in September and being skipped next February into 4A, which was the beginning of the grammar school proper.[3]

Graham was a stellar student throughout grammar school, although, by his own admission, he spent much of his time reading books entirely unrelated to the school curriculum. Characteristic of an insatiable intellectual hunger, such extensive "nonrequired reading,"[4] as he described it, became a lifelong habit. From his early schooldays through his forty-two-year Wall Street career, reading on a wide variety of topics (in an assortment of languages) became his primary passion. Moreover, during Graham's twenty-year semiretirement, when he had both the time and resources to engage in the hobby of his choice, he eschewed golf, yachting, and the like for time alone in his office reading, translating, writing, and otherwise engaging in the intellectual delights of the written word. As literary critic and University of California at Berkeley professor Seymour Chatman wrote in his introduction to Graham's posthumously published memoirs: "Graham's memoir also documents what many teachers suspect: that the best, and perhaps the only, durable education is self-education."[5]

Graham's intellectualism, both inside and outside the classroom, was evident to his family and classmates alike. Unfortunately, his remarkable mental faculties stood out in marked contrast with his physical awkwardness. Although he had little aptitude or interest in athletics, he (like all other students at the grammar school) was compelled to "participate fully in games and exercise of all sorts."[6] This caused considerable embarrassment for the young and somewhat sensitive Benny Grossbaum: "I did as much as anyone else, only I did so less successfully. Thus my ego was constantly being bruised."[7] In a particularly revealing passage, Graham writes of his reaction to external criticisms regarding his lack of physical coordination and apparent carelessness from his classmates and brothers:

> I was incurably absentminded, constantly given over to meditation or mere daydreaming. Hence, the angry cry from others that sounded so often in my ears: "Why don't you watch what you're doing!" or "Why don't you look where you're going?" These were rhetorical questions. If I ever had tried to explain that a little boy might have his head full of many intriguing ideas entirely peculiar to himself, and that these ideas prevented him from noticing the physical world around him—no doubt I'd have been treated as young Joseph the Dreamer was by *his* brothers, and perhaps I'd have deserved it.[8]

Nonetheless, despite the ongoing mental distraction of "ideas entirely peculiar to himself" (a nuisance of his youth that would prove to be the singular strength of his Wall Street career), Graham continued to perform brilliantly on his assignments and examinations. However, his absentmindedness proved to be an academic handicap in one notable instance: in Graham's sixth year of elementary school, the dreaded Maxwell examinations—the brainchild of New York's superintendent of schools, whom Graham recalls as "a forbidding character named Dr. Maxwell"[9]—were held across the New York City educational system. Graham's apprehension surrounding these examinations seemed to have been shared by others at the time. A 1905 letter to the editor of the *New York Times* from a W. S. Clinton condemned the rigors and structure of these examinations by observing that "cramming and a liberal education are altogether incompatible."[10] Graham proceeded to complete and hand in the five-question exam while other students were still working through the questions.

Unfortunately for Graham, it turns out that the exam actually had *seven* questions, not five. Thoroughly engrossed with the five questions on the blackboard in front of him, Graham failed to notice that the sixth and seventh questions were written on a blackboard at the back of the room. Of course, the teacher announced to the students that the last two questions were posted behind them but, by that time, it's likely that Graham was too captivated by the first question to even realize that the teacher was speaking. (From my interview with his third son, Benjamin "Buz" Graham Jr., it seems that this pattern of being physically in one place but mentally elsewhere lasted well beyond his schooldays: "He was a little preoccupied much of the time"[11]). Despite omitting two of seven questions from his exam, Graham's perfect score on the five questions that he did answer gave him a grade of slightly over 70 percent, which, incredibly, was the highest Maxwell examination score in P.S. 10!

The principal of the school called Graham in for a meeting and with a regretful tone admonished nine-year-old Benny Grossbaum with the following words: "If you had only *answered* those other two questions, you would have made a name for yourself—and for the school."[12] Indeed, if Graham had, it is likely that he would have scored the highest in the entire New York City public school system on the dreaded Maxwell examinations. Considering that quantitative analysis and writing were integral elements of his Wall Street career, it is also notable that the two subject areas of these exams in which he led his school were mathematics and English. Not surprisingly, this bittersweet success preceded yet another grade-skipping for a ten-year-old Graham who, uncomfortably, found himself in a 7A class surrounded almost entirely by twelve-year-old boys. Graham recalls that his classmates were not averse to ridiculing their younger "whiz kid" classmate.

More positively, Graham's extraordinary aptitude in mathematics was proving to be a lucrative skill (quite a number of years before it helped make his fortune on Wall Street). After tutoring his friend Chester Brown, whose mother hired Graham to tutor him three times per week, tutoring in mathematics (and other subjects) would be an important source of income for Graham for a number of years to come: Graham continued tutoring "more or less steadily until I ended tutoring the son of General Leonard Wood and of other officers at Governors Island."[13] He also continued to expand the volume and scope of his reading.

> I didn't care for the street life in the evening; the boys struck me as coarse and uninteresting. Thus I had plenty of time to read, and the amount I did seems prodigious. Each two weeks I would take four or five books out of the library, and in addition I consumed a number of proscribed but relatively innocent books that passed from hand to hand.[14]

He enjoyed classic authors of various origins and eras (Homer, Virgil, Shakespeare, Dickens, Alger, etc.), lighter and more contemporary works (e.g., the Nick Carter detective stories) as well as historical works about great men of the distant (e.g., the Roman emperor Hadrian) and less distant (e.g., Benjamin Franklin) past. As before, although the vast majority of this reading was extracurricular, it didn't seem to detract from his consistently stellar academic performance. Considering Graham's prolific literary output as an adult, it is also worth noting that, due to his outstanding academic performance, he was appointed editor of the school magazine, in which he published a "longish poem."[15] Graham proceeded to graduate elementary school as valedictorian of his class at P.S. 10, which was a matter of great pride to the eleven-year-old boy: "I was a proud boy when I made my Valedictorian's Address at the graduation exercises."[16] It's especially remarkable when one considers that almost all of his fellow graduates were at least two years *older* than him!

As the top graduate of P.S. 10, Graham was admitted with ease into the prestigious Townsend Harris Hall High School at Lexington and 23rd Street. Graham's class was one of the first to be placed in Townsend's accelerated program, initiated in 1904, in which the traditional four-year high school curriculum was to be covered in only three years. Over one hundred years later, Townsend (now located in the borough of Queens) is still one of New York's top-ranked high schools.[17] Despite its lofty reputation, Graham seems to have been unimpressed by the caliber of instruction. Of the two Townsend teachers that Graham could recall in his memoirs, only one was remembered for being a great teacher: "Eduardo San Giovanni, a holy terror of a Latin teacher, who really taught me that complicated language."[18] Graham's mastery of Latin and Greek (which he was also learning at Townsend) would further deepen his lifelong passion for Hellenic wisdom and literature: "The classical languages have given inestimable value to my inner life."[19]

In a synopsis of Graham prepared for Columbia University, Jason Zweig, a noted young value investor who contributed to the most recent (2003) edition of *The Intelligent Investor*, wrote that "one of Graham's favorite hobbies was translating Homer into Latin and Virgil into Greek."[20] Indeed, even Graham's investment books were laced with the wisdom of the ancients. Among the most prominent of his frequent classical references are the openings to *The Intelligent Investor* ("Through chances various, through all vicissitudes, we make our way,"[21] quoted and translated from Virgil's Latin poem *Aeneid*) and *Security Analysis* ("Many shall be restored that now are fallen and many shall fall that now are in honor,"[22] quoted and translated from Horace's Latin treatise *Ars Poetica*).

Aside from the Latin teacher, the other teacher whom Graham recalled from this time, a quiet and hilariously ineffectual geometry teacher by the name of Morris Raphael Cohen, was only unforgettable because of what he accomplished some years *after* he taught Graham: Cohen became a philosopher of some renown, whose classic work, *Reason and Nature*, the philosophically inclined Graham probably read at some point in his life. However, the "teacher" who made the most significant impression on the adolescent Graham was Constance Fleischmann, an eighteen-year-old college freshman who was staying with the Grossbaum family (during the time when Graham's mother was renting to boarders). She enjoyed giving French lessons to Graham for free: "No one could be kinder to a bashful boy than Constance was to me."[23] Notably, Graham's translation of one of the French poems he used to read with her sparked a new passion for him: "I have found much private satisfaction in making numerous translations from Greek, Latin, French, and German."[24]

Meanwhile, the twelve-year-old Graham was also studying the Hebrew portion for his upcoming Bar Mitzvah ceremony. Graham's recollection of his religious studies is a revealing exploration of his spiritual journey: He recounts that, in his youth, he once embraced many aspects of Judaism and then had quite a fascination with Christianity ("Jesus became my hero"[25]) but, ultimately, neither could meet Graham's standards of consistency and logic. So he dispensed *almost* entirely with both. From my interviews with his surviving children and relatives, it's clear that he did not observe any Jewish customs, which is reflected in the fact that two of his four long-term romantic relationships were with non-Jewish women (one of whom was a moderately observant Catholic). His values, like those of his children (and, perhaps not coincidentally, the Presbyterian-born Warren Buffett), were those of a thoroughly secular liberal Democrat. However, he still retained some feeling of affiliation with the Jewish people. As was told to me by Dr. and Mrs. Hamburger, a similarly nonobservant Jewish couple with whom he socialized in La Jolla (in the San Diego area) toward the end of his life: "He was not religious at all but he was still Jewish."[26]

Perhaps the most interesting aspect of Graham's reflections on his Bar Mitzvah is the fact that the usually well-behaved Graham (John Train describes the youthful Graham as "an industrious student and almost too good a boy"[27]) disobeyed his religious instructor's orders. In a rather brazen act of defiance, Graham stuck to a "stubborn refusal to deliver the usual speech of gratitude to parents and solemn commitment to the glories and observances of Judaism."[28] Judging from his memoirs, this reluctance did not stem from any resentment toward his mother but, rather, a widening gap between the precepts of Judaism and his own conclusions regarding theology. By his early teens, Graham seems to have already embraced a form of agnosticism in place of the religion of his birth. This is particularly remarkable considering the time period and considering that he was born into an *Orthodox* Jewish family.

Regardless of which religion one is born into, such questioning of one's "family faith," if it occurs at all, tends to take place considerably later in life. Clearly, Graham was already processing even the most sacrosanct and commonly-held beliefs that surrounded him through the rigorous and dispassionate analysis toward which his mind seemed to be inclined. Those ideas and conceptual systems that passed logical muster (according to him) were retained and those that didn't were discarded regardless of what those around him believed or how unconventional his conclusions might be. Graham's lucid passage rejecting religious dogma but accepting of some form of divine power, thereby placing him in neither the religious nor atheist camp, is illustrative in this regard:

> The contrast between man's undoubted need for religion and the dubious character of his religions is striking. It is hard to deny the existence of the Divine in the universe; but it is equally hard to accept any of the numerous conflicting doctrinal ways in which the Divine is said to have revealed itself to man.[29]

Clearly, Graham's observations regarding religion reveal the same intellectual courage and independence that would go on to set him apart from his peers in the realm of investment finance.

When, for various logistical and financial reasons, the Grossbaum family made yet another move (this time to the Bath Beach neighborhood of Brooklyn), the commute to Townsend in Manhattan became impractically long. So Benjamin transferred to Brooklyn's Boys High. This was a bit of a blow to Graham who, due to Townsend's three-year program (coupled, of course, with several skipped semesters), was on track to graduate from high school at fifteen! However, Graham came to realize that Boys High had its advantages as well. As Graham recalls, the school "had long enjoyed one of the highest reputations in the country for scholastic excellence, and I was fortunate indeed in being able to go there."[30] In its early twentieth-century heyday, the school produced such distinguished graduates as Isaac Asimov, Norman Mailer, and Abraham Maslow. Indeed, considering that Graham, who had become accustomed to topping his class, was "only" ranked third at Boys High, it was probably the most rigorous academic environment that he had yet encountered.

Aside from an unfortunate scheduling conflict that prevented him from continuing his Greek studies, Graham reflects that he had "two fruitful years at Boys High."[31] His continued scholastic excellence won him election to Arista (the honor society for New York high schools), and his literary endeavors took another step forward with the publication of one of his short stories in Boys High's annual bound volume of the school's best literary works. However, Graham, who was likely still smarting over his past humiliations in school sports, was proudest of a surprisingly significant athletic victory: beating out the captain of the school's tennis team. Graham actually won the school tennis tournament! Underscoring how much of an upset this was, when the athletic director presented Graham with his medal, instead of "Congratulations" he said, "How did you do it?"[32] Graham considered this athletic victory to be a "great personal triumph"[33] and he would go on to enjoy tennis for decades to come.

Having completed his courses at Boys High, Graham spent the summer of 1910 (just prior to his final year at high school) as a hired hand on a farm in New Milford, New York. It seems that Dr. Weaver, Graham's math teacher at Boys High, believed that a summer of manual farm labor was an enriching experience for "city lads" (especially, one presumes, bookish ones) like Benny Grossbaum.[34] So, for room and board, along with $10 per month, Graham set out for the farm of an intriguing man by the name of Jacob Barman. A German-born elderly man who had immigrated to the United States as a youngster, Barman had served with the Union Army and, as such, was a bona fide Civil War veteran. As the two months he spent on the farm in upstate New York contrasted so dramatically with the urban setting of his life before and (to a great extent) since that summer, Graham's memories of this time are especially vivid: "It was the complete change in my way of life, coming at an especially impressionable age that explains the sharpness and persistence of these recollections."[35]

Among the most memorable of these pertains to a cow named Lucy. It seems that Lucy was in heat and Graham was asked to take her to a bull on a nearby farm that would, as Mr. Barman characterized it, "freshen her."[36] A still-innocent Graham was asked to bring Lucy to that farm for the mating. His embarrassment was palpable as he stammered out an explanation to a young woman at the farm who asked what he had brought the cow for. Then, to add potential injury to insult, when he finally brought the cow to the bull, it was stamping around in its pen so feverishly that Graham was terrified for his life and headed straight back home with a very irate Lucy! Generally, that summer seems to have been an arduous ("I put in between sixty and sixty-five hours of steady work each week"[37]) yet not unsatisfying transitional period of Graham's life.

Aside from harvesting hay, milking cows, feeding chickens, and studying Greek literature after dinner, Graham's primary concern that summer was whether or not he would receive the Pulitzer scholarship. He had his heart set on attending Columbia University but, since the Grossbaum family was still destitute at this time, the scholarship was his only hope of being able to afford the tuition. Shortly before the end of his stay at the Barman farm, he was pleased to learn that he had placed seventh in all the greater New York City area on the Pulitzer examinations that he had written several months earlier. Considering that there were twenty Pulitzer scholarships available, the upcoming interview with the then editor-in-chief of the Pulitzer dailies seemed like a mere formality and he felt assured of his place at Columbia in the fall. Shortly after returning to New York City at the end of August, the interview was held at the Pulitzer offices on Park Place and, as far as Graham could tell, it was a success: "The interview went off very well, I thought, and I found it hard not to appear cocksure of the result, when I reported it to my family."[38]

So, when Graham discovered that he was *not* chosen, the news was, as he recalls, "more than a disappointment, it came as a horrible blow."[39] Graham's longtime hopes of being a Columbia Ivy Leaguer were utterly dashed. Furthermore, since he had friends who placed far below seventh on the exams that *were* accepted, Graham came to the logical (but, as events would prove, erroneous) conclusion that something went terribly wrong during the interview. On the surface, the interview seemed to have gone well and the interviewer even complimented Graham on his choice of favorite book, Gibbons's classic *The Decline and Fall of the Roman Empire*. So the sixteen-year-old Graham deduced that the interviewer must have detected the "secret deformity of my soul and awarded my scholarship to someone purer and better than myself."[40] In plain English, Graham believed that masturbation is what denied him his Pulitzer scholarship and, by extension, his entry to Columbia.

Especially since the passing of his father seven years earlier, Graham had become his own harshest disciplinarian. So, as a test of his own "strength of character,"[41] he refrained from these "bad habits"[42] for some years to come. This prohibition, coupled with the fact that, according to Graham's first cousin, Rhoda Sarnat (maiden name Gerard), his mother encouraged her three boys to "have a lot of affairs,"[43] helps account for the extent of Graham's infidelity once his first marriage began to founder. This behavior, of course, further complicated and undermined that marriage, and Graham's unfaithful tendencies would persist in subsequent marriages. Ironically, it seems distinctly possible that Graham's "character test" contributed to his most significant character *flaw* as an adult. This is unfortunate since, in all other respects, Graham's life stands as a model of exemplary, almost extreme, ethical conduct.

Having in his mind learned the moral lesson of this most painful rejection, Graham proceeded to enroll at the College of the City of New York (CCNY), which was considerably less prestigious than Columbia, considering the woeful financial state of the Grossbaum family. The fact that it was both local and free would render it the most attractive of the remaining postsecondary options. However, in fairly short order, finding himself at CCNY after almost ten years of consistently brilliant academic performance proved to be an unbearable humiliation:

> It was a free college, attended for the most part by poor students with rather low social standing and often lacking in polish. Also, they were preponderantly Jewish. To go there, instead of to Columbia, meant the acceptance of inferiority, the admission of defeat.[44]

In 1910, roughly two hundred students attended Columbia (the student body has grown almost eightyfold since!). Of this select group, few Jews were admitted. The data from 1910 is not available, but in the class of 1900 (a year in which New York City was roughly 15 percent Jewish), there were ninety-seven students, of which six were Jewish.[45] In fact, the student body was comprised almost entirely of the highest echelons of white Protestant stock (of predominantly English, Scottish, Dutch, and German ancestry). Such was the case at Harvard, Princeton, and all Ivy League institutions of that era. This was partly due to class and ethnic discrimination and partly to the fact that Jews and southern and eastern European (as opposed to French and Irish) Catholics were relative newcomers to America (at that time, Muslims and Hindus had yet to arrive in noticeable numbers, although a modest-sized Asian Buddhist community was present).[46] As such, these groups were not as well situated, in terms of social standing and finances, for Ivy League admission. That's why, among the less favored groups (of which Graham, being poor, fatherless, and Jewish, was certainly a member), Ivy League admission was prized as a mark not only of scholasticism but also of successful *Americanization*. As Graham wrote, "My own acceptance of these distorted values intensified my feeling of humiliation."[47]

Shortly after enrolling, Graham's discontent intensified to the point where he decided that he'd rather not be a student at all than continue to suffer the humiliation of studying at what he saw as a second-rate institution. So Graham looked through what was then the "Boy Wanted" section of the Sunday *New York Times* and found work on an electric doorbell assembly line. He found the work distastefully dull ("I took to reciting poetry to myself while I worked"[48]), so he opted for more interesting and lucrative employment at the L. J. Loeffler Telephone Company. The company manufactured phone systems for the upscale apartment houses that were being built on Fifth Avenue, Riverside Drive, and other prestigious Manhattan locales. The work was varied and somewhat challenging: "We shaped the heavier metal parts . . . polished hard-rubber push buttons . . . assembled elaborate wiring systems . . . [and] painted the thin film of gold."[49] Graham came to enjoy this work and, as someone with a reputation for being maladroit, took some pride in mastering these intricate manual tasks. Moreover, his natural inquisitiveness soon had him studying the operation and assembly of the company's telephone systems in considerable detail.

On a day when Mr. Loeffler was away, an electrical contractor called with a fairly complex question pertaining to the wiring system. Having studied the installation blueprints, the sixteen-year-old Graham was able to resolve the issue for him over the phone. As Graham writes, "From that time on I was Loeffler's fair-haired boy."[50] While Graham certainly felt more contented working at Loeffler's than studying at CCNY, he had not given up all hope for Columbia. In the fall of 1910, he had sent an inquiry to the school about applying for a scholarship to enroll in February. Columbia replied that there were no such scholarships for the second semester, but he was welcome to inquire in the spring of 1911 about a scholarship for September enrollment. So Graham waited patiently, working at Loeffler's throughout this time. Then, in April 1911, shortly after Graham sent in his second inquiry, he received a personal invitation from the dean of Columbia to meet at the dean's residence the following evening. As the dean did not give the slightest indication of what he wanted to discuss, Graham was both intrigued and, still having high hopes for being a "Columbia man,"[51] more than a little anxious:

The next afternoon I cleaned my grimy hands as well as I could with grease solvent, took the West Side subway from Fulton Street to 116th Street, and walked over to the Dean's residence not far away. With a thumping heart I rang the bell.[52]

Dean Frederick F. Keppel turned out to be a pleasant man who showed a genuine interest in Graham's work at Loeffler's. Several minutes later, he shared a startling revelation with the nervous teenager: Benjamin Grossbaum *did* win a Pulitzer scholarship the previous year for Columbia. According to the dean's explanation, the problem was that Graham's cousin, Louis Grossbaum, had been at Columbia for three years on the same Pulitzer scholarship. Apparently, the same last name (at a time when such names were relatively uncommon at Columbia) and the same scholarship led someone at the registrar's office to confuse the two applicants and deny Graham his scholarship because "they couldn't give a scholarship to a boy who already had one, so they gave yours to the next fellow in line."[53] The dean proceeded to assure a shocked Graham that they would award him an equivalent scholarship for the following academic year. In other words, the door to Columbia had been pried open once again!

The interview was over. I returned home in great excitement. There was boundless rejoicing in our Kelly Street household. But Mother repeated over and over as she wiped away her tears, "I'll never be able to forgive them for causing so much heartache to my Benny."[54]

Graham continued to work at Loeffler's all the way up to September, when he commenced his studies at Columbia. Not surprisingly, Graham "hit the ground running" and, instead of completing his four-year degree in three years (which was his initial goal, to make up for his lost year), he completed it in two and a half. Notably, while the alumni scholarship awarded to Graham covered tuition, he needed to rely on himself for pocket money, textbooks, and the like. Consequently, Graham's experience of college, particularly during the first two years, seems to have been a flurry of intense scholastic activity and various part-time jobs but little else:

> I had always dreamed of college life as the halcyon period of youth, a wonderful combination of education, friendship, romance, athletics, and all-around fun. Alas! Looking back at my own college career, I recall no such happy interlude.[55]

While it may not have been fun, Graham's time at Columbia was a seminal period of intellectual development that would yield considerable "dividends" (financial and otherwise) for the rest of his life. In this respect, Graham's most fateful decision at the Ivy League institution was electing to major in mathematics for his bachelor of science degree. He proceeded to take many courses in this area, and he so impressed his primary mathematics professor, Herbert Hawkes (who would later become Columbia's dean), that Professor Hawkes offered Graham a teaching position in the field upon his graduation (which, at the time, was not an uncommon practice for outstanding undergraduates). Although Graham's value-investing system does not involve or require the advanced level of mathematics he studied at Columbia, Graham's numbers-oriented (as opposed to rumor-oriented) approach to security analysis served him extraordinarily well. Moreover, his almost unique ability to strip away the obfuscation and superficiality of some financial reporting by formulating his own methods to arrive at more meaningful numbers has at least some of its roots in Graham's intensive mathematics coursework at one of the world's finest universities.

Aside from mathematics, Graham shined especially bright in German and English. His mastery of the latter would, like mathematics, become central to his future endeavors. Although his writing style has been criticized (unfairly, in my view) as overly "Victorian," Graham's talent for writing lucid and engaging English prose helped spur the dissemination and the adoption of his ideas on investment finance (and, to a lesser extent, macroeconomics). There's no question that Graham was a brilliantly original thinker but, had he not been able to communicate his original thoughts effectively, the impact of his contributions would have been greatly diminished. Certainly, it takes an inventive and independent thinker to formulate a principle like the margin of safety, but it takes a strong writer to convey such a principle in a manner that can be readily understood by "a dentist in Pocatello, Idaho, or a lawyer in Austin, Texas"[56] (as Warren Buffett described the intended readership of *The Intelligent Investor* to me). Indeed, it is doubtful that *The Intelligent Investor* would have sold over a million copies if Graham hadn't succeeded in that regard.

Meanwhile, he was also able to write other publications in a more technical style for more advanced students and practitioners of investment finance (*Security Analysis* is still the textbook of choice for some investment finance courses almost eighty years after its original publication). These abilities, coupled with the fact that he livened much of his writing with references to English (and classical) literature, demonstrate that his Columbia training in this regard served him well. For example, one of the English classes Graham took at Columbia was called "Daily Theme," in which each student was obligated to write a one-page composition on a particular subject due the following day. As Graham writes, "This was grueling work, but it certainly taught us how to write English."[57] The superlative quality of Graham's writing in these and other assignments did not go unnoticed by the professor, a man by the name of Algernon Duvivier Tassin (who would later become both a friend and a financial associate of Graham's). Professor Tassin told Graham: "I have never encountered so much insight and such power of precise, succinct expression in anyone your age."[58] Upon his graduation, another English professor, Professor John Erskine (an academic of considerable renown) offered Graham a full-time faculty position in Columbia's English department.

As for German, Graham became the first person to be awarded an A+ in a course covering the works of Goethe, Schiller, and Lessing— all read and discussed in the original language. Indeed, Graham's admiration for German culture reached its zenith at Columbia. He admired "its combination of scientific efficiency with poetic sentimentality."[59] A few years later, with the onset of World War I, he began to adopt a different view: "I conceived a violent dislike for the German 'Volkspsychologie.'"[60] By the end of that war, Graham had all but abandoned "a language and a literature which had once claimed my deepest interest."[61] However, Graham's son, "Buz," who lived with his father from 1947 until the early 1960s, told me that while the writers of ancient Greece and Rome were his father's favorites, Graham still enjoyed reading Goethe and other German authors from time to time. Regarding Greek and Latin, although Graham did not take classics courses at Columbia, he continued to read many of these works in his spare time (although one marvels at where he found any spare time). As a bachelor of science student with a penchant for the classics, he once got a friendly scolding from Dean Keppel:

> "Up to now," he remarked, "we had a saying around here that there was only one thing certain about a Columbia Bachelor of Science degree—that the owner didn't know Latin. Because of you, that's no longer so."[62]

Aside from mathematics, English, and German, Graham also took a variety of other courses and seminars, including a few in philosophy—one of his more recent passions. Once again, he must have made an outstanding impression on his professor, who, in this instance, also happened to be chairman of the department. In fact, Professor Frederick Woodbridge was the first of the Columbia faculty to offer Benjamin Grossbaum a teaching position in his faculty. In what seems like a superhuman feat of both discipline and intellect, Graham not only completed a four-year Ivy League degree in two and a half years, but he did so with such brilliance that three entirely unrelated faculties sought his talents as a full-time faculty member. That is remarkable enough as it is, but considering that Graham was working thirty-nine hours per week as a movie-theater cashier during his freshman year then forty or more hours per week in various positions at US Express for nearly the remainder of his time at Columbia (as well as less regular jobs such as tutoring and advertising sales), such an academic performance is the mark of an unusually, almost freakishly, quick and powerful intellect.

In light of all this academic and professional activity, it's not entirely surprising that Graham does not recall forging any strong friendships at Columbia. What is surprising is that Graham himself ascribes this lack of friends not to excessive work but to some kind of inscrutable personality quirk:

> I made no close friends at Columbia. Was it because I was too busy studying and working, or had something happened to my emotional life that precluded male chums or cronies? No doubt the latter; for this same deficiency was to mar all the years to come.[63]

True to another pattern that would characterize "all the years to come," Graham *did* manage to find time for women. A bit of a "late bloomer" in romance, it seems that Graham's first set of dates were arranged through his brother Leon. Unlike Graham, Leon was a smooth talker with a certain swagger that women found irresistible: "From time to time he had more girls than he could handle, so naturally he turned some over to me."[64] However, aside from a few innocent dates here and there (walking along the Coney Island boardwalk or seeing a movie), encounters with these women proved romantically uneventful, with one very notable exception:

One of those that Graham met through his brother was Hazel Mazur, a young Brooklyn girl who, just a few years later, would become his first wife. However, unlike the other women, Leon was actively courting Hazel, after an unsuccessful pursuit of her sister, and certainly did not intend to "turn her over" to his younger brother. Nonetheless, she seemed to fancy both Grossbaum boys and enjoyed the added thrill of flirting with the two brothers, quite literally, at the same time. Dr. Bernard Sarnat, whose family was close with Graham's family in the 1950s and who lived across the street from the Grahams in Beverly Hills, told me about when both Leon and Victor were over for dinner at the Grahams' house. Naturally, the three brothers reminisced about their early life in New York City. Dr. Sarnat recalled that the whole table got a good laugh from hearing Leon and Benjamin recount their mutual courting of Hazel: "She would walk down the street smiling, holding hands with Leon on one side and Ben on the other."[65]

To add to the confusion, according to Graham's memoirs, it seems that their Cousin Lou also fell under Hazel's spell after ridiculing the two brothers for "this double courting of the same girl."[66] Under such circumstances, it is hardly surprising that nothing of substance developed between the mischievous young Hazel and *any* of her bewildered suitors, including Benjamin. As well, soon thereafter, Hazel left for Boston for a full year. During that year, Graham finally had what he humorously describes as a "more concentrated romance."[67] Judging from his memoirs, it was Alda Miller, not Hazel, who was Graham's first true love: "I shall always remember Alda with deep affection and some compunction."[68] Several decades before the advent of "free love," premarital dating rarely involved sex, particularly among those who considered themselves "respectable" (and Graham was certainly eager to maintain respectability). However, it seems that Graham's relationship with Alda was not entirely innocent. As Graham writes: "There were, however, some experiences in the Miller hammock whose details the reader must imagine, though we remained virgins."[69]

At that time, Graham assumed that he would be going to law school for three years following the completion of his bachelor of science degree. At that time, marriage before gainful employment was almost as taboo as premarital sex. So, to Graham, continuing the relationship with Alda under such circumstances would be an unbearably frustrating distraction. As he wrote in his breakup letter to Alda,

> Desires were sharpening that we had no hope of satisfying. I wrote that she was so much in my thoughts and blood that I could not do justice to my college work.[70]

Following Alda, there was what Graham describes as a "shallower"[71] relationship with a "less interesting girl,"[72] possibly an allusion to losing his virginity. Then Hazel returned from Boston, and so began the prelude to their long, fruitful, but ultimately tragic union.

Graham concluded his studies at Columbia (and what would turn out to be his final year of formal schooling) in a flurry of honors and employment offers. Aside from graduating second in his class, he was elected to Phi Beta Kappa (the academic society honoring excellence in the liberal arts), nominated for Sigma Xi (the academic honor society for sciences—this was kept from him due to a misunderstanding about how long he had been at the school), and, as mentioned above, he was offered full-time teaching positions at Columbia's Mathematics, English, and Philosophy Departments. Intrigued by the possibilities of an academic career but concerned about the relatively low starting salaries, Graham decided to consult with Dean Keppel, a man he both trusted and respected, regarding such matters. Considering that Graham had withdrawn from the only economics course he ever enrolled in just a few weeks after its commencement (as for finance courses, they hardly even existed at that time), it's likely that a Wall Street career was not even "the last thing on his mind," but, rather, was not on his mind at all.

However, in a truly fateful concurrence of events, shortly before his meeting with Benjamin Grossbaum, Dean Keppel had been meeting with Alfred Newburger, the senior member of the Wall Street firm Newburger, Henderson, and Loeb. As Irving Kahn and Robert Milne describe in *Benjamin Graham: The Father of Financial Analysis*:

> By coincidence, a member of the New York Stock Exchange came in to see Dean Keppel about his son's woeful grades and, in the course of the interview, asked the Dean to recommend one of his best students.[73]

So, in the spring of 1914, the newly minted Columbia graduate began his full-time professional career as a junior bond salesman for a modest-sized Wall Street firm—humble beginnings for the man who would be lionized as "the Dean of Wall Street." However, in remarkably short order, Graham's extraordinary skills in quantitative analysis would enable him to scale the heights of investment finance. Some of Graham's most essential methods of quantitative analysis will be explored in the following chapter, "Numbers Don't (Usually) Lie."

CHAPTER 4

NUMBERS DON'T
(USUALLY) LIE

It would be difficult to overestimate the importance of Graham's choice of major at Columbia. After all, the core of his value-investing approach is a rigorous "numbers don't lie" quantitative analysis of issuing companies' (those companies issuing the security—i.e., stock or bond—under consideration) financial statements. All parameters that may reflect upon the true financial health of a company and, by extension, its issued securities, are quantified as thoroughly and accurately as possible. Due to his comfort with numbers, Graham was willing to "roll up his sleeves" and dig deep into annual reports, historical financials, and other documents that other investors might either ignore or eschew for just a few "headline" numbers. Graham's more extensive quantitative analysis often uncovered internal facts and dynamics that would indicate that those headline numbers were, in fact, much worse or much better than they seemed on the surface.

As an Ivy League mathematics graduate, Graham had a facility with numerical analysis that was uncommon on the Wall Street of that era. Interestingly, when John Train discussed what kind of investor is likely to enjoy success with Graham's methods, he highlighted three traits: "common sense, a mathematical bent, and patience."[1]

Of course, as the *original* value investor, Graham also had sufficient courage and inventiveness to leverage his numerical-analysis skills to develop his own investment-selection methodology, one entirely at odds with the prevailing wisdom of "the Street." While other analysts of his time were looking at securities' price trends (i.e., the fluctuations in the price of particular bonds or stocks), Graham was more interested in the true underlying value of those securities, as determined by his own analysis. For example, most Wall Street firms might have looked at the pattern of stock prices for ABC, Inc., stock to determine whether or not it would be a good time to buy more of that stock. Instead, Graham would look at ABC, Inc.'s financial statements and any other information he could get his hands on. He would, in a sense, "diagnose" the underlying health or sickness of ABC, Inc., as a business, examining its earnings, debts, management, and other factors, regardless of the stock price. He would proceed to estimate a value for ABC, Inc., based upon that analysis.

Graham would proceed to convert that value into a per-share estimate of value. Then, as described in chapter 2 ("The Margin of Safety"), if that analysis yielded an estimated per-share value of $4.00 and ABC, Inc.'s stock was selling for $2.00, he would urge his firm to buy. Conversely, if that ABC, Inc., stock was selling for $6.00, he would urge his firm to not buy and, possibly, to sell any holdings of ABC, Inc., that the firm had acquired before. As touched upon earlier, Graham knew that the way the market priced a security at a given point often had little to do with the underlying value of the business that the stock or bond represented. So, regarding those who claimed to be able to project specific prices (or ranges thereof) over specific future periods, Graham was very skeptical. After all, if the present price is based on a mix of unpredictable factors, many of which pertain more to emotion and mass psychology than anything else, how could anyone expect to predict future prices accurately? As Graham and Dodd write in *Security Analysis*:

The placing of preponderant emphasis on the trend is likely to result in errors of overvaluation or undervaluation. This is true because no limit may be fixed on how far ahead the trend should be projected; and therefore the process of valuation, while seemingly mathematical, is in reality psychological and quite arbitrary. For this reason we consider the trend as a qualitative factor in its practical implications, even though it may be stated in quantitative terms.[2]

QUANTITATIVE VERSUS QUALITATIVE

Regarding the distinction between qualitative and quantitative factors, Graham's position was clear but nuanced: the strength of brand name, the state of customer/employee relations, and other intangible accounting items (often grouped within the term "goodwill"), as well as quality of management were not immaterial, but they were also not sufficiently quantifiable and reliable to be given much weight in assessing a company's value. As Thomas Kahn (current manager of acclaimed value fund Kahn Brothers, a contributor to the fourth [1973] edition of *The Intelligent Investor*, and one of Irving Kahn's three sons) told me when he was interviewed for this book:

> Graham did not like to meet managements. He would say, "So, I meet the guy and he has a moustache and I don't like people with moustaches. It just puts me 'off the scent,' it confuses me."[3]

As far as Graham was concerned, the most meaningful "scent" to follow in investment analysis is the issuing company's published financial statistics. Nonetheless, while such data was, in his view, the most significant, he was not blind to its limits.

In the modern age of automated stock screens, where one can enter various parameters and then have a terminal or an online system spit back a laundry list of results, Graham's nuanced view is important to bear in mind. As Lawrence Cunningham cautioned, the modern value investor does not want to become an unwitting "bottom fisher,"[4] that is, an investor who identifies "very low priced businesses"[5] that, despite carrying a strong margin of safety and other favorable quantitative characteristics, are actually "dying fish"[6] that provide little of the long-term appreciation enjoyed by successful value investors. As Graham (and Spencer B. Meredith) wrote in *The Interpretation of Financial Statements,* security selection "requires a skillful balance between the facts of the past and the possibilities of the future."[7] Assessing the latter, of course, can involve more than merely projecting beyond past performance indefinitely to predict future performance. So, while Graham believed that a company's recorded financial performance must meet certain standards even to be worthy of consideration, the final selection may entail other factors. Expressing this principle in the form of a mathematical precept, Graham and Dodd wrote that "a satisfactory statistical exhibit is a *necessary* though by no means a *sufficient condition* for a favorable decision by the analyst."[8]

Graham's primary "gatekeepers" for both stock and bond selection were all quantitative due to his belief that such factors are much more conducive to a mathematically sound investment-selection approach than factors that were difficult to measure in any kind of standard (and therefore, comparable) manner. Graham recognized that quality of management, brand recognition, and other such factors could be of great significance. However, he felt that such factors would already be reflected in the company's financial performance. For example, if an enterprise suffered from incompetent management, sooner or later that would translate to declining sales, declining profitability, high levels of debt, and other "symptoms" of poor management that would find ample expression in that company's balance sheet and income statement. So, according to Graham, even if one were to make the dubious assumption that one could determine a numerically sound method of weighing such factors ("The standards by which they are measured are to a great extent arbitrary and can suffer the widest variations in accordance with the prevalent psychology"[9]), such a weighting would essentially be redundant.

INDEPENDENT QUANTITATIVE ANALYSIS

Particularly in an era in which one can obtain almost endless amounts of secondhand investment analysis with a couple keystrokes and mouse clicks, Graham's admonitions about doing one's own homework seems almost prescient. The following quote from the (original) 1934 edition of *Security Analysis* is likely to resonate with those who, like me, have suffered the experience of investing in a heavily promoted "no-brainer" only to end up feeling like one: "The public buys issues which are *sold* to it, and the sales effort is put forward to benefit the seller and not the buyer."[10] Applying Graham's independent quantitative analysis is an excellent way of filtering out those aggressively sold securities that, despite their popularity, are fundamentally unsound. However, the greater danger (particularly for the value-oriented investor who, for the most part, has already developed a healthy aversion to "hot stocks"[11]) is not the siren call of suspect stock promoters. Rather, it is the body of professional opinion offered by allegedly credible investment and economic "experts."[12]

As Charles Brandes wrote in the 2004 edition of *Value Investing Today*, "Be wary of adopting *others'* optimistic views on particular companies even if those others are professional analysts."[13] Brandes goes on to clarify that "analysts have, on average, predicted an earnings growth rate nearly three times the actual rate."[14] As well, there is solid empirical data establishing that, overall, those investment analysts who publish rosier reviews and recommendations earn higher salaries and enjoy more frequent job advancements than their more subdued counterparts. An extensive *Journal of Finance* study published in 2003 (in the wake of various dot-com analyst coverage controversies) concluded that the brokerage houses that employ many of these allegedly independent professional analysts tend to prefer "relatively optimistic analysts presumably because they help promote stocks and hence generate investment banking business and trading commissions."[15]

Notably, an earlier study, published in the *RAND Journal of Eco-*

nomics, demonstrated that similar financial and career advantages were held by those analysts who engage in "herding"; that is, those who avoided "forecasts that differ markedly from the consensus."[16] Since the consensus (particularly in the dot-com era) often proved to be disastrously incorrect, the fact that analysts are incentivized to adhere to it is troubling. However, even in instances where analysts appear to be completely independent, it is likely that the publication or program that communicates their views relies on advertising dollars from brokerage firms and other entities that, in general terms, would prefer that people buy as many securities as possible. As well, it is impossible to ascertain what other personal relationships, biases, and other such factors (all unrelated to the fundamentals of the issuing company's business) may be influencing an analyst's views. So Graham recommended sticking as closely as possible to the original sources: "The analyst should consult the original reports and other documents wherever possible, and not rely upon summaries or transcriptions."[17]

GRAHAM'S ESSENTIAL QUANTITATIVE COMMON STOCK SCREENS

Graham believed that investors can be divided into two primary categories: defensive investors and enterprising investors. While the former are primarily concerned with minimizing risk and earning a satisfactory return without expending much time and effort, the latter are less risk averse and more willing to invest significant time and effort for a return that is somewhat better than satisfactory. That is why Graham wrote that the defensive investor could also be thought of as a "passive"[18] investor and the enterprising investor as "active or aggressive."[19] Since both the objectives and the capabilities of defensive and enterprising investors differ in significant ways, Graham customized a set of quantitative screens for each.[20] As a general rule of thumb, if you do not intend to devote more than two or three hours to your investments each week, it's advisable to stick to a defensive strategy. Otherwise, you may choose to adopt the somewhat riskier and more time-intensive approach of an enterprising investor.

SCREENS FOR THE DEFENSIVE INVESTOR

Graham's screens, as articulated in *The Intelligent Investor*, are highlighted below and applied to leading toymaker Mattel's data (as of December 20, 2011):

- **Size:** Investors should look at companies with at least $550 million in annual sales (roughly the current equivalent of the $100 million cutoff Graham suggested in the last [1973] edition of *The Intelligent Investor* that was published during his lifetime). However, it should be noted that, according to noted value investor Jason Zweig's commentary in the most recent (2003) edition of the book, the modern defensive investor "should steer clear of stocks [of companies] with a total market value of less than $2 billion."[21] Mr. Zweig also suggests that the modern defensive investor can circumvent Graham's original restrictions on investing in small companies by "buying a mutual fund specializing in small stocks."[22] I am more partial to the first modification than the latter. However, I will leave it to the reader's discretion to determine if it is best to remain absolutely faithful to Graham's original size screen (adjusted for inflation) for the defensive investor or to adopt one or both of the modifications suggested by Mr. Zweig. Applying this criterion to Mattel, its market capitalization is $9.43 billion,[23] well in excess of both Graham's and Zweig's requirements.
- **Financial Condition:** The current assets figure on the balance sheet (representing all of the company's assets that can be con-

verted into cash within one year—cash, inventory, marketable securities, etc.) should be at least double the current liabilities figure on the balance sheet (representing all of the company's short-term debts that are due within one year—such items as short-term bank loans, accounts payable, etc.). Applying this test to Mattel, the result is 2.39,[24] which means that the company passes this first test of financial health.

Another important test of financial health is ensuring that the long-term debt figure on the balance sheet (representing all debt obligations maturing beyond a one-year time frame: various forms of notes payable, bonds, etc.) is not larger than the working capital (alternatively referred to as net current assets) figure (calculated by subtracting the current liabilities figure from the current assets figure). Mattel's long-term debt is $950 million;[25] slightly over half of the value of its working capital figure of $1.877 billion.[26] So Mattel passed both tests of financial health for the defensive investor.

- **Earnings Stability:** The issuing company must have generated positive earnings in each of the past ten years (i.e., it has shown no losses for at least ten years). Earnings summaries of the past ten years reveal that Mattel meets this requirement as well.[27]
- **Dividend Record:** A consistent record of uninterrupted dividend payments over the preceding twenty-year period. A review of Mattel's record of dividend outlays confirms that the company passes this test as well.[28]
- **Earnings Growth:** Over the past ten years, per-share earnings should have increased by at least one third (33.33 percent). In order to smooth out anomalous years, Graham insisted that the beginning and end figures (upon which this screen is applied) are the three-year average earnings figures of years 1 through 3 and years 8 through 10 respectively. Regarding Mattel, a comparative view of its earnings per share (EPS) in 2010 relative to its 2000 EPS indicates earnings growth of 161 percent[29]—several times the required 33.33 percent minimum.

- **Moderate Ratio of Price to Assets:** The market price for the stock under consideration should not exceed the net book value figure (representing the issuing company's total tangible assets minus its total liabilities) per share by more than 50 percent. Mattel's stock price is $27.83,[30] and its book value per share is $7.71.[31] Therefore, its price to assets ratio is 3.61—80 percent higher than the maximum of 2.0 stipulated by Graham.

- **Moderate Ratio of Price to Earnings:** The price to earnings (P/E) ratio should not exceed 15. In other words, the stock should not be priced at more than fifteen times its earnings per share. So, if the earnings per share of a particular company is, for example, $1.00, the stock price should not exceed $15.00. The reader will recognize that both this screen and the preceding screen have their roots in the margin-of-safety principle addressed in chapter 2. Mattel, with a P/E of 13.75,[32] passes this requirement.

These screens are designed to filter out stocks marred by any or all of the following weaknesses: insufficient earnings, poor financial health (i.e., lacking liquidity, carrying too much debt, etc.), and excessive price relative to intrinsic value. As Graham clarifies in *The Intelligent Investor*, these screens are deliberately rigorous and exclusionary: "They will eliminate the great majority of common stocks as candidates for the portfolio."[33] Even Mattel, which passes all but one of the above tests, is not considered to be sufficiently safe for the defensive investor.

SCREENS FOR THE ENTERPRISING INVESTOR

As one would expect, the screens for the enterprising investor (who, by definition, is less risk averse and more willing to devote the time and effort to making more frequent portfolio decisions) are both fewer and less severe than those for the defensive investor. Perhaps the most notable omission for the enterprising investor is a minimum size requirement, thereby enabling such investors to invest in smaller and less-established companies. However, even for the enterprising investor, the ever-cautious Graham still insisted on some significant tests of safety, strength, and value. These screens are highlighted below and applied to ITT Corporation's ("a diversified leading manufacturer of highly engineered components") data (as of December 21, 2011):

- **Financial Condition:** The current assets figure on the balance sheet should be at least 1.5 times the current liabilities figure on the balance sheet. At 1.6,[34] ITT's ratio of current assets to current liabilities meets this requirement. Regarding debt, total long-term debt should not exceed 110 percent of the working capital figure. ITT's long-term debt is 1.354 billion,[35] only 82 percent of the value of its working capital figure of $1.649 billion.[36] Clearly, ITT's financial health is satisfactory for the enterprising investor.
- **Earnings Stability:** The issuing company must have generated positive earnings in each of the past five years. A review of ITT's earnings performance confirms that it has met this requirement.
- **Dividend Record:** There must be some current dividend paid on the stock, but dividend history is not considered. ITT meets this requirement as well.
- **Earnings Growth:** The most recent annual earnings figure must be greater (by any percentage) than that of seven years ago. A comparative view of ITT's performance in 2010 (the last fiscal year) and 2003 indicates that the company passes this test.
- **Price:** The market price for the stock under consideration must be less than 120 percent of the company's tangible book value per share. In the instance of ITT, its stock price is $19.50,[37] considerably less than its tangible book value per share of $36.87.[38]

So, ITT passes all five tests for the enterprising investor.

It is important to note that despite the greater appetite for risk among enterprising investors, Graham's suggested screens for this group ensure that such investors' activities stay well within the realm of investment (as opposed to the speculative transactions they may be tempted to engage in). In Graham's view, the defensive and enterprising investor alike must be "willing to forego brilliant prospects,"[39] that is, the (generally) vain and self-defeating hope that a particular investment will "hit the jackpot." Instead, as discussed earlier, by making a series of prudent purchases of attractively priced securities with strong growth potential, the enterprising investor is well-positioned to profit from the market.

GRAHAM'S ESSENTIAL QUANTITATIVE BOND SCREENS

Graham's screens for bond selection are appropriate for all lay investors, defensive or enterprising. As stated in *Security Analysis*, the safety of bonds, a form of debt issued by companies to provide them with additional capital, "depends upon and is measured entirely by the ability of the debtor corporation to meet its obligations."[40] Indeed, the issuing company must demonstrate that it has sufficient resources and earning power to cover interest payments on its bonds and other "fixed charges" (i.e., expenses that recur consistently as part of the regular course of business, such as insurance payments and the like). That is why Graham lists the screens for bond selection in *The Intelligent Investor* as "coverage standards."[41] It is important to note that these screens are applicable only to "investment-grade" bonds; that is, bonds that are generally rated triple A or double A by the major ratings agencies (i.e., Moody's and Standard & Poor's). Despite the shortcomings of these ratings systems (especially evident in the aftermath of the 2008–2009 financial crisis), it is probable that Graham would have still recommended their use—but only as an initial screen. The following coverage standards are then applied to these highly-rated "investment-grade" bonds.[42]

MINIMUM "COVERAGE" FOR BONDS

FOR INVESTMENT-GRADE BONDS

Minimum Ratio of Earnings to Total Fixed Charges:

- The total fixed charges (i.e., fixed and recurring expenses such as interest payments on bonds) of bond-issuing utilities must be covered at least four times by earnings before taxes (calculated as the figure arrived at by taking the average of the earnings before deducting income taxes for each of the past seven years or, alternatively, for the poorest year in the past seven years). For railroads, fixed charges must be covered at least five times (seven-year average) or four times (poorest year). (Due to a number of changes that have reshaped the transportation industry, relative to Graham's time, railroad bonds are both scarce and pricey. Although sound railroad-bond investment opportunities still exist, the focus on these securities in *The Intelligent Investor* and *Security Analysis* is somewhat anachronistic from an early twenty-first-century perspective.)
- For industrial bonds (i.e., those issued by industrial businesses such as General Motors, General Electric, Coca-Cola, etc.), the minimum requirements are seven (seven-year average) and five (poorest year), and for retail businesses (such companies as Walmart, Nordstrom's, McDonald's, etc.) five (seven-year average) and four (poorest year).
- For after-tax earnings (i.e., after deducting income taxes from annual earnings), the coverage requirements are 2.65 (seven-year average) and 2.1 (poorest year) for utilities, 3.2 and 2.65

for railroads, 4.3 and 3.2 for industrials, and 3.2 and 2.65 for retail businesses.

Regarding industrial bonds specifically (which, for most readers, is likely to be the primary focus of bond selection), Graham believed that, aside from sufficient coverage requirements, the company should be of "dominant size"[43] within its particular industry. In order to fulfill this requirement, the issuing industrial company does not need to be the undisputed leader of its industry, but it should be *among* its leaders in overall "business volume"[44] (as opposed to one of the second- or third-tier competitors that, as Graham recognized, are generally less well-protected "against adverse developments"[45]). A healthy stock/debt ratio is another primary bond screen. This consists of the market price of the issuing company's common stock relative to its debt; this ratio helps assess the degree of protection that the company's more "junior" securities (i.e., common stock) provide to its more "senior" securities (i.e., bonds and preferred stocks). Graham and Dodd advised a minimum ratio of 1:1.[46] While earning power, not assets, is the central measure of safety for industrial and retail bonds, property value (as represented by balance-sheet asset figures) is an important measure of safety for bonds issued by public utilities, and real-estate and investment companies.

These are some of the most essential screens. Applying the primary industrial bond screens to the agricultural/food-processing giant Archer Daniels Midland (ADM), one arrives at a fairly strong indication of whether or not ADM's bonds pass Graham's rigorous safety tests. Examining ADM's data as of November 2011,[47] a seven-year average of ADM's ratio of before-tax earnings to total fixed charges is 5.8, and the ratio for its poorest year was 4.65. Both of these metrics fall short of the required levels of 7 and 5, respectively, preferred by Graham. Regarding its *after*-tax earnings to total fixed charges ratio, ADM's 4.02 (seven-year average) does not pass the minimum 4.3, but its 3.2 figure for its poorest year is just sufficient to meet that requirement. Certainly, with respect to dominant size and business volume, the Fortune 500 stalwart is more than adequate. However, with common stock valued at $6.64 billion and long-term debt valued at $8.27 billion, ADM falls far short of Graham and Dodd's minimum 1:1 stock/debt ratio. So, despite passing three important tests (poorest year of after-tax earnings, dominant size, and business volume), overall, Graham would consider ADM's bonds to be unsatisfactory for the standards of a prudent investor.

However, according to Jason Zweig's commentary to the 2003 edition of *The Intelligent Investor*, Graham's advice regarding individual bond selection is not quite as widely applicable as it was when the fourth edition was first written:

> In 1972, an investor in corporate bonds had little choice but to assemble his or her own portfolio. Today, roughly 500 mutual funds invest in corporate bonds, creating a convenient, well-diversified bundle of securities. Since it is not feasible to build a diversified bond portfolio on your own unless you have at least $100,000, the typical intelligent investor will be best off simply buying a low-cost bond fund and leaving the painstaking labor of credit research to its managers.[48]

ONLINE SCREENING TOOLS

In Graham's time, conducting a thorough screening of the market, or even a particular segment thereof, was a fairly arduous process. Fortunately, modern technology has simplified and expedited this process to a remarkable degree. Utilizing free screeners provided by the major search engines (Google, Yahoo!, and MSN/Bing) and some financial publications (such as *Kiplinger's*), one can usually construct a passable Graham screening mechanism. Paid services, such as those provided by value-oriented investment resources (AAII.com, ValueLine.com, Morningstar.com, etc.), make it much easier to apply a more comprehensive set of value criteria. For example, AAII.com (the website of the American Association of Individual Investors) has a number of Graham-derived screens (with some minor adjustments) that can help one apply the screens above with greater speed and less effort. Nonetheless, such online resources, whether paid or free, are best used as intended—that is, as *screens* only, not as security-selection mechanisms.

DIVERSIFICATION AND THE DEFENSIVE INVESTOR

Regarding Graham's classification of lay investors into defensive and enterprising: for those readers who place themselves in the former category, a word of caution is in order regarding the next step in the value-investing process. According to Graham, it is imperative that the defensive investor conduct the multifaceted screening that he formulated for such an investor in *The Intelligent Investor*. However, as opposed to the enterprising investor, whose next objective will be finding the most promising individual opportunities among the successfully screened securities, Graham believes that the defensive investor would be better served by minimizing such work and opting for diversification instead:

> This matter of choosing the "best" stocks is at bottom a highly controversial one. Our advice to the defensive investor is that he let it alone. Let him emphasize diversification more than individual selection.[49]

In his commentary in the 2003 edition of *The Intelligent Investor*, Jason Zweig recommends that modern defensive investors place 90 percent of their investment funds in an index fund (a fund modeled after a market index such as the S&P 500), leaving 10 percent with which to select their own individual securities. Such an approach is probably sensible for most defensive investors despite the fact that all components of an index do not necessarily adhere to Graham's principles. Nonetheless, since all represented companies tend to be large and well established, indexing generally provides a strong measure of both safety and diversification. Moreover, as a "passive" form of fund management (in the sense that an index fund merely replicates the composition of an existing market index (such as the S&P 500) and does not need to hire professionals to make independent investment-allocation decisions), index-fund management fees are considerably less expensive than those of actively managed mutual funds.

However, the defensive versus enterprising dichotomy is really more of a spectrum than a strict binary "either/or" classification. So, over time, the defensive investor may consider raising the percentage of personally directed investment funds well above 10 percent. After all, as more experience (and, hopefully, confidence) is gained with the value-investment selection process, it can be both educational and profitable to build on that momentum in a prudent, but steady, manner.

SCREENING, THEN *STUDYING*

The screens summarized above compose the part of Graham's approach to investing that is likely to be of greatest relevance to the nonprofessional investor. Graham developed many other screens, and the finer points of their application take up many of the 699 pages (including appendices) of *Security Analysis*. Certainly, if one is intent on becoming a full-time investor dealing with a wide variety of equity and debt investment scenarios, a thorough reading of this additional information would be worthwhile. Otherwise, the screens highlighted in this book are a suitable starting point for those eager to apply Graham's methods to the current field of investment opportunities. It is also important to clarify that the application of these screens is only the first step in the value-investing process. As connoted by the term "screens," Graham formulated them to identify which securities should be kept *out* of subsequent analysis.

So, even if the screening process eliminates almost all options and leaves the investor with very few securities to choose from, that does not necessarily mean that any or all of the remaining candidates are worthy of investment. What it does mean is that those securities that have failed to meet the screening criteria are definitely *not* worthy of any further consideration, let alone investment. Indeed, the screens save time and effort by providing a filtered list of stocks. Subsequently, the enterprising value investor can then apply more rigorous analysis on the screened securities in order to determine the final selection of promising opportunities or whether, in fact, there are any worthy candidates at all.

WHEN NUMBERS *DO* LIE

Graham's independent mind, coupled with his Ivy League training in mathematics, equipped him with both the inclination and the ability to pierce through the "smoke and mirrors" that can cloud important elements of corporate financial reporting. Of course, when undetected, such distortions of the enterprise's real financial picture can be costly to the investor. However, the *intelligent* investor can usually, as Graham put it, "avoid being deceived by these devices."[50] That is, if the investor is willing to follow Graham's example and take the time to look beneath some of the more malleable financial statement figures to determine their true substance. As Graham and Dodd wrote in *Security Analysis*:

> Deliberate falsification of the data is rare; most of the misrepresentation flows from the use of accounting artifices which it is the function of the capable analyst to detect.[51]

Indeed, much of *Security Analysis* pertains to deciphering financial statements. Graham's 1937 publication, *The Interpretation of Financial Statements* (cowritten with Spencer B. Meredith, then a security-analysis instructor at the New York Stock Exchange), addresses this issue (among others) item by item. According to its preface, the purpose of the book is to enable one to read the financial statements of a business "intelligently"[52] so that one becomes "better equipped to gauge its future possibilities."[53]

For example, when discussing the potentially misleading reporting of a company's intangible assets (i.e., nonphysical resources such as goodwill, intellectual property, etc.), Graham writes that "little if any weight should be given to the figures at which intangible assets appear on the balance sheet."[54] Instead, Graham counseled that "it is the earning power of these intangibles, rather than their balance sheet valuation, that really counts."[55] Similarly, Graham assails corporate reporting of property values ("the same misleading results which were obtained before the war by *overstating* property values are now sought by the opposite stratagem of *understating* these assets"[56]), the "book value" item on the balance sheet, meant to represent the value of all of the assets available for the security in question ("if the company were actually liquidated the value of the assets would most probably be much less than the book value [of the stock]"[57]), reported earnings figures ("look out for booby traps in the per-share [earnings] figures"[58]), and more.

Throughout his investing-related writings, Graham illustrates the chicanery behind some of these figures to devastating effect. A fine example of Graham's "quantitative diagnostics" can be found in the appendix of the first (1934) edition of *Security Analysis*. The problem of bond issuers massaging figures in order to "beautify" their debt offerings is highlighted through examining a mortgage leasehold bond issued by Waldorf-Astoria (the former hotel company). As Graham and Dodd demonstrate, by treating its heavy (and *fixed*) rental charges to its landlord as operating expenses, the company helped obfuscate the highly unfavorable (but certainly *material*) fact that the $11 million bond issue had roughly $23 million of "prior claims"[59] (i.e., debt that had a more senior claim on the company's assets than the more "junior" bond issue being sold to investors) in front of it!

In the 1973 edition of *The Intelligent Investor*, Graham devotes several enlightening pages to the multiple accounting "magic tricks" that he identified in ALCOA's 1970 earnings report. As the aluminum company's numbers tinkering is brought to light, Graham's sarcastic skepticism finds frequent expression. He puts forth the "question" of whether someone at ALCOA has been manipulating the books: "but always, of course, within the limits of the permissible?"[60] Graham was well aware of how some companies were intent on stretching their unethical accounting practices just up to, but not beyond, their legal limits. This tendency on the part of some corporations is why Graham's (and subsequent value investors') dissection of questionable stated figures is a vital element of the value-investing framework. In the case of ALCOA circa 1970, through a number of questionable "special charge-offs"[61] (i.e., management estimates of various "anticipated costs"[62] that, as Graham observed, "charged off before they actually occur, can be charmed away, as it were, with no unhappy effect on either past or future 'primary earnings'"[63]), the company was overstating its earnings by a significant margin. However, its books were so deliberately vague regarding the timing of these charge-offs (i.e., to which year they belonged), that it wasn't even possible for *Graham* to determine the company's true earnings for the year!

Another fine example in this regard is found in the fourth (1962) edition of *Security Analysis*. Graham (along with coauthors David Dodd and Sidney Cottle) scrutinizes Dynamics Corporation of America's stated earnings for the decade of 1951 through 1960. Among other flagrant distortions of Dynamics's financial performance during this time, Graham and his coauthors identified multiple "important items"[64] amounting to roughly $6.5 million (of the company's $13.5 million in stated earnings) that should have been deducted from income (which would have also reduced earnings) but were charged to "earned surplus" (profits that were not distributed as dividends) instead. The authors concluded that "in effect, its true earnings per share for the decade were only half the reported earnings."[65] While Dynamics is a somewhat extreme example, it helps underscore

Graham's focus on *true* earnings, the determination of which often entailed adjustments to a company's *reported* earnings.

Graham was similarly concerned with deciphering a company's true book value, that is, the value of all assets available (i.e., assets minus liabilities) to the security under consideration. In *The Interpretation of Financial Statements*, Graham and his coauthor Spencer B. Meredith illustrate the potentially dramatic difference between book value and what Graham calls *net* book value:

> If you had not deducted the intangibles and had simply divided the $1,800,000 by the 17,000 shares you would have found the book value per share to be $105.88. You will note that there is quite a difference between this book value and the *net* book value of $76.47 a share.[66]

Financial "detective" that he was, Graham was able to look beyond first appearances (stock price, stated numbers, etc.) and, with his exceptional grasp of mathematics, identify the numerical "criminals" and determine the *real* state of a business's earning power and financial position.

While Graham's time at Columbia helped solidify this facility with numbers, it was his time at his first postgraduate employer, the investment house of Newburger, Henderson, and Loeb, that enabled him to develop, apply, and refine this unique form of quantitative analysis. In so doing, Graham not only founded the value "school" of investing but, as the very first security analyst (or *financial analyst*, as it has been known since 1947), Graham also founded a profession that would transform the investment world permanently. Meanwhile, other dimensions of Graham's life were also evolving rapidly as his "star" began to rise on Wall Street. This seminal period of Graham's professional, intellectual, and personal development is illuminated in the next chapter.

CHAPTER 5

THE ORIGINAL
SECURITY ANALYST

J ust a few months prior to Ben's graduation, the Grossbaum family abandoned their original Germanic-rooted surname for the Scottish-rooted (and more "American") Graham. Certainly, there are some Germanic names, like Goldstein or Rosenberg, that are usually more associated with Jews than with Christian Germans. As a general rule, Grossbaum belongs in the former category. (Of course, such generalizations don't always apply very well when one considers that one of history's leading "Nazi ideologues"[1] and administrators was the Lutheran-born Alfred Rosenberg.) Although the United States did not enter World War I until 1917, by 1914, anti-German sentiment across the country was rife as America began to provide all manner of munitions and supplies to British and French forces. Consequently, many Americans of German descent (the overwhelming majority of which were not Jewish) did, in fact, "Anglicize" their names to avoid discrimination. So Graham's later contention that his family changed its name primarily due to anti-German (as opposed to anti-Semitic) sentiment is plausible if not entirely believable.

Graham's memoirs reveal that, in stark contrast to his generally harmonious relations with gentiles as an adult, as a youth he felt that societal animosity toward Jews was palpable: "The problems experienced by Jews during my early years, even in America, were all too manifest,"[2] and he even wrote that "I cannot help thinking that on the whole it has been a great misfortune for Jews to be born Jewish."[3] Another fact that belies Graham's explanation for the name change is that, throughout the early twentieth century, even many Jewish immigrants with *non*-Germanic surnames were exchanging them for "nonethnic" names.[4] So, along with eliminating the stigma of a German surname during the "Great War," obscuring their *Jewish* identity by becoming "all-American" Grahams probably appealed to the Grossbaums on some (conscious or, more likely, subconscious) level.

While Graham's family may have been able to alter its "foreignness" easily enough, the more menacing and immediate problem of poverty could not be signed away with a stroke of Dora Graham's pen. However, due primarily to the considerable work of her three sons in various capacities, the Graham family had emerged from its previous destitution. Nonetheless, Graham described his postgraduate financial situation as "weak,"[5] and despite being a natural academic, he turned down three prestigious Columbia teaching offers for the first job opportunity that held greater financial potential. Between his application to law school and his enthusiastic acceptance of a starting Wall Street position, there can be little doubt that the trauma of extreme poverty was still fresh in Graham's memory. The depth of Graham's interest in literature, philosophy, and, most especially, the classics (i.e., the works of ancient Greece and Rome) suggest that, had his family not suffered economic ruin during his formative years, Graham probably *would* have accepted a position in academia.

With a tinge of regret (perhaps suggesting that some part of him wished that he had become a classics professor after all), Graham recalls how his family circumstances almost compelled him to become more materially oriented than the makeup of his personality would have otherwise preferred:

> My natural inclination, I believe, was always away from the material and towards the intellectual and even the spiritual side of life.

But the difficult conditions of my childhood affected me no less than my brothers; I became too conscious and respectful of money.[6]

Moreover, as Warren Buffett and Charles Brandes (both billionaire value disciples of Graham) confirmed when they were interviewed for this book, Graham was far from the typical "show me the money" Wall Streeter. Though dedicated to attaining a measure of financial security, Graham was not preoccupied with amassing tremendous wealth. Mr. Buffett said that

> Ben was really not fascinated with business to the extent that I am or some people I know are. It was one of many interests for him and one that he became particularly well known for. But it wasn't something that occupied his thinking all day, every day, at all.[7]

Similarly, Mr. Brandes recalls that

> the monetary interest, I think throughout Graham's whole life, was secondary. More of his interest was in knowledge and learning new things, looking at new potential techniques in investing.[8]

Perhaps most tellingly, Dr. Bernie Sarnat, who knew Graham especially well on the personal level, confirmed this view when I asked him about his former neighbor and family friend: "The thing about Ben is that he was basically not that interested in making lots of money. It was more intellectual for him."[9] Immersed in Wall Street, Graham soon developed a sincere interest in, even a passion for, the intellectual exercise of investing. This was immediately evident to those who were fortunate enough to attend his investing lectures, as it is to the modern reader of *The Intelligent Investor* and Graham's other classic writings in the field. However, while an eight-year-old Warren Buffett had already begun reading everything he could about investing, an *eighteen*-year-old Ben Graham had never even picked up a single book on the subject and had dropped out of the only economics course he had ever registered for at Columbia! So there's no question that, at its outset, the 1914 "marriage" of Graham and Wall Street was driven by financial necessity.

The Wall Street of roughly one century ago would still be recognized by citizens of the twenty-first century. A narrow street lined by towering buildings and filled with crowds of financial-services professionals making their hurried way back and forth, much of its essential character has remained the same. In fact, although Wall Street (as a city street) was established by the British some two hundred years earlier, and although the origins of the New York Stock Exchange can be traced back to 1792, the area that we are familiar with today began to take shape in earnest during the early years of the twentieth century. It was not until 1903 that the stock-exchange building moved into its present location on nearby Broad Street (in the same financial district where Wall Street is found today). Moreover, the early 1900s constitute the first period when truly gigantic fortunes were being made on "the Street." This is best exemplified by the likes of J. P. Morgan and other "blue-blooded" New York bankers. Although it was still several years before the "Roaring Twenties," 1914 is well within the period bookended by the 1907 panic (when multiple banks underwent bankruptcies due to en masse withdrawals by nervous depositors) and the 1929 crash. So, when Graham stepped onto Wall Street, America's financial center was in the midst of a generally positive era of long-term growth.

However, it is interesting to note that 1914 still stands as the most tumultuous year in the history of the New York Stock Exchange.[10] The exchange was entirely closed from August 1 to December 12—over one third of the year! Aside from the regular holiday and weekend closings, the exchange has only closed one other time before in its 196-year history. However, that instance, a reaction to the panic of 1873, lasted a mere ten days. With the outbreak of World War I in Europe at the beginning of August 1914, a more severe panic gripped Wall Street. With so many US securities held by Europeans, in the wake of a massive European war, a mass Wall Street sell-off began. To prevent further hemorrhaging, the New York Stock Exchange

(NYSE) governors proceeded to close the exchange temporarily. Graham recalls these extraordinary events and how, within a few months, due to the war orders coming in to the United States from France and Great Britain, "the economic picture changed quickly from gloom to boom."[11]

Although Graham's employer was not among the largest firms on the street, Newburger, Henderson, and Loeb, founded in 1899, was sufficiently well established to provide Graham with a strong entrée into the world of high finance. A 2009 *New York Times* piece on a then ninety-nine-year-old Bob Newburger (son of original partner Alfred Newburger), confirms that the firm, aside from launching the career of "the Dean of Wall Street," attained a significant level of recognition on Wall Street, independent of its association with Graham (who is not even mentioned in the article).[12] Closing in 1970, the firm was a sizable, if not a formidable, presence on Wall Street for seventy-one (mostly) successful years. It seems that its ultimate demise was due, at least in part, to compromising the generally conservative principles that the firm's original partners upheld (at least during Graham's seven-year tenure at the firm).[13]

From the outset of his employment, the firm inculcated the impressionable newcomer with a cautious view on the allocation of investment funds. For example, at his very first meeting with Alfred H. Newburger, the most senior partner of the firm, Mr. Newburger concluded the interview with some sage advice: "One last warning, young man. If you speculate, you'll lose your money. Always remember that."[14] Of course, the value-investing approach that Graham would become famous for is the antithesis of speculation. Due to both experience and necessity, financial conservatism was already second nature to Graham. Nonetheless, he was fortunate to have secured employment at a firm where this prudence would (albeit with some vexing exceptions) be reinforced and occasionally well rewarded.

After a few weeks of training, Graham was working as a bond salesman for the firm. It seems that he was assigned to sell bonds (primarily of railroad companies) to businessmen in and around

Manhattan's financial district. Graham proved to be poorly suited to selling bonds but exceptionally well suited to *analyzing* them. Hardly the backslapping salesman, Graham was much more comfortable conducting independent analysis behind a desk than pitching financial products to a wide assortment of clients and prospects. As he told his employer, he just wasn't "cut out for a bond salesman."[15] In short order, he was also assigned the duty of describing each bond in what were then called "thumbnail descriptions." True to his inquisitive nature, he got his hands on any reading material that he could find regarding bond analysis, most notably *The Principles of Bond Investment* by Lawrence Chamberlain. A masterfully comprehensive text on bonds, Chamberlain's was the definitive volume on the topic until it was permanently supplanted by Graham and Dodd's *Security Analysis* in 1934. Graham aptly describes *The Principles of Bond Investment* as "a ponderous tome in every sense."[16] Especially from a twenty-first-century perspective, Chamberlain's work is impressively thorough but somewhat dated in its style (e.g., "no other form of security is so readily convertible into coin of the realm"[17]).

Frustrated with his lack of success as a bond salesman, Graham informed Alfred Newburger's colleague and brother, Samuel, that he would leave the company to work at the "statistical department" (the early twentieth-century equivalent of an investment research department) of another firm. Considering how poorly he was performing as a salesman, he was shocked to find that, instead of being relieved, Samuel Newburger was offended by his intention to leave the company. Graham insisted, "I'm sure I'd do better at statistical work."[18] To his surprise (and, presumably, delight), Mr. Newburger responded, "That's fine. It's time we had a statistical department here. You can be it."[19] His primary duty from that point forward would be assessing the relative strengths and weaknesses of varied investment opportunities for the benefit of his employer and its clients. So began Graham's career as a full-time analyst of Wall Street securities.

As Irving Kahn and Robert Milne recount, it didn't take long for Graham to distinguish himself in this area: "Ben's career as a distinctive professional Wall Street analyst dates back to the 1915 plan for the dissolution of the Guggenheim Exploration Company."[20] The dissolution was due to the decision of the Guggenheim family (the controlling interest of the company) to extricate itself from this business. Not surprisingly, the soon-to-be-dissolved company was viewed negatively by Wall Street and the price of its common stock suffered accordingly. However, Guggenheim actually held significant stakes in a number of NYSE-listed copper-mining enterprises—enterprises that, unlike the company, were in no danger of dissolving for the foreseeable future.

Graham brought to the attention of his superiors at Newburger, Henderson, and Loeb that the value of the pro rata shares of these enterprises to be distributed to Guggenheim stockholders upon dissolution offered an excellent arbitrage opportunity; that is, the market value of Guggenheim stock was less than the value of the copper-mining shares that it held so there was money to be made by purchasing the former (at its market price of $68.88[21]) while selling the latter (with an aggregate market price—i.e., the market price of each of the related copper-mining shares and other assets—of $76.23[22]). In other words, it was roughly equivalent to purchasing a basket of nine one-dollar bills for eight dollars. When the dissolution was executed in January 1916, the firm's one-man "statistical department" proved correct. Following Graham's advice, the firm itself had taken a substantial position in Guggenheim, as had a senior employee of the firm who paid Graham 20 percent of his profits from this transaction. That is why, according to Kahn and Milne, in the wake of the Guggenheim dissolution, "Ben's reputation and his net worth both grew."[23]

During his first few years at Newburger, Graham began developing his thorough and methodical approach to security (i.e., bond and stock) analysis and valuation. Unlike some financial theorists, Graham's thinking was never based on mere abstractions that read well on paper but had little bearing on reality. For Graham, a good approach was one that worked; after all, his job depended on it. As discussed in previous chapters, he had a facility with numerical analysis that was uncommon on the Wall Street of that era. As well, he had the requisite courage and innovative spirit to leverage his numerical analysis skills to develop his own security-analysis approach. Such an approach (which he later codified and refined to a much greater degree) was a far better way of selecting securities because it was based on extensive research and analysis of more tangible and significant factors than the stock price alone. Seymour Chatman, who wrote the introduction to Graham's memoirs, put it best when he wrote that Graham was "inclined to research at a time when research was not a serious project in brokerage houses."[24]

Indeed, it was Graham, the individual *Fortune* magazine credited with "inventing security analysis,"[25] who played a central part in making it a "serious project" (although some of what has since passed for "research and analysis" strays some distance from Graham's methods). Of course, such a research-intensive system involved more work than just noting stock/bond price trends, but Graham proved the soundness of his methods time and again with a series of safe but profitable transaction suggestions (such as the Guggenheim arbitrage opportunity) for his employer. These suggestions were the fruit of an analytical approach that even the Wall Street veteran partners of Newburger, Henderson, and Loeb marveled at. As Graham recounts in his memoirs, the timing for his then-unique investment approach was propitious:

> If I was fortunate in the assortment of talents I brought to financial analysis, I was equally fortunate in the epoch in which I entered Wall Street. When I started, investment was almost entirely limited to bonds. Common stocks, with relatively few exceptions, were viewed primarily as vehicles for speculation. Nonetheless, a considerable amount of window dressing began to be arrayed around common stocks, to impart some aura of respectability to what was previously considered a near relative of the gambling casino. Detailed information on operations and finances was beginning to be supplied by corporations, either voluntarily or to conform with stock exchange requirements. The financial services had begun

to present this material in convenient forms in their manuals and current publications.[26]

In other words, had he begun working at Newburger (or one of its competitors) even a few years earlier, Graham would have lacked the "detailed information on operations and finances"[27] that was the most essential ingredient of his "secret sauce." In fact, considering that Graham was a poor bond salesman and that he saw little merit in what other "statistical departments" were doing at that time, one wonders how long Graham would have remained on Wall Street if those were the only options available to him. Knowing that he lacked the gift for sales and seeing no way to make his mark in "price trending" methods that, in his view, were far too haphazard for successful consistent application, Graham developed his own approach (i.e., conducting an independent assessment of a security's intrinsic value and *then* looking at its market price). He must have known that what he developed required a level of intellectual energy and emotional discipline that few of his Wall Street peers possessed. So, once he had demonstrated that his approach worked, he must have sensed that he was no longer a mere employee but an indispensable asset to his employer.

Indeed, just as he leapfrogged his way up the academic ladder to an early graduation, Graham continued to win successive promotions, raises, and bonuses at Newburger with tremendous speed. By September 1916, Graham's weekly salary had risen steadily from his 1914 starting salary of $12 a week to $50 a week—at the time a *very* handsome weekly salary for a twenty-two year old. In a 1958 address to the Financial Analysts Society, Graham provides an illustrative example of another excellent investment suggestion that he provided to Newburger during this time. In early 1916, Graham strongly recommended the purchase of Computing-Tabulating-Recording, Corp., to Alfred Newburger personally. "C-T-R" stock was being sold for around $45, but according to Graham's calculations, its book value (i.e., the per-share value of its net assets, as indicated on the company's balance sheet) was in the neighborhood of $130. Moreover, its earnings were strong and it paid a healthy dividend as well. However, as Graham recounted to an audience of financial analysts, Newburger would have none of it:

> Mr. A. N. looked at me pityingly, "Ben" said he, "do not mention that company to me again. I would not touch it with a 10-foot pole." . . . So much was I impressed by his sweeping condemnation of Computing-Tabulating-Recording that I never bought a share of it in my life, not even after its name was changed to IBM in 1926.[28]

What is particularly interesting about this example is how the essence of Graham's system of independent fundamental analysis (i.e., examining a company's assets, earnings, and dividends to arrive at an assessment of value independent of market price) was already in practice some eighteen years prior to the publication of Graham's (and coauthor David Dodd's) *Security Analysis*. Of course, the example also illustrates that at that very early stage, Mr. Newburger was still skeptical of some of his twenty-two-year-old employee's ideas. However, the fact that his employer had more than quadrupled his salary within roughly two years is a strong indication of just how highly prized Graham (also known as "the statistical department") had become at Newburger, Henderson, and Loeb. So, with his financial situation relatively secure, in November 1916, he was engaged to Hazel, whom he had been seeing regularly for over two years. However, America's official April 1917 entry into the "Great War" seemed like it might delay the planned June wedding indefinitely.

Given Graham's strong sense of duty and as-yet unblemished record of admirable conduct, it is hardly surprising that he immediately set about gaining entry into the officer-candidate training camp being established in Plattsburg, on the northeastern edge of New York State. With characteristic thoroughness, he collected recommendations from the high-ranking generals whose children he had tutored over the years and "an especially enthusiastic one"[29] from the current assistant secretary of war, who happened to be none other than the former dean, Frederick Keppel! With such impressive recommendations in hand, Graham was certain that he would be admitted. However, since he was still a British subject and only US citizens were eligible for officer positions, the army rejected him as a matter of policy (it was not until 1920, when Graham's application for citizenship was accepted, that he became a naturalized US citizen).

This military rejection came as a blow to Graham, who "strongly felt the sense of patriotism which makes young men fight for their country."[30] After all, despite all the difficulties encountered by the Grahams in America (many of which stemmed from the tragically premature death of Jacob) and despite a measure of ethnic/religious discrimination, the country *had* fulfilled its promise of providing opportunity to this industrious immigrant family. Graham did not fail to realize this: "I considered the United States to be three-quarters my country then, and England to represent the other quarter."[31] His officer ambitions thwarted, Graham could still have joined the army as a private. As the primary breadwinner in the Graham household (his two brothers "earning comparatively small sums at the time"[32]), Graham could not have kept the family household afloat on a private's wages as opposed to the more substantial officer's wages, which would still have involved a drastic pay cut relative to what he was earning at Newburger.

So, claiming a legitimate exemption as his mother's "support,"[33] he continued working at Newburger while both of his brothers served in the army. However, as Irving Kahn and Robert Milne recount, Graham did join "Company M" of the New York State Guard, in which his "most active participation was marching to the Guard's band led by [the then-famous musician/conductor] Victor Herbert!"[34] Despite his concerted effort to enter the war as an officer, Graham's inconsequential participation in such a consequential war would be a source of personal embarrassment for many years to come. As he wrote decades later, "I have an unbanishable feeling that the part I played in World War I was far from credible."[35] At least his fiancé was pleased that the wedding could proceed as planned at her family's apartment on June 3, 1917, followed by a honeymoon in Virginia.

By 1920, Graham was the proud father of his first son, Isaac, generally referred to by his middle name, Newton (hereafter referred to as Newton I—to distinguish him from another Newton whom Graham would father some years later), and his first daughter, Marjorie. Even when describing these early and relatively happy years of his marriage with Hazel, Graham reveals where the fault lines were beginning to form. For example, when recounting the brief time during which his mother stayed with his new family and the friction that was generated between the two women in his life, he describes his wife as "energetic, conscientious, and dictatorial."[36] Notably, this description of Hazel correlates perfectly with what Marjorie Graham Janis recalled when I asked her about her late mother:

> She was a very bossy person but she was a self-taught moviemaker and photographer. She later helped many World War II refugees through her work at Hadassah [the Women's Zionist Organization of America]. She was really quite marvelous but she was difficult for me personally. When I was growing up, she would just be dashing everywhere and demanding this and that and the other thing, telling everybody, including her kids, what to do all the time.[37]

Fortunately, Marjorie got along much better with her father—"I absolutely adored him. I used to call him my walking encyclopedia"[38]— and her older brother, Newton—"he was a wonderful person and, as his younger sister, I felt that he would be there to protect me from anything that went wrong."[39] Moreover, despite her mother's overbearing nature, Marjorie recalls that her parents' marriage and the overall atmosphere in the home during those early years seemed to be reasonably happy. To be fair, by Graham's own admission, his long working hours would, like Hazel's bossiness, eventually prove to be a contributing factor to the failure of his first marriage. Indeed, when one considers how much Graham achieved during his Wall Street career, one wonders how he found the time for *any* kind of romantic relationship, let alone a marriage that would produce five children. Not only did he apply himself diligently to the investment business itself but, judging from his prodigious output, he must have spent a great many evenings and weekends during this period of his life writing and lecturing *about* investing.

Prior to the end of World War I, Graham's first official publication pertaining to investment finance was printed in a periodical known as the *Magazine of Wall Street*, a fairly prominent and widely read trade publication of the time. (However, Graham had already become a published author two years earlier when a piece that the twenty-one year old wrote about calculus was published in the *American Mathematical Monthly*.[40]) As Kahn and Milne wrote in 1977, Graham's first article on investing examined "the disparities among the prices of a number of quite comparable issues."[41] In other words, it helped the reader identify underpriced securities relative to their value. It's worth noting that this piece of quintessential Graham value investing, entitled "Bargains in Bonds," predates *Security Analysis* by fifteen years and *The Intelligent Investor* by no less than thirty years.

While continuing to work diligently for his full-time employer, Graham also became a regular contributor to the *Magazine of Wall Street*. His exceptional writing ability was also finding growing expression at the investment firm. In 1920, Graham wrote three pamphlets for Newburger, Henderson, and Loeb that he collectively titled "Lessons for Investors," one of which marked the (written) introduction of the "Margin of Safety" concept, the quintessential Graham principle. (At a speech that he gave several decades later, Graham reflected amusedly on the youthful hubris of publishing his "Lessons for Investors" pamphlets while still in his midtwenties![42])

As well, throughout most of his tenure at Newburger, Graham was the lead writer on a number of "circulars" (i.e., research reports that were *circulated* among current and prospective clients). As Milne and Kahn wrote, these circulars examined "one or more securities in detail,"[43] and the partners at Newburger were very impressed with the thoroughness of Graham's research, the soundness of his conclusions, and the unusual clarity of his writing style. As for the *Magazine of Wall Street*, the periodical was so impressed with Graham's fascinating and well-written insights on investing that its owner offered him a substantial salary to become the magazine's editor! Once again, Graham was tempted to leave Newburger but, to keep its rising star, his employer decided to make him a junior partner.

As a partner of Newburger, Henderson, and Loeb, along with his high salary, Graham was granted "a 2.5% interest in the profits, without any liability for losses."[44] These profits had a significant impact on his income, and he soon moved his young family out of the city to Mt. Vernon in affluent Westchester County, New York. The senior partners of the firm felt that this additional compensation for their young hire was a worthwhile investment. After all, they recognized that Graham had mastered a unique and surprisingly lucrative way of profiting from the mania of Wall Street. They were also impressed by his unquenchable thirst for additional knowledge with which to further "sharpen" his methods.

For example, once Graham began to appreciate the enormous impact of taxes upon the financial data that he was reviewing, Graham engaged in extensive independent study of this increasingly complex field. As he recalls in his memoirs, "After World War I, US tax laws and regulations—blessedly simple before—became increasingly complicated as well as onerous."[45]

Graham proceeded to become one of the most learned investment professionals in the field of American tax law as well as in other spheres of knowledge with a substantive impact upon investment data. Equipped with this kind of sophisticated investment knowledge, Graham began to engage in more complex investments involving arbitrage and hedging (taking both "long" [i.e., betting that an asset's market price will rise] and "short" [betting that it will decline] positions in the same asset so that, if the price declines dramatically, the loss may be at least partially offset by the other position) transactions.

For example, he would purchase convertible bonds (i.e., bonds that can be converted into the issuing company's common stock) while selling call options (i.e., the right to buy the common stock at a specified expiration data for a specified "strike" price) on the same common stock. Without delving into the intricacies and inverse relationships of these financial instruments, such an arrangement enabled Graham to make money as their prices fluctuated in either direction. With very few exceptions, such transactions proved highly profitable for the firm. In short order, Graham was assigned to work directly on behalf of a number of his firm's clients.

It was rare for senior partners to delegate that degree of responsibility to a junior partner, but Graham's performance was so extraordinary that they felt compelled to make maximum use of his moneymaking prowess with important clients. Moreover, Graham was beginning to bring in some significant clients of his own. For example, in 1920, a school friend of Graham's who was working at a prominent "bond house" of the era, introduced him to a young Japanese man by the name of Junkichi Miki. Mr. Miki represented a large Japanese investment bank that was interested in Japanese government bonds that had wound up in various European countries during Japan's 1906 war with Russia. There was considerable profit to be generated from purchasing such bonds in Europe and then reselling them to a more enthusiastic Japanese market. Through Newburger's connections in London, Paris, and Amsterdam, Graham was able to help both his firm and his new friend Mr. Miki by facilitating the purchase of the bonds and then shipping them to Japan: Newburger's 2 percent commission on these transactions amounted to $100,000 (roughly $2 million in current funds). Graham has fond memories of inviting Mr. Miki home to enjoy his wife's "Jewish cooking"[46] and, in return, being treated to his first Japanese meal at the Nippon Club in Manhattan: "To my own amazement, I found myself swallowing varieties of raw fish dipped in numerous sauces."[47]

Another personal relationship that would have significant financial and, eventually, professional consequences for Graham during this early period of his Wall Street career was his longstanding friendship with his former English professor at Columbia, Algernon Tassin. A few years earlier, impressed by his former student's burgeoning success with clever investments, Mr. Tassin proposed supplying Graham with $10,000 of capital (a very significant sum at that time) the profits/losses of which would be split evenly between the two men. At first, this arrangement worked out tremendously well, with both "partners" enjoying several thousand dollars of profits each. Graham, who enjoyed a close relationship with his brothers and was always eager to help them out, invested his profits in an Upper West Side phonograph store to be run and co-owned by his audiophile brother Leon.

When overall security prices took a steady drop throughout 1917, Graham's Tassin account was "called in for margin"[48] (when the price of a particular security, or group thereof, declines below a certain point, a *margin call* is made, at which point the account holder must either deposit additional funds or sell off assets). The problem was that Graham, who had anticipated better results for both the Tassin account and what proved to be a difficult (and ultimately short-lived) music retail enterprise, did not have the funds to meet the shortfall. This put Graham in the extraordinarily awkward position of having to inform a friend (one who had put his trust in Graham's investment skill and moral integrity) that he was unable to cover his share of the loss. More significantly, such an admission would also indicate that the investment-management approach he had executed for his former professor "had failed abjectly."[49] For Graham, this was nothing short of a nightmare scenario, and the emotional fallout was severe.

Graham's shame and anxiety proved so unbearable that he came perilously close to ending his own life: "I recall spending one of my lunch hours walking around the financial district in bleak despair. At that moment I thought, more or less seriously, of suicide."[50] The fact that he considered the ending of his own life to be less painful than the acute sense of failure and embarrassment that had engulfed him reveals much about Graham's character. Although he was not arrogant, there's no question that Graham had a strong sense of pride. To his credit, unlike others on Wall Street, Graham's pride was tied not only to his financial performance but also to a strong sense of responsibility and fair play vis-à-vis his employer and clients, and, in later years, his partners and employees as well. So his shame stemmed not only from a financial failure but also from a moral one. After all, Graham was unable to repay his share of the losses—a responsibility that was an essential element of the verbal agreement with his trusting friend and benefactor. Graham's strong (some would even say puritanical) sense of conscientiousness with regard to other people's money would characterize the whole of his forty-two-year Wall Street career.

Fortunately, Graham regained his courage and, instead of throwing himself in the Hudson River, he threw himself on the mercy of Algernon Tassin. Fortunately, Graham's friend, though shocked and dismayed, was sufficiently empathetic and forgiving to work out a payment plan to recoup Graham's share of the loss. Within two years, this debt had been repaid and, as recounted in his memoirs, "Tassin retained his confidence in me. . . . In later years I was able to build his fortune to quite a respectable figure."[51] True to Friedrich Nietzsche's oft-quoted maxim "what does not kill me, makes me stronger,"[52] the Tassin near disaster provided Graham with the necessary emotional fortitude against much worse circumstances a number of years later. Then, facing similar adversities on a much larger scale, instead of contemplating suicide, he was able to keep a level head and focus on minimizing the damage as much as it was in his power to do. However, he would still retain the same commitment to do right by his clients, and, like Mr. Tassin, all those who kept their faith in Graham ultimately found their loyalty *very* well rewarded.

As for Newburger, Henderson, and Loeb, they also found that their trust in their new partner was well placed. Aside from doing a spectacular job handling the duties of a "statistical department" (which now included a junior "statistician" assigned to work under the "senior" twenty-four-year-old Graham) and orchestrating increasingly complex and profitable transactions for the firm, Graham was bringing in a significant stream of additional business to the firm. According to Milne and Kahn, as Graham's reputation for profitable investments grew, "several clients opened accounts that allowed him, as sole manager (of these accounts), a 25 percent share in the cumulative net profits."[53]

However, as evidenced by the Tassin account, Graham's decisions were not always profitable. Although he already had demonstrated an unusual proficiency for shrewd and prudent investing, he was not always immune from the poor judgment (driven by emotion and incomplete analysis) that his Wall Street peers succumbed to more frequently. One of the best (and, fortunately, few) examples in this regard is Graham's investment in Pennsylvania Savold, a company that allegedly had the exclusive rights to a "patented process for retreading automobile tires"[54] across every US state except New York and Ohio. Encouraged by his friend Barnard Powers, who had just made a fortune on an oil stock, Graham put in a considerable sum of his own money as well as that of his former schoolmate Maxwell Hyman and Max's two brothers. Not only did Pennsylvania Savold fail to perform, but eventually Mr. Powers learned that "the arch-promoter who had managed all these flotations [issuances of stock] had diverted our money to other uses."[55] Later, Graham discovered that Pennsylvania Savold may not have ever even existed!

Although he had read and heard of many such incidents during his first couple of years on Wall Street, the Savold fiasco was the first time Graham had experienced this kind of brazen fraud himself. It must have hardened his natural skepticism and caution even more. In Graham's own words, he had allowed himself to get snookered into the Savold deal, "in spite of my innate conservatism."[56] In fact, the stock promoter's "fleecing" of Graham in this incident is mainly noteworthy as the exception that proves the rule, the "rule" being Graham's general prudence and extensive due diligence to check out thoroughly each and every investment opportunity—especially with respect to funds entrusted to him by his clients. That is why, in just a few short years, he was able to attract some significant clients to his money-management services with only word-of-mouth advertising. The growing number and size of these accounts was a significant boon to Newburger's bottom line because the firm would earn all the brokerage fees on these transactions. Moreover, as a junior partner, he considered it part of his duty to bring in additional clients to "his" firm.

From both a personal and a financial perspective, perhaps the most noteworthy of Graham's clients was Uncle Maurice Gerard (formerly Gesundheit). As discussed earlier, despite his rocky relationship with Graham's more unruly brothers (when Maurice's sister and her three sons had to move in with him many years earlier), Maurice always got along very well with Graham. Dr. Sarnat, Maurice's future son-in-law, recalled that "the two of them were close. They were a couple of intellectuals and I think they had a lot in common. So, although it was an uncle and nephew, it was really more like a friendship."[57] Maurice, who had long admired his nephew's extraordinary intellect, had been tracking Graham's impressive Wall Street career with great interest. As early as 1918, he had invested several thousand dollars into a Newburger account managed by Graham and had seen it appreciate handsomely. Then, in 1920, Maurice came to Graham with a "startling proposal."[58] He would add $20,000 (over $230,000 in today's money) to his account and retire, expecting to live off the combined power of his capital and his nephew's financial genius. His confidence in Graham's competence and probity was so immense that he never questioned any of his nephew's decisions regarding the account despite the fact that, according to Graham, his uncle was usually "a most interfering man."[59]

From business development to investment strategy, Graham was certainly making his mark at Newburger. As he recalls, by the early 1920s, his responsibilities as junior partner had expanded considerably:

> In addition, I handled all the operations of the firm for its own accounts (these being limited to arbitrage and hedging); I was the tax expert; I did the over-the-counter trading (including the Japanese bond operation); I was in charge of insuring the efficiency of the office systems; and, of course, I had a growing number of customers of various kinds who paid substantial commissions to the firm.[60]

Considering the range of vital functions that he was serving, as a partner with a 2.5 percent stake, it's hardly a surprise that Graham would soon consider establishing his own investment firm! After all, he had certainly proven (not least of all to himself) that he could handle both the administrative and the strategic dimensions of running such a firm quite well.

Finally, on July 1, 1923, a new business by the name of the Grahar Corporation was incorporated in the state of New York. (Note that, curiously, in his memoirs, Graham (or whoever typed Graham's notes for publication) refers to his joint venture with Lou Harris as the Graham Corporation while the account in Milne and Kahn's biographical sketch states that "the new business was incorporated as Gra*har* Corporation (Louis Harris being the major investor)."[61] Considering that Harris's other company was the Harris Raincoat Company, I find the latter name combination scenario to be more likely, which is why the venture is referred to as the Grahar Corporation in this book.)

Nine years after commencing work at Newburger, Henderson, and Loeb, and partially backed by his friend Lou Harris (a raincoat company owner whom the Grahams had befriended in Mount Vernon), Graham was now a founding partner and manager of his own investment firm. While he was happy with the change, there's no question that Newburger was the ideal launching pad for Graham's Wall Street career: the firm was large enough to possess the requisite resources for a wide range of investment opportunities but small and open-minded enough to provide a creative thinker like Graham with an unusual degree of independence and, eventually, authority. The principals at Newburger probably realized that this was the only way to keep such an independent-minded operator for as long as they did. However, his overall success over the next thirty-three years would demonstrate that, as far as business was concerned, Graham was most comfortable (and effective) leading (or coleading) from the front. After all, the constraints imposed by even the most accommodating employer could never be accepted permanently by an intellect as expansive and independent as Graham's.

No longer an employee, Graham was now a major stakeholder and primary manager at Grahar Corporation. As a business owner and manager himself, it became even easier for Graham to see securities and their issuers from the perspective of a private business owner (instead of merely a holder of stock), a paradigm that lies at the heart of value investing. After all, earnings, expenses, taxes, and other "accounting items" become far less abstract when they pertain to one's own business. This essential paradigm of Graham's (and later Buffett's) investment-selection approach is the focus of the next chapter.

CHAPTER 6

ALL OR NOTHING—
INVESTORS AS
BUSINESS OWNERS

I n the last chapter of *The Intelligent Investor*, Graham wrote that "investment is most intelligent when it is most businesslike."[1] Warren Buffett describes this pithy adage as the "nine most important words ever written about investing."[2] Indeed, the nine-word phrase encapsulates the investment-selection framework through which Graham, Buffett, Munger, Ruane, Schloss, Brandes, Kahn, and others all made their fortunes. Along with the margin of safety and "Mr. Market" (discussed in chapter 8), this concept is another essential dimension of what Lawrence Cunningham calls "Graham's foundational insight that price and value are different things."[3]

While almost all other market participants were basing their investment decisions upon near-term predictions of upward or downward movements in *price*, Graham looked at the businesses behind the securities as a prospective buyer would of the whole business. From this standpoint, he was concerned about the *value* of the issuing company, as reflected in its income statement and balance sheet. Only once he ascertained that did he look at the current price to determine what course of action (i.e., buy, sell, or hold) would be the most advantageous. Only if it made sense, hypothetically, to purchase the entire business at that price did Graham consider purchasing some shares to thereby own a piece of the business at an advantageous price. Similarly, with respect to selling shares, the decision revolved around the value of the business relative to the current market price. As Robert Hagstrom wrote, "In Graham's view, the appropriate reaction for an investor is the same as a business owner's response when offered an unattractive price: Ignore it."[4]

At least ninety years after Graham first applied it to his own investments, this business-owner's paradigm has continued to define the value-investing approach. As Pat Dorsey, an exemplar of a younger generation of value investors, told me,

> To me, the core insight of Benjamin Graham is that you view a stock as a piece of a business and, by doing so you remain focused on the cash the business will generate and on its balance sheet as opposed to the opinions of other investors in the market. The importance of that hasn't changed since Graham's time.[5]

In other words, instead of looking at ABC common stock and wondering whether or not to "buy a couple of shares" because one believes that the stock may "see some action" next week, Graham believed that it is better to view ABC common stock from the hypothetical viewpoint of whether or not you, as a business owner, would want to purchase *all* of ABC, Inc. Such a perspective is a remarkably effective filter, as it compels the investor to focus more on a company's income statement and balance sheet than on its stock chart. Moreover, although considering whether or not to purchase the entirety of such companies as Merck (current market capitalization of $101.39 billion), Coca-Cola ($152.04 billion), and Google ($188.45 billion) might seem like a bizarre abstraction, it's actually an invaluable mental process for conservative investors. The following example will help illustrate this principle.

Larry, an acquaintance of yours, owns an independent auto shop that has been in operation for over twenty years. He wants to sell a 10 percent interest in his business to you for $40,000 in investment capital. As a savvy businessperson, before parting with $40,000 of your hard-earned money, it is likely that you would want to obtain more than enthusiastic assurances about how "great" his business is. You would want to see precisely what the shop's profits have been over the past couple of years (i.e., income-statement information) and you'd probably also take an interest in the value of his assets and how much debt his business carries currently (i.e., balance-sheet information). So, even though you are not considering the purchase of Larry's entire business, you are likely to consider it from that perspective. If the economics are favorable from that vantage point, you know that the purchase of a partial share is worth considering. Conversely, if purchasing the entire business is likely to be a money loser, you will then extrapolate down to the 10 percent piece that you are considering acquiring.

When faced with a scenario like a prospective $40,000 investment in Larry's Auto Shop, most people are likely to delve fairly deeply into the earnings history and capital position of such a private business. Yet many of these same individuals will place significant investments of $1,000 or more in public companies based on nothing more than a thirty-second buy recommendation on a cable television program, an e-mail forwarded from a friend (which, at some point, originated from a stock promoter), or, most ominously, a "gut feeling." Neither Graham nor Buffett nor any of the other value-investing millionaires and billionaires made their fortunes by investing on such flimsy pretexts.

Instead, whether purchasing a fraction of 1 percent or (as Buffett and Munger's Berkshire Hathaway has done several times in recent decades) 100 percent of a company, these investors see themselves, first and foremost, as business owners, and they analyze the prospective investment opportunity accordingly. As Jason Zweig wrote in the 2003 edition of *The Intelligent Investor*, the leading value investors "are, mentally, always *buying the business, not buying the stock*."[6] He goes on to write that "their attitude, whether buying all or a tiny piece of a business, is the same."[7] In other words, the true value investor would deliberate on whether or not it is an opportune time to buy a couple of shares in Merck with the same degree of thorough business analysis that most people would apply only to a private business–investment scenario like Larry's Auto Shop. That, of course, is a primary reason why the investment history of "most people" is far less successful than that of dedicated value investors.

THE DECOUPLING OF PRICE AND VALUE

As is widely known, the fundamentals-based valuation approach illustrated above has long been standard for prospective buyers of private businesses (in whole or in part). What is less well-known is that, prior to the First World War, this businessperson's (or "businesslike") approach was also the norm for those who purchased shares of publicly listed companies. As Graham and Dodd wrote in *Security Analysis*:

> Another useful approach to the attitude of the prewar common-stock investor is from the standpoint of taking an interest in a private business. The typical common-stock investor was a business man, and it seemed sensible to him to value any corporate enterprise in much the same manner as he would value his own business.[8]

This change is reflected in Graham's own writings. In his very first published work on investing, the September 1917 *Magazine of Wall Street* article titled "Curiosities of the Bond List," Graham wrote that "as accurate as markets are, they cannot claim infallibility."[9] Writing at the end of World War I, Graham's observation about the market's general (but occasionally imperfect) accuracy was correct. Then, during the war boom and the ensuing "Roaring Twenties," this dynamic was altered dramatically and permanently. Whereas, prior to the war, the collective behavior of these investing businesspeople usually kept security (particularly common stock) prices well-anchored to a value reflective of the issuing companies' business fundamentals, the collective behavior of the postwar "speculative public"[10] left many security prices dangerously untethered to their underlying (or *intrinsic*) values, as they remain to this day.

So, like a balloon released into the air, security prices have since veered up, down, and sideways for a multitude of reasons, the vast majority of which are not material to the issuing company's long-term business fundamentals. Graham observed and recognized the decoupling of market price and underlying business value remarkably early. As early as November 1918, in such *Magazine of Wall Street* articles as "Hidden Assets of Consolidated Gas," Graham was writing about emerging divergences between business value and price that presented attractive investment opportunities. In that article, he wrote of how the lack of "speculative enthusiasm"[11] for public utility stocks had kept the prices of these securities (Consolidated Gas in particular) lower than the prices warranted by their long-term business fundamentals.

Similarly, almost fourteen years later, in an article for *Forbes* magazine written in the midst of the Great Depression, Graham observed that

> in good times the prices paid on the stock exchange were fantastically high, judged by ordinary business standards; and now, by the law of compensation, the assets of these same companies are suffering an equally fantastic undervaluation.[12]

Writing in 1932, the "good times" that Graham was referring to were the heady years of post–World War I Wall Street in which stratospheric prices, entirely indefensible from a business-fundamentals perspective, became the norm among common stocks. Not surprisingly, the same shortsighted investment public that facilitated such an irrational inflation of prices stampeded in the opposite direction after the 1929 crash and *de*flated many prices to well below their business values.

With relatively few market participants motivated primarily by long-term fundamentals, the news of the moment tends to obscure the more meaningful data. For example, short-term earnings reports often have a wildly exaggerated impact upon security prices. As stated in *Security Analysis*, security prices are "governed more by their current earnings than by their long-term average [earnings]."[13] The authors then highlight how such a dynamic diverges sharply from sound valuation practice among nonlisted companies:

> A private business might easily earn twice as much in a boom year as in poor times, but its owner would never think of correspondingly marking up or down the value of his capital investment.[14]

Applying that principle to your hypothetical 10 percent investment in Larry's Auto Shop, if after investing your $40,000 the shop manages to double its usual $100,000 earnings to $200,000 in such a "boom year," does that mean that the fundamental value of your 10 percent share has now doubled from $40,000 to $80,000? Such a dramatic reappraisal, based on only one year of unusually high earnings, would be unthinkable in the realm of private business.

However, in the stock market, such reappraisals occur for events that are even less substantial than that. Unexpectedly strong (or weak) quarterly earnings, high-profile lawsuits, public-relations fiascos (or triumphs), product recalls (major and minor), regulatory violations, and a variety of other events are all circumstances that tend to have a much greater impact on the fleeting whims of the investing public than on the long-term fundamentals of the issuing companies themselves. This is particularly well-illustrated by a 2005 study published in the *Quarterly Journal of Business and Economics* in which the extent and duration of impact of (nonautomotive) product recalls on stock prices were examined. Just as Graham would have anticipated, the average price impact was found to be both negative and statistically significant, but, from a long-term investment perspective, the duration of this negative price impact was less than sixty days.[15]

For the likes of Graham, Buffett, and others, a two-month-long price dip has little consequence because, as *investors* (not speculators), such a time frame is entirely *in*significant. As value-investor-extraordinaire Charles Brandes wrote in 2004, "Any contemplated holding period shorter than a normal business cycle (typically 3 to 5 years) is speculation."[16] As well, contrary to what many assume about the world's most famous Graham acolyte, Warren Buffett, is similarly detached from the market's short-term movements. As acclaimed author and investor Robert Hagstrom observed, Buffett "has no need to watch a dozen computer screens at once; the minute-by-minute changes in the market are of no interest to him."[17]

The problem with these minute-by-minute changes is that they are rarely anchored in events of long-term consequence. Once a negative or positive direction on a particular security has been set in motion by short-term earnings reports, product-recall announcements, and other seemingly earth-shattering (but, from a long-term perspective, largely inconsequential) news items, a herd mentality often sets in. For example, due to a recall of one of its many products, ABC, Inc., common stock declines by 5 percent initially. Then, as news of the recall and the initial selloff circulate further, ABC is down by 30 percent two weeks later.

However, within a year or two, ABC releases a particularly strong earnings report. Having examined the company's financial statements, the value investor has known all along that ABC is still a fundamentally strong business, and despite the earlier product recall, its customers are still purchasing massive volumes of high-margin products from ABC. However, to the same short-sighted investors who sold ABC due to the product recall, the positive earnings report is now a green light for everyone to pile on once again, but this time in the opposite direction. Consequently, the stock price ramps up from far below to far *beyond* its true business value.

Worse yet, with the advent of electronic computer networks (ECNs), day trading, and, more recently, high-frequency trading (HFT), the gulf between security prices and the underlying business realities that they are supposed to represent has widened even further in recent decades. In his 1999 book, *The Day Traders*, finance (and education) writer Gregory Millman devotes a chapter to what he observed at a day-trading "boot camp." In a particularly revealing passage, he recounts how the instructor advised the class to essentially ignore even *short-term* news and "wait and trade in the direction it (the stock price) goes. It's uncanny how often good news drives a stock down and bad news pushes it up."[18] As Lawrence Cunningham wrote, such trades are "related more to the motives of the trader than to the business value of the company."[19]

As for HFT, a 2009 study regarding its impact on US markets concluded that this form of trading accounted for as high as 73 percent of all US trades for that year.[20] Such trades are based entirely on whether or not a tiny profit can be made in trading a particular security over the next few seconds. The present power of the computers and algorithms being utilized in this approach enables what the *New York Times* describes as "a handful of high frequency traders"[21] to execute sufficient numbers of these microprofit trades to earn large profits. As with day trading, the calculus behind such trades, motivated only by the next anticipated micromovement of the stock quote, is hardly concerned with the long-term fundamentals of the issuing company's business. Clearly, the rapid technological transformation of the market has further marginalized the impact of long-term business fundamentals on the ticker chart.

However, throughout the recent decades in which these changes have taken place, value investors have still managed to prosper by viewing each security as a long-term business investment instead of as a stock quote that may decline by three cents in twenty seconds. Graham was always skeptical of methods that claimed to anticipate market movements with any degree of long-term reliability. The vast majority of those who have investigated such systems tend to agree with Graham on this point. For example, toward the end of *The Day Traders*, Millman concludes that "day trading is a very competitive, high-risk game. . . . With sufficient preparation, discipline, and capital, it is just barely possible to make slightly more winning trades than losing trades."[22]

Indeed, horror stories of day traders earning large sums of money only to lose much larger sums are just the modern-day equivalent of what Graham observed in the Wall Street of his time. Cautious and conscientious in money matters, Graham could never be comfortable with entrusting anyone's capital (especially his clients') in such a haphazard manner. Instead, he learned to purchase pieces of good businesses at reasonable prices (or not-so-good businesses at fire-sale prices) and ignore the day-to-day gyrations of the ticker chart as meaningless noise. A 2006 *USA Today* piece regarding the growing popularity of day trading among those looking for a quick and easy way to earn money surmised that "the chances of suffering big losses are much greater than the ability to generate gains over the long term."[23] That scenario is the mirror opposite of Graham's more prudent, business-oriented framework in which, from a long-term perspective, one is much more likely to wind up "generating gains" than "suffering big losses."

VALUE VERSUS VOLATILITY

The frequent divergence between price (as quoted by an often volatile and irrational market) and value (as determined by the investor's valuation of the underlying business) that Graham first wrote about almost a century ago is likely to remain a defining characteristic of the market for the foreseeable future. However, although he often wrote of the gulf between Wall Street's prices and underlying business realities with a blend of disdain and cynicism ("they are in no sense business valuations; they are products of Wall Street's legerdemain, or possibly, of its clairvoyance"[24]), this divergence was nothing less than the "rock" upon which Graham and his disciples built the value "church."

After all, if the market *had* maintained the link between share prices and their corollary business values, profitable value investing would be impossible. As Graham wrote in *The Intelligent Investor*, the value investor's purpose is to capitalize upon "a favorable difference between price on the one hand and indicated or appraised value on the other."[25] So, if the two become more or less the same (as they once were), both the number and the size of these price-value gaps would shrink considerably. Such a scenario, of course, would serve to undermine, even nullify, the profitability of value investing.

Indeed, the fact that security prices remain frequently (and sometimes wildly) disconnected from business valuations (or *intrinsic* value) is why the value investor can profit so handsomely from applying the margin-of-safety and valuation techniques highlighted in the second and fourth chapters of this book. As Pat Dorsey told me, "Mean reversion is the essence of value investing."[26] Each time a value investor decides to capitalize upon a significant price-value gap, that investor is placing a bet that the price will, sooner or later, make its way back up to a level that better represents the underlying business value (and often exceeds it). Regarding the interplay between market price and business value, Robert Hagstrom wrote that "those who can see the latter before the former catches up are in a good position to profit from their astuteness."[27]

As will be highlighted in subsequent chapters, one of the most impressive aspects of the value-investment method's historical performance is how consistently superior its gains are relative to more speculative investment approaches. While the latter revolve around the notoriously risky timing of price movements, Graham's approach bypasses this fool's errand altogether by purchasing businesses that the market has set at prices that are irrationally low and then letting the market reconnect with reality whenever it chooses to do so. So much of the "delta" between value investing and rival approaches pertains directly to this concept of investment decision making from a business owner's perspective.

By leveraging the contrast between the business owner's approach and the more speculative attitude of the wider market, the value investor is well-positioned to profit from the market. As Graham wrote in *The Intelligent Investor*,

The holder of marketable securities actually has a double status, and with it the privilege of taking advantage of either at his choice. On the one hand his position is analogous to that of a minority stock-holder or silent partner in a private business. Here his results are entirely dependent on the profits of the enterprise or on a change in the underlying value of its assets. He would usually determine the value of such a private-business interest by calculating his share of the net worth as shown in the most recent balance sheet. On the other hand, the common stock investor holds a piece of paper, an engraved stock certificate, which can be sold in a matter of minutes at a price which varies from moment to moment—when the market is open, that is—and often is far removed from the balance sheet value.[28]

SHAREHOLDER = BUSINESS OWNER

With the sly wit that he was known for off-screen (his on-screen persona in Marx Brothers films never spoke), Harpo Marx, when asked if he played the stock market, is rumored to have said, "I prefer the casinos in Las Vegas—the women are better-looking and the drinks are free." (Considering that his brother Zeppo met his wife while she was working at a Las Vegas casino,[29] the Marx Brothers seemed to have lived by those words!) This view of securities investing as thinly disguised gambling has become widespread. Like many commonly held beliefs, there is a kernel of truth to it. However, it fails to account for some critical differences between placing $50 on a roulette wheel and purchasing shares in a publicly traded company for the same amount.

One of the most essential and often-overlooked distinctions is that, while both transactions involve a hopeful bet on some kind of positive future development, only the latter option purchases a share in a living, breathing, revenue-generating enterprise. In other words, it purchases a legal ownership in an incorporated business enterprise, its future disbursements, and the (potential) appreciation of its assets. As Graham and Dodd noted in *Security Analysis*, this legal fact is often overlooked by market participants: "It must never be forgotten that a stockholder is an *owner* of the business and an *employer* of its officers."[30] This realization permeated Graham's entire conception of Wall Street. Among his writings, the best example of Graham's attitude on this matter can be found in another article that he wrote for *Forbes* in 1932 titled "Inflated Treasuries and Deflated Stocks: Are Corporations Milking Their Owners?"[31]

That article includes an emphatic, almost disparaging, warning regarding shareholders' failure to see themselves as business owners. Not only did such a failure impair these investors' understanding of the securities they owned, but it also engendered a dangerous passivity in the face of managerial decisions at many US companies that, in Graham's view, were contrary to shareholders' interests:

> Evidently stockholders have forgotten more than to look at balance sheets. They have forgotten also that they are *owners of a business* and not merely owners of a quotation on the stock ticker. It is time, and high time, that the millions of American shareholders turned their eyes from the daily market reports long enough to give some attention to the enterprises themselves of which they are the proprietors, and which exist for their benefit and at their pleasure.[32]

Throughout his life, Graham reminded investors that *they*, not the corporations' management, are the rightful owners of these enterprises and deserve to be treated with the respect and consideration that owners of a private enterprise would expect from its management. In fact, even if one owns a single $8.45 share of a publicly listed company, ownership of that share confers the status of business owner upon the purchaser. As such, it makes eminent sense to approach each prospective share purchase from the perspective of a business owner. Like almost all effective principles, the business owner's investment paradigm is consistently successful because it is fundamentally *true*. Nonetheless, this notion, so contrary to the view of most market participants, is difficult for many to internalize.

As Warren Buffett told me, Graham's "most important idea is

looking at stocks as part of a business."[33] Yet, in his sixty years of investing, Buffett has noticed that, despite the proven logic and power of this simple fact, it "escapes people with IQs all the way up to 170 or so."[34] (Perhaps its simplicity confuses those who are convinced that superior returns can result only from something more complex.) This concept of business ownership is one of the "Holy Trinity" of Graham's precepts (along with the margin of safety and "Mr. Market")— all three of which Buffett still views as indispensable. He told me that the business owner's approach is "so fundamental that, unless it's ingrained as part of your basic philosophy, you're going to get in trouble in life when you do investments."[35] As it was for his mentor, such an owner orientation is the primary paradigm through which Buffett judges each investment opportunity.

However, beyond investment selection, Buffett also considers this owner orientation to be an integral element of Berkshire's unique corporate culture and, ultimately, its superlative success. Moreover, he seems to have employed it effectively to help align the interests of managers with those of shareholders (which, as highlighted above, was a matter of great concern to Graham). As Buffett wrote in a February 2011 chairman's letter (to Berkshire Hathaway shareholders):

Our final advantage is the hard-to-duplicate culture that permeates Berkshire. And in businesses, culture counts. To start with, the directors who represent you think and act like owners. They receive token compensation: no options, no restricted stock and, for that matter, virtually no cash. We do not provide them directors and officers liability insurance, a given at almost every other large public company. If they mess up with your money, they will lose their money as well. Leaving my holdings aside, directors and their families own Berkshire shares worth more than $3 billion. Our directors, therefore, monitor Berkshire's actions and results with keen interest and an owner's eye. You and I are lucky to have them as stewards. This same owner-orientation prevails among our managers. In many cases, these are people who have sought out Berkshire as an acquirer for a business that they and their families have long owned. They came to us with an owner's mindset, and we provide an environment that encourages them to retain it.[36]

DIVERSIFICATION AND OWNER ORIENTATION

Another important aspect of an owner orientation is that it enables the more actively engaged value investor to employ some flexibility with respect to traditional diversification practices (i.e., no more than x percent in one company, no more than y percent in one sector, etc.). Instead, confident that a business is being sold by the market for less than its true value, the value investor has greater latitude to operate outside of the bounds of standard diversification practices. However, what's essential is that, regardless of whether the value investor's portfolio consists of ten securities or two hundred, each must be selected with an owner orientation. For example, Warren Buffett once said the following about the late Walter Schloss, his former colleague at Graham-Newman and an outstanding value investor in his own right: "Walter has diversified enormously, owning well over 100 stocks currently. He knows how to identify securities that sell at considerably less than their value to a private owner."[37]

Although Buffett prefers not to own as many stocks as Schloss did, that difference is almost cosmetic relative to the value-investing fundamentals on which both Graham disciples have built their fortunes. An essential element of this irreducible core of value investing is the owner orientation, and Schloss was in full agreement with Buffett (and, of course, Graham) on this point. In fact, when Walter Schloss wrote down sixteen bullet points that summarized his investment approach, owner orientation was listed second: "Try to establish the value of the company. Remember that a share of stock represents a part of a business and is not just a piece of paper."[38]

Jason Zweig wrote about the range of diversification practiced by the leading value investors: "Some of them hold portfolios with dozens of stocks; others concentrate on a handful. But all exploit the difference between the market price of a business and its intrinsic value."[39] Indeed, the success of Walter Schloss and others (detailed in chapter 12) demonstrates that some very successful value investors prefer purchasing shares of a relatively large number of businesses. Nonetheless, other value investors have enjoyed considerable success by pursuing a much less diversified investment strategy. Of course, Berkshire Hathaway exemplifies the more focused approach. Despite its formidable $372.23 billion in assets, Berkshire owns relatively few companies: Buffett and Berkshire's vice chairman Charlie Munger prefers to place very large bets on a select number of especially attractive businesses.

For Graham, what was paramount was that all investments were logically sound from a business owner's perspective (regardless of how large the investment was or how many or few securities were in a portfolio). So he would have approved of the approaches of both Schloss and Buffett (and that of any other successful value investor) since they all center around what he summarized in *The Intelligent Investor* as "the value of a business to a private owner."[40] However, there is a particularly illustrative example of a Berkshire-style "all-in bet" on a famously underpriced business in Graham's own investment record.

CASE STUDY: GOVERNMENT EMPLOYEES INSURANCE COMPANY

In 1948, a few well-connected people with a "special situation"[41] for sale called on Graham's investment entity (which, by then, was known as the Graham-Newman Corporation). The opportunity was none other than the Government Employees Insurance Company, more commonly known as GEICO (yes, the very same insurance company that has since become synonymous with competitive rates and reptile-themed advertising). Through a simple but ingenious optimization of the traditional automobile-insurance business model, GEICO cut out insurance agents and their often-hefty commissions by selling its policies directly to consumers (at that time, through direct mail). GEICO also saved money by selling only to government employees, a relatively low-risk group of drivers. For these reasons, they were able to offer insurance coverage to drivers at highly competitive rates and, consequently, enjoyed considerable growth. Founded in 1936, by 1948, the company had, as Milne and Kahn wrote, "exceptional growth during its first dozen years."[42]

True to the business-oriented approach that he espoused, Graham conducted a fundamental analysis of GEICO, its earnings, and its balance sheet. As Graham recounts in the 1973 edition of *The Intelligent Investor*, although he was "impressed by the possibilities"[43] of GEICO's unique business model, what was "decisive" for him and his partner was "that the price was moderate in relation to current earnings and asset value."[44] In fact, he and his then-partner Jerome Newman considered the value to be so exceptional that roughly one quarter of the partnership's assets were devoted to the purchase of an astonishing 50 percent of GEICO's shares. The Graham-Newman Corporation's stockholders' letter for that period reveals that the company paid $736,190.95 for the half-ownership of GEICO on July 6, 1948.[45] It is interesting to note that when the GEICO transaction took place, Graham-Newman was, in the literal sense, purchasing a large share of a private business (although it was understood that the hitherto private company would go public on the New York Stock Exchange later the same year).

During his lifetime, Graham, who became a member of GEICO's board of directors in 1949, lived to see the value of these shares reach "two hundred times or more the price paid for the half-interest"[46] And today, GEICO, a wholly owned subsidiary of Buffett's Berkshire Hathaway, boasts $28 billion in total assets[47] and annual premium revenue in excess of $14 billion.[48] Of course, as with all successful decisions, Graham's placement of the modern equivalent of just less than $7 million to purchase one-half of a company like GEICO seems like a "no-brainer" in retrospect. Yet, the question remains: Why was this deal, the most lucrative of Graham's (and later, one of the most lucrative of Buffett's) career, "turned down by quite a few important [Wall Street] houses"[49] before Graham-Newman went "all in" and bought *half* the company? Apparently, since the insurance industry was out of favor with the investment community of the late 1940s, those on Wall Street whose primary concern was what kind of "market action" GEICO stock would see when it went public had reason to be pessimistic. Graham, who had little interest in the market's short-term pricing behavior, allowed his business-oriented framework to take precedence over such concerns. In characteristic "tortoise and hare" fashion, he came out the winner.

It's interesting that when GEICO stock fell into temporary disfavor almost thirty years later, it was Warren Buffett who swept in and purchased large portions of the company. After decades of successful growth, due to a number of macroeconomic and legislative factors, GEICO faced some choppy waters in the mid-1970s. By 1976, the company's stock had hit an absurdly low price of $2 (from $60 just three years earlier)! The overall market was spooked by its short-term losses and was driving the price well below the company's intrinsic value. Despite its difficulties at the time, Buffett (who had been purchasing GEICO stock since the early 1950s) reexamined the business and was elated to be presented with the opportunity to own more of it for such a bargain. So he proceeded to purchase one-third of GEICO. As Nikki Ross wrote in *Lessons from the Legends of Wall Street*, within only three years of Buffett's large bet on GEICO, circa 1976, the company "was showing a profit of more than $220 million. The stock began moving up and about a decade later it was selling for more than $60 a share."[50]

SCREENING, *THEN* OWNING

As discussed in chapter 4, Graham's screens are designed to help narrow one's focus to securities of sufficient safety and quality for the intelligent investor to then consider more closely. As such, each is only a filter, not a selection mechanism. Then, surveying the list of filtered (or "vetted") investment opportunities, the value investor considers which (if any) of the remaining companies are worthy of ownership. This involves some consideration of the company's industry, its current competitive position within that industry, and, as Charlie Munger characterized it, the economic "moat"[51] around the company; that is, a sustainable competitive advantage that helps preserve long-term pricing power and profitability. Buffett defined this well in 1993 when describing the Gillette Company (the shaving accessory/personal care company that has since merged with consumer-products giant Procter and Gamble) and Coca-Cola, Ltd., both important holdings of Berkshire Hathaway:

> The might of their brand names, the attributes of their products, and the strength of their distribution systems give them an enormous competitive advantage, setting up a protective moat around their economic castles. The average company, in contrast, does battle daily without any such means of protection. As Peter Lynch says, stocks of companies selling commodity-like products should come with a warning label: "Competition may prove hazardous to human wealth."[52]

FROM INVESTOR TO OWNER

Once the owner orientation is understood and internalized, the market starts looking less like Harpo Marx's favorite casino and more like a bazaar where some goods are priced appropriately, some exorbitantly, and some are practically being given away. Graham's analytical tools, highlighted in chapters 2 and 4, are what empower the value investor to distinguish between the three categories. As Graham observed, "The stock market often goes far wrong, and sometimes an alert and courageous investor can take advantage of its patent errors."[53] However, it's not just any kind of courage that Graham is referring to in that quote from *The Intelligent Investor*. Rather, it is the serene confidence that results from knowing that the intrinsic value of the business (which Graham and Dodd once described as "that value which is justified by the facts"[54]), as ascertained from a business owner's perspective, is substantially higher than what the market, from a speculator's perspective, is selling that business for.

This is one of the main concepts that enabled Graham to scale the heights of Wall Street success and "Jazz Age" opulence, as discussed in the next chapter.

CHAPTER 7
DIZZYING HEIGHTS
AND SHUDDERING DEPTHS

T he year 1923 proved to be an auspicious time for Graham to launch the Grahar Corporation with Lou Harris. As Allen Weinstein and David Rubel wrote in *The Story of America*, "From 1923 to 1929, volume on the New York Stock Exchange quadrupled, while prices rose nearly as sharply to keep pace with the expanding investor demand."[1] While this unprecedented stock-market advance was rooted partly in sound factors (i.e., rising GDP [gross domestic product] and a larger percentage of Americans investing in the market), much of it was fueled by speculative excesses. Most ominously, these included widespread use of leverage (i.e., the use of borrowed funds in order to amplify anticipated gains), a practice that helped inflate the market well beyond true business values (and set the stage for the spectacular collapse that would follow). However, for Graham, the growth and strength of the market during the 1920s presented him with an outstanding opportunity to apply the methods that he had been developing during his time at Newburger, Henderson, and Loeb.

Among Grahar's most successful transactions was the simultaneous purchase of Du Pont shares (highlighted in chapter 2) while "shorting" (i.e., betting on a *decline* in the price of) General Motors stock. Graham's extensive quantitative analysis revealed that the former was underpriced relative to its intrinsic value (hence the large margin of safety) while the latter was considerably overpriced (hence the opportunity to profit through a short sale). Generally, such transactions proved highly profitable. However, a notable exception was Graham's shorting of the overpriced Shattuck Corporation, which, instead of falling in price, appreciated by over 40 percent! As Graham wrote, "It is an inconvenient characteristic of these popular and therefore overvalued issues that they sometimes grow more overvalued than ever before they drop to a normal and proper price."[2]

While its methods were not foolproof, the Grahar Corporation prospered admirably during the period from 1923 to 1925. Although specific figures are not available, Graham recalls that Grahar "was a successful venture and returned a high percentage on the capital."[3] However, his business relationship with Lou Harris did not fare quite as well. During this time, many "customers' men" (as they were called) were given greater authority to manage discretionary accounts without having to obtain clients' approval on specific transactions. Yet Graham found himself subjected to a series of generally irrelevant and unproductive investment "tips" from his raincoat-tycoon partner. Worse yet, most money managers were now earning a full 50 percent of profits, considerably larger than the 20 percent cut that Graham was being paid.

Driven by reasonable demands for a compensation scheme that was more aligned with those of his peers on Wall Street, Graham proposed a new structure to Lou Harris. Going forward, he would forfeit his salary and, as before, beyond the first six percent earned on capital, he would be paid 20 percent of the additional 20 percent earned. However, if over 30 percent was earned, he would expect 30 percent of all additional profits and he would expect a full 50 percent cut on all profits earned beyond a 50 percent return on capital. However, this proposed structure (which was not unreasonable relative to the compensation of other "customers' men" of the mid-1920s) did not go over well with Harris. "Lou Harris was horrified at the idea that I would want as much as half of any profit, even after 50 percent had been earned on the capital."[4]

Consequently, 1925 proved to be the final year of the short-lived but successful Grahar Corporation. On New Year's Day 1926, Graham initiated the "Benjamin Graham Joint Account," with the no-salary and graduated profit-sharing structure that had been rejected by Lou Harris. The capital providers in this new arrangement were several of Graham's closest friends at that time, including the aforementioned Hyman brothers, Bob Marony (a successful and feisty business executive who, according to Graham, had a tendency to "get his Irish up from time to time—but always against someone other than me"[5]), and Fred Greenman and Douglas Newman (who had both been schoolmate friends of Graham's).

The total pool of funds from these friends and from Graham himself amounted to $400,000 at the outset of the Benjamin Graham Joint Account. Within three years, the account's capital had reached $2.5 million. While much of that increase was due to the accumulation of reinvested profits, some was due to the addition of new clients. Notably, this early business growth resulted solely from positive word-of-mouth, as Graham did not engage in any active solicitation of additional clients (let alone paid advertising): "I made no effort to attract additional investments; in fact, I refused to accept money from people whom I did not know personally. But the number of my acquaintances kept growing."[6] The most important of these acquaintances was Douglas Newman's younger brother Jerry.

Despite having graduated from the highly prestigious Columbia Law School, Jerry Newman decided to work at his father-in-law's successful cotton-mill enterprise, where he had risen to a very well-paid managerial position. However, he found his father-in-law to be difficult to work with, and he was eager to work at a similarly rewarding position with someone more agreeable. Presumably, he was impressed by Graham's management of his brother's money (and, by that time, some of his father-in-law's money and a portion of his own funds). So, as 1926 was winding up, he proposed taking some of his cotton-industry profits to partner with his brother's competent, driven, but even-tempered friend, Ben Graham. This partnership would prove unusually successful and enduring. As Kahn and Milne wrote, "Jerry Newman remained as an ever more active and valuable associate for the next 30 years until Ben retired in 1956."[7]

By Graham's own admission, Jerry's managerial experience and natural talents in the operational and promotional spheres of an investment business were invaluable assets to the nascent Graham-Newman Corporation (as the Benjamin Graham Joint Account would later be renamed):

> He had a quick intelligence and an excellent head for business in all its practical aspects. He was much better than I at the details of a commercial operation. He was shrewd and effective at negotiating deals of all sorts and was completely honest and dependable— qualities essential for lasting success in Wall Street.[8]

Most critically, Jerry's involvement enabled Graham to focus on his talent (likely unparalleled at that time) for identifying both underpriced and overpriced securities and determining the most profitable mechanisms for capitalizing upon them. Thirty-four years old when Jerry came on board, Graham had already spent almost fifteen years on Wall Street, the last five of which demonstrating his superlative skill as an independent money manager. As such, he was already viewed as a fairly seasoned finance expert among his ever-widening circle of acquaintances and associates. So it was an opportune time to partner with someone who brought superior operational and sales skills (along with a sizable sum of additional capital) to the enterprise.

Graham's willingness to seize the opportunity reflects well on both his judgment and his character. Like those of Benjamin Franklin (one of Graham's heroes), Graham's memoirs reveal that the author was not immune from pride (particularly during an era in which he was "too young to realize" that he had "a bad case of hubris"[9]). However, to his credit, even as a relatively young man, Graham had sufficient humility to recognize his limitations. For this reason, he was able to appreciate the value of partnering with someone who brought a complementary skill set to the business. Jerry did not contribute to Graham's investment methodologies and writings, which, ultimately, are the achievements for which Graham is most remembered. However, it is highly unlikely that either of the two partners would have attained the level of financial success that they did without the other's expertise. As with most successful business partnerships, the "whole" of Graham-Newman was greater than "the sum of its parts."

Perhaps the most notable of Graham's transactions in the early stages of his post-Grahar career concerned the Northern Pipe Line Company. Some fifteen years earlier, the US Supreme Court had ruled that John D. Rockefeller's Standard Oil had been in violation of the Sherman Anti-Trust Act. As Ron Chernow recounts in his biography of Rockefeller, what followed next was "the federal government's 1911 dismemberment of Standard Oil into dozens of constituent companies."[10] Among these companies was Northern Pipe Line, one of eight companies operating pipelines that transported crude oil to Standard's refineries. In a report that Graham obtained from the Interstate Commerce Commission (ICC) for the purposes of researching a railroad, he was intrigued by the figures reported for these pipeline companies. As Kahn and Milne recount, for each of the eight companies, there was only "a one line 'income account' and a very abbreviated balance sheet."[11] However, the ICC had more extensive information available for these companies.

Being the consummate financial detective, the presence of more detailed data about these former Standard Oil affiliates piqued Graham's curiosity. So, the very next day, Graham took the train to Washington, DC, and obtained the desired details at the ICC's record room. He was astonished to find that all eight pipeline companies had significant ownership positions in premium railroad bonds. Northern Pipe Line's balance sheet was particularly impressive. The $65-per-share company held $95 (on a per-share basis) in railroad bonds (and other liquid assets)! Moreover, these assets had no bearing on the company's business and could be distributed to shareholders without any disadvantage to the operation of Northern Pipe Line. It was, almost literally, equivalent to paying $2 in exchange for $3 of invested monies. Moreover, each $65 share of this still-profitable company paid a healthy $6 annual dividend. It didn't take long for Graham to realize that one of his greatest triumphs was imminent: "Here was I, a stout Cortez-Balboa, discovering a new Pacific with my eagle eye. . . . After all these years, I'm still amazed that no one in the brokerage business thought of looking at the ICC data."[12]

While Graham had found extraordinary "treasure" hidden in the shares of the former Standard Oil affiliate, he was about to learn the first of many lessons regarding the failure of some companies' management to serve the interests of shareholders (or, as discussed in the previous chapter, *owners*) on a consistent basis. Throughout the remainder of 1926, the Benjamin Graham Joint Account purchased 5 percent of Northern Pipe Line's shares. (Notably, the only entity that owned more of these shares was the Rockefeller Foundation, a private foundation endowed by John D. Rockefeller himself soon after the 1911 breakup of Standard Oil.) Upon acquiring a sizable stake of this outrageously mispriced company, Graham set about convincing its management to, in his words, "return a good part of the unneeded capital to the owners, the stockholders."[13] Much to his surprise and chagrin, management was not immediately responsive to this most reasonable request. "Naively, I thought that this should be rather easy to accomplish."[14]

Indeed, Northern Pipe Line's New York–based management did its best to thwart Graham's request to distribute $90 of the company's $95 per-share surplus of liquid assets to shareholders. As Graham indicated, the company was generating annual revenues of $300,000 while carrying $3,600,000 in railroad bonds that were unrelated to Northern's normal course of business. So, distributing most of these assets to their rightful owners (i.e., the shareholders) made eminent sense. Nonetheless, as Kahn and Milne recount, Northern's management was eager to stall such a payout as long as possible, and it proceeded to present a number of "specious arguments"[15] to counter Graham's efforts. Finally, Northern's exasperated management had been worn down to their final and weakest line of defense:

> "Look, Mr. Graham, we have been very patient with you and given you more of our time than we could spare. Running a pipeline is a complex and specialized business, about which you can know very little, but which we have done for a lifetime. You must give us credit for knowing better than you what is best for the company and its stockholders. If you don't approve of our policies, may we suggest that you do what sound investors do under such circumstances, and sell your shares?"[16]

Of course, Graham was not one to be deterred by such nonsense. Almost eighteen months later, after completing a series of legal maneuvers (including petitioning support from other large shareholders), Graham finally prevailed: "$70 per share was eventually distributed, and the aggregate value of the new Northern Pipeline stock plus the cash returned ultimately reached an aggregate of more than $110 per old share."[17] It is also worth noting that, in the midst of his herculean efforts to compel management to accede to his request, he became the first elected director of a Standard Oil affiliate who had never been a Standard Oil "insider." Understandably, Graham recalls being "mighty proud of my exploit."[18] As well, he later learned that John D. Rockefeller Sr.'s foundation eventually approved of the distribution and, in time, forced the other seven pipelines to follow suit. In fact, during Graham's career, he would meet the world's first billionaire (and, adjusting for inflation, the wealthiest individual in recorded history[19]) three times.

Another mark of distinction for Graham at this momentous period of his career was his association with Bernard Baruch, the preeminent American financier cum statesman of the first half of the twentieth century. In 1927, Graham's expanding investment partnership had outgrown the small independent office space available at Newburger, Henderson, and Loeb that he (and, at times, a few employees) had been using for the past four years. So he set up an office at what was then known as the "Cotton Exchange Building" on nearby Beaver Street in the financial district. H. Hentz and Co., the global commodity firm that Baruch and one of his brothers purchased in 1907, happened to be headquartered in the same building. Graham encountered Hentz's two managing partners at that time— Jerome Lewine and Bernard's brother, the physician turned stockbroker Dr. Herman Baruch, "both of whom I came to know well."[20] The Hentz partners were intrigued by Graham's methods and, fairly soon, began participating in some of his transactions.

For example, Hentz followed Graham's lead in purchasing a large stake in National Transit, another entity that had been spun off from Standard Oil. Flush from his success with Northern Pipe Line, Graham found that National Transit was yet another of Standard Oil's progeny with significant "hidden treasure" (dormant cash assets, in this case) within its shares. Facing a reluctant management yet again, Graham's plan to distribute the surplus cash to National Transit shareholders, backed up by the Rockefeller Foundation, finally prevailed. Soon thereafter, Graham discovered that Dr. Baruch had also made a significant personal investment in National Transit when Graham did and had profited very handsomely from the transaction. Feeling indebted to this gifted young man with a unique perspective on the market, Dr. Baruch gave Graham (and five friends of Graham's choosing) full use of the Hentz manager's fully staffed yacht for eight days. This proved to be a memorable experience for him: "So my work and success in the National Transit matter led to eight glorious days as honorary skipper of Dr. Herman Baruch's luxurious *Reposo*."[21]

Through his brother and others at Hentz, Bernard M. Baruch himself had become intrigued with Graham's uncanny knack for identifying lucrative investment opportunities. The legendary financier and presidential adviser began following Graham's lead regarding a number of securities that Graham favored. Among the most notable of these investments was the Unexcelled Manufacturing Company.

Graham and his new partner Jerry Newman had been presented with an opportunity to buy a large block of Unexcelled shares through one of the "over-the-counter houses—those dealing in issues not listed on any stock exchange."[22] America's most prominent fireworks manufacturer of the era, Unexcelled boasted strong working capital and healthy earnings relative to the stock price. Its shares (as sold through this special block) were being sold for $9. That was less than the company's per-share working capital, and, considering that per-share earnings were $1.50, Unexcelled had an unusually low P/E (price-to-earnings) ratio as well. So Graham and Newman decided to purchase ten thousand shares of this favorably priced block, and Bernard Baruch purchased the remainder.

Aside from Bernard Baruch's personal involvement in a major transaction led by Graham, the Unexcelled episode is also notable for an entirely unrelated reason. As the company's primary motivation for putting up a large block of shares was to transfer control of the company from its current president to a new management team, Graham was offered a salaried position as vice president of the nation's largest fireworks company. It is probable that such an offer was a "sweetener" for the prospective purchaser of the shares. In any case, once it was clear that the position would require only a part-time commitment, Graham accepted without hesitation: "The whole thing appealed to me greatly, not the least attraction being election as officer in a fair-sized corporation."[23] Due to a number of macroeconomic and legislative developments, the fireworks industry as a whole would not fare well in the coming years, so Unexcelled (an appropriate name in retrospect!) never fulfilled its promise and, despite all its surrounding fanfare, the investment proved to be among Graham's *least* successful.

Fortunately, Unexcelled was "the exception that proves the rule," and almost all of Graham's collaborations with Bernard Baruch proved to be highly lucrative for both. Generally, they were quintessential Graham operations: most involved securities that, due to transient dynamics of the company and/or the sector in which it operated, were temporarily out of favor with the general investor community. Yet, relative to their current market prices, these securities tended to have considerable earnings and a strong cash position. For example, Graham recommended the purchase of the then-prominent rope-making company Plymouth Cordage at $70 per share at a time when he appraised Plymouth's working capital at roughly $100 per share.

Regarding the series of recommendations that he offered to Bernard Baruch, Graham summarized their common characteristics in the following manner: "All were selling below their minimal value as judged by the ordinary standards of a private business, and at ridiculously low levels in comparison with the prices of most popular stocks at the time."[24] Unlike his more generous brother Dr. Herman Baruch, Bernard, according to Graham, "had the vanity that attenuates the greatness of some men."[25] Bernard did little for Graham in return for all of these highly profitable suggestions. Nonetheless, Graham was grateful to him for facilitating (brief) encounters with two of the greatest statesmen of the twentieth century—Winston Churchill ("Winston, allow me to present my young friend, Ben Graham, a very clever fellow"[26]) and, a number of years later, General Dwight D. Eisenhower.

Although Bernard Baruch never repaid Graham as tangibly as the latter had thought appropriate, in 1929, he paid him what can only be construed as the ultimate compliment from a man of such stature. As Graham recalled,

> He told me that he was going to make a proposal to me that he had never before offered to anyone. He would like me to be his financial partner. "I am now fifty-seven years old," he said, "and it's time I slowed up a bit, and let a younger man like you share my burdens and my profits."[27]

Although Graham was not yet well known among the investing public, there's no question that, among the highest echelons of American finance, Graham was revered greatly. After all, the fact remains that Bernard Baruch, soon-to-be economic advisor to President Franklin

Delano Roosevelt, made a *partnership* offer (as opposed to an employment offer) to only one Wall Street professional, Benjamin Graham.

Certainly, the fact that both men were Jewish and that Graham had already developed a positive rapport with Bernard's brother (and others at Hentz) may have influenced Bernard's decision in some way. However, Bernard Baruch was a man governed by logic, not sentiment. So, on some level, it is likely that he believed that there were few, if any, Wall Street professionals of that time who were likely to deliver the kind of consistently profitable investing skill that Graham had already demonstrated to him across multiple transactions. As amazed and flattered as Graham was by Baruch's offer, he declined with little hesitation (a decision that, as the Depression wore on, he would come to regret).

Although he had great admiration for Bernard Baruch's intellect and accomplishments, as alluded to earlier, Graham had some reservations about his personality. More critically, in pre-Crash 1929, Graham's business was already scaling the heights of Wall Street success without Baruch's involvement. To illustrate, for the previous year, Benjamin Graham's pretax income exceeded $600,000. That is a very large sum by today's standards, but it was an *enormous* figure for annual personal income more than eighty years ago—roughly equivalent to $7 million! Indeed, Graham's rapid ascent during the "Roaring Twenties" provided him and his wife with more than ample means to support a growing family.

In 1925, Benjamin and Hazel welcomed their third child, Elaine Graham, to the family. Although Elaine's surviving (and elder) sister was ninety-one years old when she was interviewed for this book, Marjorie Graham Janis could still recall with great clarity the day that her sister was born:

> I still can remember waiting [*laughs*] under the Steinway piano at our apartment in New York, waiting for mother to come back from the hospital with the new baby. I was five and a half and it turned

out to be Elaine. I was very happy and excited that she was born. Then I became jealous of her because she was very beautiful. She had wonderful golden curls, I had dark straight hair. I had freckles and she had beautiful big blue eyes. She was also very talented. She could dance and I was never very good at dancing. Anyway, she was definitely the one that I grew closest to in the family.[28]

It is evident from his memoirs that Graham thought very highly of his first three children (particularly Newton I and Marjorie) and that they were generally happy and well-adjusted additions to the family. Indeed, for several years, the Grahams enjoyed a relatively harmonious family life, and Benjamin and Hazel's marriage, at least on the surface, seemed to be reasonably strong. However, in retrospect, an older Graham considered the marriage to be fundamentally flawed from its outset: "Our marriage was doomed to failure—nay, was already a fundamental failure—before either Hazel or I suspected that there was anything radically wrong."[29] For the first decade of their marriage, the Grahams were able to keep their marital tensions more or less hidden beneath a veneer of upper-class contentment. However, on April 20, 1927, a tragedy occurred that shattered this veneer and, more significantly, left a deep, lasting (and, according to some, festering) emotional wound in Graham's psyche.

In March 1927, Newton I was diagnosed with mastoiditis, a bacterial infection of a portion of the skull behind the ear. After undergoing an operation meant to remove the infection, Graham's first and favorite child was afflicted with spinal meningitis. Considering that it wasn't until the early 1940s when such conditions were treated with penicillin, a diagnosis of bacterial meningitis was usually a death sentence for children in the 1920s. (To illustrate, Boston Children's Hospital data from that decade pertaining to two forms of bacterial meningitis reveal that the mortality rate was 98.7 percent for one and 100 percent for the other.[30]) Tragically, not only did Isaac Newton Graham pass away just days before his ninth birthday, but, as the infection consumed and debilitated him in progressive stages, the last weeks of his life were an unspeakable horror for his parents. As Graham wrote in his memoirs, "Many painful incidents connected with Newton's illness and death are engraved on my memory, but I don't have the courage to recount them—for which the reader may indeed be grateful."[31]

Perhaps the most striking aspect of the Graham family burial plot north of New York City is the fact that Graham himself is not buried next to his mother, one of his brothers, or his second son, Newton II (who, like the first Newton, passed on long before his father did). Instead, in their own small row somewhat apart from the other Graham family members, Graham and his first son are buried side by side. It is not entirely clear whether this burial arrangement was a provision of his will or the decision of others who were close to him at the end of his life. In either case, Graham had a very special bond with his first child that was severed in a most unexpected and unsettling manner. It is interesting that Newton I's headstone reads "SWEETEST, BRAVEST, MOST BELOVED BOY," whereas, in his memoirs, Graham mistakenly recalls the last word as "CHILD."[32] Moreover, after transcribing those words in his memoirs, Graham added, "He was all that, and more."[33]

When I brought up the matter of her (first) late brother, the emotion that stirred in Marjorie's voice and demeanor was evident as she spoke: "That was a terrible blow for everybody. The tragedy of it, the sadness of it. . . . It was awful losing him for me and for everyone in the family. That marked the beginning of the deterioration of their (Ben and Hazel's) relationship as well."[34] To a considerable extent, Graham seemed to concur with this assessment: "Hazel and I felt closely united in our grief, but this sense of union indicated to us more clearly than we had realized how we had been drifting apart."[35] Graham describes lunching with Hazel shortly after losing their son and, in the context of a resolution to overcome their anguish and start anew, she made a revealing confession to her husband: she had needed more "warmth and understanding"[36] than Graham, who was "too immersed"[37] in his career, could provide. So, she had filled the void with a friendship (but "nothing more"[38]) with their family doctor.

At least on the conscious level, Graham believed in the innocence of Hazel's relationship with the doctor. However, considering that he would initiate his first extramarital affair just a few months after hearing his wife's "innocent" confession, one wonders if, on some level, Graham had suppressed his true feelings and suspicions on the matter (which then found expression in a physical affair with another woman). Despite these festering tensions and deceptions between husband and wife, within a year of Newton I's death, a new boy, Newton II, was welcomed into the Graham household. The new addition to the Graham family was a beautiful baby. Unfortunately, he soon proved to be a deeply troubled child and, at least in terms of character, the polar opposite of the late brother he was intended to replace.

In a cruel irony, the most significant similarity between the two Newtons would be tragic death at a young age—each would deliver a devastating emotional blow to their father. Buz Graham sees these deaths, particularly that of Newton I, as transformative events in his father's life, which, on some level, may have impaired his ability to relate to others on a deeper level:

> He was not exactly close to people. . . . I think that he struggled a bit. It may have had to do with the death of his son, the first Newton, and, later, the second Newton. He might have built up a kind of defense mechanism after being hurt so deeply. I would think that, by having two of your kids die so young—I am sure that affected him in some ways and set some tone for his relationships.[39]

While the family's emotional dynamics were deteriorating in the late 1920s, its material position had never been stronger. The family purchased a home in the upscale New York suburb of Mount Vernon and then moved back to the city, taking up luxurious accommodations on Manhattan's tony Riverside Drive. In both cities, the Graham children were sent to the best schools and enjoyed music lessons, dancing lessons, and other trappings of bourgeois life. As well, the family took winter vacations in Lake Placid and rented a summer residence on the Atlantic coast of New Jersey, just a short drive from a casino. Clearly, the Grahams were enjoying the fabled Jazz Age in all its opulence, an exclusive "Great Gatsby" lifestyle that very few Americans experienced during that time.

Always a scholar and a teacher at heart, once Graham had attained a certain level of financial security, he began pursuing an academic career along with his burgeoning investment-management practice. In 1928, Graham began teaching a security-analysis course at the Extension Division of Columbia University. Later, he also taught advanced security analysis—a class he took great pleasure in teaching. One of his first students in the late 1920s was David Dodd, an avid and enthusiastic "disciple" of Graham's, who later became a coinstructor of the security-analysis course and, eventually, the coauthor of the classic investment tome named after that course. Another one of Graham's students was Irving Kahn, who later became his full-time assistant for his classes and a devoted friend.

When I interviewed the 106-year-old Mr. Kahn, he reminisced about the early days of Graham's legendary course with surprising clarity: "This was the first time that such a course was ever offered. Ben soon realized that it was much more popular than he expected."[40] Indeed, as Milne and Kahn recount in their 1977 tribute to Graham, "By 1929, the class reached its peak attendance of over 150 students, a fairly important fraction of the working statisticians or analysts then on Wall Street."[41] The fact that so many financial professionals committed themselves to attending a class held quite a distance from Wall Street on a weekday afternoon reflects upon Graham's strengths as both a lecturer and a theoretician (after all, the ideas and examples that he was imparting were all his own original material). As Kahn told me,

> Graham would come up after the market closed at 3:00 and read
> from his notes and then, month to month, gave exams to make sure

that they understood what Ben was trying to teach. He realized that he needed an assistant because he wrote up the lectures on the very day that he lectured on. So he didn't have any time in between. After a few years, it was evident that he needed a full-time assistant. So Ben asked me to help him full-time.[42]

Graham would continue teaching at Columbia (and later at the New York Institute of Finance) until he left New York almost three decades later. Aside from Warren Buffett and Walter Schloss, other luminaries whose approach was, to a great extent, formed through attending one or more of Graham's classes include Gus Levy (future chairman of Goldman Sachs), Marty Whitman (of the Third Avenue Funds), Bill Ruane, and many others. Asked to list Graham's notable pupils, Kahn responded that "there were so many, it would take me quite a long time to list them out for you."[43] While *The Intelligent Investor* helped spread Graham's "gospel" of value to the general investing public, these security-analysis courses (and later, the *Security Analysis* book, the contents of which were drawn from these courses) disseminated Graham's ideas directly to some of the best minds of the investment world. These legendary investment courses, coupled with his prodigious body of published work in the field, are why Graham is still known as "the *Dean* of Wall Street."

In 1929, the "Dean" was well aware of the dangerously bloated state of the market and the likelihood of some sort of market correction or decline. However, by his own admission, he did not appreciate the full implications of such a decline vis-à-vis his investment partnership. Yet, in fairness to Graham (and Newman), very few fund managers anticipated such a crash. As Warren Buffett replied when I asked him about Graham and the Depression:

He was riding high in the late twenties and he was doing things that made sense but he just found out how crazy markets could become then. How extreme, really, the economic reaction, the economic behavior, was in the thirties, compared to anything that we've seen before. So he developed a very cautious streak, and he certainly developed a great aversion to borrowing money that a lot of people developed in that period. But, in the late twenties, because he was buying stocks that were so cheap, some borrowed money made sense, and I think that caused him a lot of grief.[44]

Along with the use of borrowed money, by 1929, the Benjamin Graham Joint Account had taken a substantial number of hedging positions involving convertible preferred stock and the underlying common stock of a wide selection of companies. That was a relatively safe strategy during the more or less consistently upward market of the 1920s, when there had been a somewhat inverse relationship between the two classes of stock. During that time, it made sense to hedge so that a drop in the value of one might be offset by an attendant rise in the other. However, as stock values (preferred *and* common) declined precipitously after the crash that brought in the Great Depression, the benefits of this strategy unraveled quickly. Since all classes of equities were being crushed by the market, there was no longer any consistent and reliable advantage to be gained from that kind of hedging.

To Graham's credit, once he had overcome the initial shock of just how steep the overall market decline was, he shifted into a defensive mode and did an admirable job of limiting losses through the remainder of the Depression. The following chart, drawn from data provided by Kahn and Milne[45] (as modified by data provided in Graham's memoirs, in one instance[46]) summarizes Graham's performance during the first (and most severe) phase of the Great Depression. The comparative figures reflect both his inadequate preparation for the initial collapse as well as his superlative performance (relative to the wider market) in 1931 and 1932. Of course, they also reinforce the fact that neither Graham nor the wider market posted any net annual gains during this calamitous period (the percentages in parentheses reflect losses):

	Benjamin Graham Joint Account	Dow Jones Industrials	S&P 500
1929	(20%)	(15%)	(7%)
1930	(50.5%)	(29%)	(25%)
1931	(16%)	(48%)	(44%)
1932	(3%)	(17%)	(8%)
1929–1932	(70%)	(74%)	(64%)

As Warren Buffett mentions above, Graham, like most Wall Street professionals of the era (including such titans as J. P. Morgan Jr.), did not see the initial crash of October 1929 for what, in retrospect, it proved to be: the onset of a protracted period of extreme economic contraction. To illustrate, between 1929 and 1933, aggregate US personal income plummeted from almost $86 billion to $47 billion, foreign trade fell from $7 billion to $2.4 billion, and the country lost almost half of its industrial production, reverting to 1913 levels of output.[47] Most dramatically, as Weinstein and Rubel wrote, "In April 1929, there were 1.6 million Americans out of work, representing just 3.2 percent of the workforce . . . by April 1932, that figure had jumped to 12.1 million (24.1 percent of the workforce)."[48] The problem for Graham (and others on Wall Street) was that the initial 1929 crash was so severe that, as John Train observed, he "was enticed back into the market before the final bottom."[49]

Revealingly, the introduction to *Security Analysis* (published in 1934), describes how, soon after the initial crash, "prices were again attractive in relation to earnings and other analytical factors."[50] Nonetheless, Graham and Dodd (the former drawing from his own unfortunate experience) point out that jumping back in the market at that seemingly attractive point "would have resulted in making repurchases too soon—as matters turned out—with consequent paper or actual losses."[51] For Graham, the losses were all too "actual," and they would take a considerable toll on his business and his peace of mind for a number of years to come. However, it was the Graham family's lavish lifestyle that was the first casualty of these losses. In short order, the Grahams let go of their servants and moved into considerably more modest accommodations.

As well, on the personal level, Graham reverted to his pre-1920s frugality. Due to his extraordinary resourcefulness, work ethic, and his determination not to relive the riches-to-rags humiliation of his childhood, Graham and his family managed to steer well clear of poverty during the Depression. However, as Roger Lowenstein recounts in *Buffett: The Making of an American Capitalist*, Graham's partnership came perilously close to bankruptcy: "Graham was ready to quit, but a relative of Jerome Newman, Graham's partner, put up $75,000 of capital that enabled the firm to survive."[52] Moreover, as his investment-management activities were becoming less profitable, Graham supplemented his income by becoming an expert witness in contentious corporate legal cases pertaining to valuation. He was hired for more than forty such cases. Not only was this work lucrative, but it also helped cement his reputation as one of the nation's leading authorities on the principles of corporate valuation.

Of course, the 1934 publication of *Security Analysis*, drawing on several years of Graham's Columbia course, strengthened Graham's stature in that regard even further. The book was a collaborative effort with David Dodd, an assistant professor at Columbia's School of Business who had been transcribing Graham's lectures there since 1928. The son of a Presbyterian minister, Dodd had become a close friend of Graham's, and he eventually became a director of the soon-to-be-formed Graham-Newman Corporation. As Graham recalls in his memoirs, "we agreed that I would be the senior author and write the entire text in my style. He (Dodd) would aid with suggestions and criticisms, would check the numerous facts and work up the tables."[53] Written in 1932 and 1933, the book was informed by the painful lessons Graham had learned from the early years of the Depression. Currently in its sixth edition, *Security Analysis* has sold extraordinarily well.

As Irving Kahn said when I asked him about the book, "I was told by McGraw-Hill that they have printed almost one million copies of *Security Analysis*, which is very unusual for a rather dry book specialty written as a sort of textbook."[54] Indeed, with such chapters as "Protective Covenants and Remedies of Senior Security Holders,"[55] it was written to be a textbook of the course it originated from; both the book and the course were intended primarily for the more avid students of security analysis (or those who were already professionals in the field). As the following example demonstrates, aside from its fairly technical subject matter, the presentation (i.e., terminology, tone, etc.) of *Security Analysis* was oriented unmistakably toward the advanced student/practitioner: "It is essential, in the case of industrial bonds at least, to supplement the earnings test by some other quantitative index of the margin of going-concern value above the funded debt."[56]

Covering all major forms of securities (in existence at the time) in considerable detail, Graham and Dodd's classic collaboration supplanted Chamberlain's encyclopedic *Principles of Bond Investment* as the most comprehensive and authoritative text for security/financial analysts. As stated in a relatively recent (2004) reissue of the 1951 edition, "No investment book in history had either the immediate impact, or the long-term relevance and value, of its first edition in 1934."[57] Although Graham intended to produce this 616-page "Bible of Wall Street" some years earlier, he later reflected that "it would have proved a great mistake to have published it earlier, for by 1934 I was able to pour into it wisdom acquired at the cost of much suffering."[58]

Indeed, the application of the value-investing wisdom detailed in *Security Analysis* soon began to pay off yet again for Graham and Newman, as they were able to buy up large shares of excellent businesses that were severely underpriced by the depressed market. In fact, as early as June 1932, when Wall Street was still mired in pessimism, Graham wrote an article for *Forbes* titled "Inflated Treasuries and Deflated Stocks," in which he made such observations as: "An amazingly large percentage of all industrial companies are selling for less than their quick assets alone."[59] (Quick assets include cash and those assets that can be converted into cash within six months.)

By buying up these "deflated stocks," Graham and Newman positioned themselves for a considerable windfall when business conditions finally began to improve. After all, Graham came to realize that the more irrational, even manic, the market became (and the late 1920s euphoria/early 1930s despair is probably the most dramatic historic example of such mania), the greater the opportunities were for intelligent (and *patient*) investors. In one of his most impressive creative feats, Graham communicated this idea through his fictitious "Mr. Market," a remarkably effective and memorable concept that is the subject of the next chapter.

CHAPTER 8

THE FOLLY OF "MR. MARKET"

Although Graham had witnessed all manner of Wall Street lunacy during the first fifteen years of his career (1914–1929), the harrowing depths of the Great Depression were how he learned, as Buffett said, "just how crazy markets could become." The modern investor community, to an extent not witnessed since the Great Depression, has also had ample opportunity to learn this same lesson in recent years—as did investors in the electronics bubble of the 1960s or the Dutch "Tulip Craze" of the 1630s! Anyone who has reviewed the history of such episodes throughout the ages would have to agree that as expressions of collective human psychology, the fundamentals of market behavior are timeless. Graham had the wisdom to recognize this and, more importantly, to capture the essential dynamic of irrational market behavior in an easily understood manner, what he characterized as "something in the nature of a parable."[1]

The parable of "Mr. Market," featured in Graham's million-selling *The Intelligent Investor*, has helped transform many investors' perceptions of the stock market from a strictly computational paradigm to one in which psychology plays a prominent role. As Graham wrote in 1949:

Imagine that in some private business you own a small share that cost you $1,000. One of your partners, named Mr. Market, is very obliging indeed. Every day he tells you what he thinks your interest is worth and furthermore offers either to buy you out or to sell you an additional interest on that basis. Sometimes his idea of value appears plausible and justified by business developments and prospects as you know them. Often, on the other hand, Mr. Market lets his enthusiasm or his fears run away with him, and the value he proposes seems to you a little short of silly.[2]

The phrase is so effective that it has won a prominent place in the vernacular of the financial community. To this day, it is often used as a colorful synonym for the market itself (and, by implication, its underlying behavioral dynamics). For example, a 2010 piece in the *Wall Street Journal* stated, "At this point, what is good for the US economy isn't necessarily good for Mr. Market."[3]

Like the stock market he represents, the bipolar Mr. Market becomes overly optimistic in good times and utterly despondent when things turn south. These exaggerated emotions lead to stock values that are either irrationally inflated or irrationally deflated, but rarely at a level that reflects the true underlying value of the business issuing the security. The latter, of course, is determined by one's own assessment of intrinsic value. This is why, according to Graham, "Mr. Market" is the value investor's best friend: due to his mood swings, stocks become grossly underpriced or overpriced relative to intrinsic value, thereby creating attractive buying and selling opportunities for owner-oriented (as opposed to market-oriented) investors. As Graham elaborated in *The Intelligent Investor*:

If you are a prudent investor or a sensible businessman, will you let Mr. Market's daily communication determine your view of the value of a $1,000 interest in the enterprise? Only in case you agree with him, or in case you want to trade with him. You may be happy to sell out to him when he quotes you a ridiculously high price, and equally happy to buy from him when his price is low. But the rest of the time you will be wiser to form your own ideas of the value of your holdings, based on full reports from the company about its operations and financial position.[4]

As highlighted in the chapters discussing the margin of safety and owner-oriented investment (chapters 2 and 6, respectively), such an approach stands in stark contrast to the market-driven behavior of most investors. Indeed, the market skepticism embodied in Mr. Market rounds out the three integral "pillars" of Graham's independent and value-oriented investment paradigm. Graham was among the first to challenge Wall Street orthodoxy regarding market efficiency. Instead of accepting the dogma that the stock market is a wholly logical computational system, Graham concluded that much of the market's behavior was not the product of dispassionate logic but, rather, the tumult and irrationality of human emotion.

THE FUTILITY OF MARKET TIMING

In his recent book *Common Sense on Mutual Funds,* Vanguard Group founder John Bogle summarized his own observations on this matter in fairly strident terms: "After nearly fifty years in this business, I do not know of anybody who has done it [market timing] successfully, and consistently. I don't even know anybody who knows anybody who has done it successfully and consistently."[5] Graham came to a similar conclusion regarding the futility of market timing early in his career, and his "Mr. Market" parable represents the fundamental cause of market-timing failures. After all, driven by something as irrational and unpredictable as human emotion, how can market (and individual security-price) movements be anticipated reliably and consistently? As the noted value investor and author Pat Dorsey wrote, "Given the proclivity of Mr. Market to plead temporary insanity at the drop of a hat, we strongly believe that it's not worth devoting any time to predicting its actions."[6]

An extensive academic study published in the *Financial Analysts Journal* seems to bear this out. In 1986, Gary Brinson, Randolph Hood, and Gilbert Beebower tracked the portfolio performance of over ninety large US pension plans over a ten-year period. Among their findings, the three asset managers discovered that, on average, pension plans' attempts to profit from market timing actually yielded a net *negative* result.[7] More recently, Dorsey wrote in 2004 (when he was director of equity research at Morningstar, a leading investment research firm) that "after talking to literally thousands of money managers over the past fifteen years or so, we've discovered that none of the truly exceptional managers spend any time at all thinking about what the market will do in the short term. Instead, they all focus on finding undervalued stocks that can be held for an extended time."[8]

TUNING OUT THE MARKET'S "NOISE"

In order to preserve one's capital (and sanity!) in the midst of market madness, Graham and his most eminent disciples learned that, while others are tracking each market movement with bated breath, the value investor is better served by adopting a more detached view of short-term market and security-price fluctuations. As noted value investor and writer Jason Zweig highlighted in his commentary that augments the 2003 edition of *The Intelligent Investor*, "When asked what keeps most individual investors from succeeding, Graham had a concise answer: 'The primary cause of failure is that they pay too much attention to what the stock market is doing currently.'"[9] This answer strikes at the heart of the widely popular efficient market theory (EMT). EMT posits that market pricing, representing the collective results of many well-informed market participants, can be relied on to be correct or "efficient."

The most authoritative test supporting this hypothesis was conducted by University of Chicago economist Eugene Fama in the 1960s (although even Fama conceded that market efficiency was a continuum and did not hold with absolute strength and consistency[10]). As noted investment-finance academic and author Lawrence Cunningham wrote, due to this alleged market efficiency, Fama "concluded that no trading rule or strategy could be derived that outperformed the market consistently."[11]

Indeed, if EMT (in its purest form) is correct, then there are no inefficiencies for *any* investment strategy, including value investing, to exploit. However, if that were true, how does one account for Warren Buffett's $44 billion in personal wealth? Noted value investor and author Howard Marks provides an excellent illustration of how brazenly *in*efficient the market can be: "In January 2000, Yahoo! sold at $237. In April 2001 it was at $11. Anyone who argues that the market was right both times has his or her head in the clouds; it has to have been wrong on at least one of those occasions."[12] The problem is that some of what drives market fluctuations is based upon meaningful changes in business fundamentals, or what Cunningham describes as "positive (efficient) information volatility."[13] This would include such developments as a major change in reported annual earnings, significant developments with respect to debt or ownership structure, or even legislation that has a substantive bearing upon a particular industry sector or business. These news items may be positive or negative in terms of their impact upon the business or sector in question, but any resulting volatility is *positively correlated* to relevant fundamental data.

However, as highlighted in chapter 6, at any given point in time there are also many factors determining price that have little (and often no) bearing on long-term fundamentals. These constitute what Cunningham describes as "negative (inefficient) information volatility."[14] This is the "noise" that all too often becomes a siren song, beckoning investors to their demise. Assuming that there is some infallible logic behind market movements, many investors follow the collective "wisdom" of Wall Street until they find themselves tumbling over the cliff with the rest of the "herd." As acclaimed value investor Charles Brandes told me,

General investing on Wall Street is very much a herd phenomenon, and everyone gets concentrated on just the markets and what's new at the moment. Unlike Graham, with his understanding of psychology and history, they never think about the longer-term history and the behavioral aspects of market movements. Of course, we still see the exact same thing today.[15]

The parable of "Mr. Market" helps lift the dangerous but common illusion that the market is some kind of dispassionate computational system that only yields perfectly accurate pricing data. Instead, by thinking of the market as a bipolar individual who tends to bounce from one extreme to another, a healthy skepticism sets in. In this manner, the investor can cultivate a certain detachment from the gyrations of market price, which, in turn, helps preserve a focus on intrinsic value (i.e., a business-owner orientation, as described in chapter 6) in the midst of moment-to-moment market mayhem. However, the successful value investor is not necessarily passive. For example, Warren Buffett tracks fundamental business developments vigorously while paying scant attention to near-term market movements. In other words, the "market noise" does not distract him from the more relevant long-term data. As he told me, a central aspect of Graham's superior investment paradigm is "buying investments where you don't care whether you look at the stock pages for a year."[16]

Due to the almost unfathomable advances in information technology that have taken place since Graham's time, it has never been easier or quicker to track the operating results of publicly traded companies. However, it has also never been easier or quicker to track the most minute market movements in real time, whether one lives in Manhattan or Manila or whether one is at home, at the office, or standing in line at the supermarket. This, from an investor perspective, is the more problematic dimension of our modern mobile information superhighway. Such instant, 24/7, global, and mobile access to market information has made it more difficult than ever to overcome the temptation to track price movements with distracting frequency. Indeed, the Internet, coupled with popular cable television channels dedicated exclusively to largely short-term-oriented (and often sensationalized) financial "news," has made it *easier* than ever to lose focus on the more relevant matter of the issuing company's business fundamentals. Meanwhile, traditional broadcast and print media (with some notable exceptions) have generally retained the same obsession with "hot stocks" and market timing that shaped much of their content in Graham's time.

However, as Graham recognized long before he coined the term "Mr. Market," screening out the deafening noise of the market, particularly in tumultuous times, makes eminent sense. Nonetheless, like many sound ideas, it is not always easy to put it into practice. As Graham and Dodd wrote in 1934, "The wider the fluctuations of the market, and the longer they persist in one direction, the more difficult it is to preserve the investment viewpoint in dealing with common stocks."[17] To some extent, it is contrary to human nature (perhaps due to the evolutionary instinct of herding for safety) to see that almost everyone is running in a particular direction and not succumb to the pull of the crowd. Certainly, if one chooses not to follow, some measure of discomfort and self-doubt is likely to materialize (i.e., Am I the only one who didn't "catch the rising tide" or, conversely, "jump off the sinking ship"?). However, when the market (or a particular element thereof) "persist(s) in one direction" for long enough, a line of thinking then arises that what is occurring now will last forever. As Howard Marks wrote, such thinking is "a source of great danger since it . . . ignites bubbles and panics that most investors find hard to resist."[18]

I witnessed the destructive consequences of such thinking first-hand here in San Diego, an area that exemplified the "boom and bust" real-estate cycle of the previous decade (which, of course, bore some relation to the stock market's behavior during the same period). In 2004, I attended a dinner party at which I met a university professor and his attorney wife from the East Coast who were telling me about how they had just purchased a home after renting for several years: "'Prices just keep going up,' I kept telling my wife, 'let's wait, they'll have to crash soon. Look how high they've risen so quickly,' but you look around and everything keeps shooting up. So, we got tired of sitting on the sidelines and we finally got in on the party." The professor's first instincts proved to be correct, as the subsequent crash in property values demonstrated. However, swayed by what everyone else (i.e., the market) was doing, the couple jumped in at the peak of a real-estate bubble in one of the country's most overheated residential property markets.

I'm not aware of the specific home that they chose, but they told me the area, and it is likely that, had they waited a few more years, they would have saved between $200,000 and $300,000 on the purchase price. Back to the stock market, similar dynamics apply to those who bought into the market at inflated 2006 levels versus the heavily *de*flated market of 2009. Yet, the former group is considerably larger than the latter. The point is that, whether its homes or securities, even highly educated (and presumably intelligent) people often succumb to market momentum instead of adhering to a more prudent independent strategy. As Zweig observed, "When it comes to their financial lives, millions of people let Mr. Market tell them how to feel and what to do—despite the obvious fact that, from time to time, he can get nuttier than a fruitcake."[19]

Often, investors obtain a false sense of confidence from having obtained a lot of "information" on a particular investment without questioning the source of that information. This is why "Mr. Market" is needed more than ever as a reminder that, although market information is plentiful, it's not necessarily *meaningful* to the serious investor. Worse yet, if it is followed blindly, it can often be as perilous as Mr. Market's dangerously extreme mood swings. By keeping this in mind through Graham's memorable and easily understood personification of a borderline psychotic market, the modern value investor is better able to maintain a healthy skepticism with respect to moment-to-moment prices. In this manner, the deceptively simple concept of

Mr. Market helps leverage the market's momentary insanity for the value investor's own gain.

MR. MARKET: MASTER OR SERVANT?

A recent 2011 *Barron's* article featured this memorable line: "Mr. Market is now like Julius Caesar deciding to give gladiators life or death with a flip up or down of his thumb."[20] That line was written in a somewhat different context, but the analogy to the Roman emperor is an apt representation of the view that the market is some kind of all-knowing/all-seeing electronic monarch. When one accepts that premise, the natural inclination is to adhere to the market's allegedly superior judgment. Instead, when one considers that the market is more akin to an emotionally troubled individual who shouldn't even be trusted with a pair of scissors, the value investor is then free to form his or her own independent judgment and *then* compare it to the market's mood of the moment (i.e., the current price).

If the market price is significantly lower than the value deduced from the independent assessment (thereby providing a large margin of safety), it can be an opportune time to buy, and if it's significantly higher, one can cash out handsomely at Mr. Market's expense. When I asked him about Graham's most essential concepts, Warren Buffett responded that "one of Graham's most important ideas is looking at the market as being there to serve you and not instruct you."[21] In *The Intelligent Investor*, Graham wrote: "Basically, price fluctuations have only one significant meaning for the true investor. They provide him with an opportunity to buy wisely when prices fall sharply and to sell wisely when they advance a great deal."[22] As the noted investor and investment writer Rob Arnott told *Forbes* editor Steve Forbes in a 2011 interview, Graham saw the market as "this nervous Nellie who was bidding up one thing and bashing down another, and that if you wait patiently and contra trade against Mr. Market you can earn a superior return."[23]

However, this view is the exact *opposite* of how most people see the market and its fluctuations. Instead, when Mr. Market seizes up and suffers a panic attack, many investors assume that he is doing so for wholly rational reasons and dive into panic selling. Conversely, when prices are absurdly high, as long as Mr. Market seems to be climbing ever higher (albeit on a rickety "ladder" of sky-high prices unsupported by business fundamentals), many investors feel encouraged to buy. The "dot-com" crash proved just how perilous Mr. Market's example can be. Yet, as demonstrated by the more recent 2008 crash (and the irrationally high prices that preceded it and the irrationally low prices that followed it), most investors have short memories. As Howard Marks wrote in 2011, "The last several years have provided an unusually clear opportunity to witness the swing of the pendulum . . . and how consistently most people do the wrong thing at the wrong time. . . . And it will always be so."[24]

The fact that the folly of the market (and the masses that follow its lead) "will always be so" is terrific news for opportunistic value investors. For example, in the wake of the fourth-quarter 2008 crash, while most investors were running scared, Buffett did not disappoint. In classic value-investor fashion, he snapped up large positions in such companies as Dow Chemical, Goldman Sachs, General Electric, and Harley Davidson during one of Mr. Market's most severe bouts of "clinical depression." All four securities have since appreciated—two by over 100 percent (as of this writing in 2011). Yet, it is worth noting that Buffett took some flack when these large bets did not pay off immediately. In fact, one financial columnist highlighted that the companies Buffett purchased in early 2009 were "all down since the news [of Buffett's purchase]."[25] With a touch of facetiousness, the author added that "Mr. Market apparently hasn't yet come around to his [Buffett's] way of thinking."[26] As has often been the case, the long-term results have proven to be highly favorable for Buffett despite the fact that the prices of those securities kept declining in the immediate aftermath of his purchases.

The serious value investor knows that, when betting on Mr. Market's insanity, it is important to exercise patience and not expect an instant payoff. Cultivating the requisite discipline and patience to put Mr. Market to work for you is at least as important as an intellectual understanding of the concept/opportunity that "he" represents. Unfortunately, the former can be difficult, particularly in tumultuous financial times. As Graham and Dodd wrote in the midst of the Great Depression, as market fluctuations grow larger and longer lasting, the investor's focus is "bound to be diverted from the investment question, which is whether the price is attractive or unattractive in relation to value, to the speculative question whether the market is near its low or its high point."[27] Graham and his most successful acolytes have learned to remain focused on "the investment question" by always keeping Mr. Market's well-chronicled history of irrational behavior in mind.

COURAGEOUS CONTRARIANS

The terms "value investing" and "contrarian investing" are often employed interchangeably when describing the Graham approach. However, the latter really represents a particular aspect of the former, one that is especially relevant to the investment approach conveyed in the Mr. Market parable. In his book *Value Investing and Behavioral Finance*, Parag Parikh, among the world's leading experts in behavioral finance, describes the essence of contrarian investing:

> What really differentiates the contrarian investor is his emphasis on looking for opportunities where consensual opinion has led to mispricing. When I say looking for mispriced bets, I mean that they are looking to exploit areas where consensual opinion is not wrong *per se* in its stand, but has led to an exaggeration. . . . This exaggeration is often the result of mass psychology that is prevalent in the stock market to varying degrees.[28]

Of course, Mr. Market is a memorable (albeit imaginary) personification of this "mass psychology" that can lead to the exaggerated perceptions and consequent price inefficiencies referred to by Parikh. As such, the concept lies at the heart of the contrarian aspect of value investing. It is telling that, when *Barron's* columnist Steven Sears highlighted the high market volatility that was surrounding a particular security during the summer of 2010, he concluded that it was "a gift from Mr. Market"[29]—that is, a market inefficiency that savvy investors could exploit profitably. Looking out for the monetary "gifts" offered by Mr. Market's erratic behavior can be a lucrative pursuit if one has sufficient confidence (and patience) to adhere to a contrarian approach.

The late multibillionaire investor Sir John Templeton once wrote, "To buy when others are despondently selling and sell when others are greedily buying requires the greatest fortitude and pays the greatest ultimate rewards."[30] Anyone who has engaged in contrarian investing is likely to agree with at least the first part of that statement. The reason why contrarian investing can be so uncomfortable is that it runs counter to the "monkey see, monkey do" instinct embedded in our primate brains. It is the financial equivalent of attending a black-tie affair dressed in polka-dot pajamas. Millions of years of evolutionary programming tend to keep us from going radically "against the grain" of what the overwhelming majority of people around us are doing. From an evolutionary context, such potentially isolating behavior can impair our ability to survive. After all, our species is a social one and survival, to a large extent, is predicated upon successful interactions with our fellow humans.

However, just as an animal crossing a highway is surely serving some sort of evolutionary instinct (e.g., it sees/smells greener pastures on the other side), it is best to analyze each of our own "animal" instincts objectively before surrendering unthinkingly to their impulses. This is especially true with respect to investing. As Howard Marks advised, "For self-protection, then you must invest the time and energy to understand market psychology."[31] Internalizing the concept of Mr. Market is among the best ways of adopting a healthy contrarian attitude toward "market psychology." Moreover, the concept helps fortify the contrarian investor's resolve when waiting for Mr. Market to correct (and often *over*correct) "his" momentary pricing errors. Investment-finance author Nikki Ross wrote, "It takes courage and discipline to invest at times when the outlook for stocks is gloomy, especially in prolonged bear markets."[32] Conversely, it also takes courage and discipline to *sell* one's holding during prolonged *bull* markets.

One of the common threads uniting Graham with successful investors like Buffett, Ruane, Brandes, Schloss, Kahn, and others is that they have all seemed to relish their "rebel" stance as contrarian investors profiting from the market's missteps. Clearly, anyone who writes that "the stock market often goes far wrong"[33] in a book titled *The Intelligent Investor* is a proud contrarian. As for Buffett, among his most frequently cited quotes is this: "We simply attempt to be fearful when others are greedy and to be greedy when others are fearful."[34] It doesn't get any more contrarian than that! Moreover, the implicit message of Buffett's statement is that market psychology is often, as Graham would say, "far wrong"—which is the essence of the parable of Mr. Market.

In his 2004 book *Value Investing Today*, Charles Brandes forges the link more explicitly by making frequent reference to Mr. Market as an integral element of a confidently contrarian stance:

> *You* decide the true value of the companies you hold, not Mr. Market. *You* decide when, and what price, you want to purchase or sell shares. . . . Trust *your* judgment. Trust *your* research. . . . Being aware of Mr. Market and his mood swings can help you be patient and help you make rational investment decisions.[35]

When placing a bet that runs counter to the prevailing notion regarding the market (or a particular element thereof), the contrarian investor draws courage from keeping in mind just how irrational Mr. Market's fleeting "notions" prove to be in the long term. Mr. Market may prove the contrarian wrong in the short term, but, as has been highlighted in multiple ways throughout this book, effective value investing requires a long-term framework.

HE WHO LAUGHS LAST . . .

This long-term versus short-term distinction is an important reason why all successful value investors are also, by definition, *contrarian* investors. The entire machinery of the market—brokerage services, stock promoters, most financial media, and so forth—revolves around the central question of "where will the market go tomorrow?" As such, the overwhelming majority of investors are chasing short-term gains. Graham considered this to be a fool's errand because, among other reasons (discussed in earlier chapters), "the work of many intelligent minds constantly engaged in this field tends to be self-neutralizing and self-defeating over the years."[36] So, aside from the inherent weaknesses involved in betting on a market that, in the short term, is prone to behave irrationally and unpredictably, the fact that "so many hunters are chasing the same rabbit" limits (and, in some instances, even nullifies) the rewards of the conventional short-term approach.

As Pat Dorsey told me, "The market for short-term returns is very competitive, but the market for longer-term returns is less competitive."[37] To illustrate, he cited the example of Harley-Davidson circa late 2008 and early 2009, an example worth delving into further because it exemplifies the contrarian approach of betting against Mr. Market when "he" is demonstrably wrong. (Of course, it is also notable as one of Buffett and Munger's most successful bets in the wake of the October 2008 crash.) In the postcrash "Great Recession" era of that time, the short-term outlook for sales of high-end motorcycles was justifiably weak. However, just how far did Mr. Market go in "pricing in" an expected *short-term* drop in Harley-Davidson sales?

On October 1, 2008, Harley-Davidson's common stock was priced at $36.73 per share, fairly representative of a stock price that had begun the year at $45.61 and had hovered between approximately $35 and $40 for most of the year. Prior to the crash, the stock's 2008 lowest level, or trough, had been a brief dip to $33.07 in July. During one of the most difficult years in recent economic history, with GDP, employment, and real-estate values plummeting all around, Harley-Davidson's third quarter results, released on October 16, were disappointing but (especially within the context of the broader economy) hardly disastrous: "Net income for the quarter was $166.5 million compared to $265.0 million in the third quarter 2007, a decrease of 37.1 percent. Third quarter diluted earnings [a more rigorous earnings measurement—earnings divided not only among common stocks but among all convertible securities (such as convertible bonds)—all of which are expected to dilute earnings per share if and when they are converted to common stocks] per share were $0.71, a 33.6 percent decrease compared to last year's $1.07."[38] Especially for a stalwart of US business that has been operating since 1903, one might think that, in the maelstrom of the October crash, Mr. Market would be wise enough to realize that when the current economic cycle turns around (as it always does), strong companies like Harley-Davidson (which was still solidly profitable) will perform very well.

Yet, just as Graham would have predicted, Mr. Market, in a full-blown panic, "slashed and burned" indiscriminately and, by November 21, 2008, Harley-Davidson shares were practically being given away for $12.04—the still-profitable and very well-established company had lost over two-thirds of its value in seven weeks! Clearly, such a dramatic discount was wildly excessive and entirely indefensible from a business-owner perspective, but it was par for the course for "Mr. Market." It was a classic example of market hysteria and myopia, precisely the sort of market mispricing that creates an opening for what Graham and Dodd describe as the "alert and courageous investor."[39] As of this writing, Harley-Davidson's share price is back in the same $35 to $40 range where it had been prior to the crash. So those who purchased it at $12 (or even $24) have earned an enviable return.

Of course, those who followed Mr. Market's lead and *sold* at $12 in November 2008 earned a decidedly *un*enviable loss. However, in late February and early March 2009, when Harley's stock sank to single-digit territory, those who had earlier sold at $12 might have felt vindicated. In the short term, their decision seemed to be correct. Meanwhile, value investors like Buffett were not particularly concerned with the dip. Remaining confident that, over the long term, the sound business fundamentals of Harley-Davidson's business would restore its stock price, veteran value investors held out for Sir Templeton's "greatest ultimate rewards." Clearly, those with the foresight, courage, and patience to purchase Harley-Davidson during one of Mr. Market's worst manic episodes had the last, best, and longest laugh (at Mr. Market's expense)!

DR. MARKET

Harley-Davidson is a fairly cut-and-dried illustration of a transaction that leveraged temporarily extreme market behavior in a highly profitable manner. However, as those who purchased certain banking stocks immediately after the October 2008 crash will confirm, betting against Mr. Market is not a guarantee of success. Just as the best doctors avoid rushing to a diagnosis without considering all the facts, no matter how patently crazy Mr. Market may be at a given point, that insanity does not mean that every plummeting stock is a sound long-term investment. That is why the masters of value investing examine all the relevant business fundamentals underlying each security in extensive detail before rendering an investment decision. It may be found that the recently lowered price provides a sufficient margin of safety for long-term value. However, it is also plausible that the underlying business is so flawed that, even at the discounted price, the security is not a sound long-term investment.

Mr. Market *can* be calm and somewhat rational when pricing securities. Yet he is known to lapse into irrational bouts of melancholy and euphoria during which he runs with his emotions. At these times, stock prices can veer away from any semblance of business value. Conversely, "Dr. Market" (i.e., the dedicated value investor) is a meticulous rationalist who insists on collecting all of the relevant owner-oriented business data and analyzing it thoroughly before writing out his "diagnosis" (i.e., his assessment of intrinsic value per share). Especially when he is calm, Mr. Market's pricing will not necessarily differ markedly from Dr. Market's calculation of intrinsic value. However, even when he has lapsed into temporary insanity, Mr. Market may still be correct (accidentally or not) with respect to certain securities—or, at least, not incorrect enough to justify a change in investment strategy. That is why the serious value investor always does the necessary homework to confirm (not just assume) that Mr. Market has, in fact, made a significant pricing error with respect to the particular security under consideration.

The masters of value investing have managed to outperform the overall market consistently, but this is not because they have learned how to avoid making mistakes. After all, avoiding any and all errors in an endeavor as complex as investing is nearly impossible. Rather, these investors have attained unusually high returns through a fundamentally sound analytical framework, of which Mr. Market is a central component, and the requisite discipline, discernment, and intelligence to apply it with maximum effectiveness. As with the margin of safety, owner orientation, and Graham's quantitative "toolbox," the value of Graham's Mr. Market is proportional to the value investor's willingness to invest the time and effort that its application demands. Of course, in light of recent events and ongoing economic instability, the Mr. Market concept has never been more potentially useful to the modern value investor.

Fortunately for Graham, in the late 1930s, after the worst economic crisis the world had ever seen, Mr. Market finally "came off the ledge." As I discuss in the next chapter, Graham's renewed Wall Street ascendancy and romantic chaos combined in one of the most eventful periods of his life.

CHAPTER 9
NEW BEGINNINGS

By 1934, Benjamin Graham and Jerry Newman were starting to see the happier side of Mr. Market, as the securities they had purchased for "less than their liquidating value"[1] earlier in the decade had begun appreciating. As highlighted previously, the original compensation arrangement for the partners included the cumulative provision that the partners would only be compensated from returns over and above a guaranteed 6 percent per annum return on invested capital (e.g., if the partnership returned 8 percent, the partners' share would only be applied to the 2 percent [8 percent − 6 percent]). Because of this, neither Graham nor Newman had earned a penny from their business for the five-year period from 1929 to 1933 (inclusive). Worse yet, due to the cumulative nature of the guarantee, even if the Benjamin Graham Joint Account (as it was then still called) performed extraordinarily well in 1934, the odds were high that the partners would still go a sixth year without compensation from the account.

Considering that, prior to 1929, the account had been the partners' primary source of income, it was a troubling situation for them. Fortunately, Guy Levy (not to be confused with Graham's student, future Goldman Sachs director *Gus* Levy), one of their more loyal investors, suggested an alternate compensation arrangement, and all but one of Graham's remaining investors (a number of investors had "jumped ship" during the account's worst years) agreed. The cumulative provision was altered, but as Kahn and Milne recount, "the terms were revised, reducing the share of Ben and Jerry to a straight 20 percent of profits earned after January 1, 1934."[2] Remarkably, by year-end 1935, Graham's selections of underpriced securities had proved so lucrative that all previous losses were recouped and the account was back in positive territory relative to 1929. Even more remarkable, Graham and Newman (who were now under no legal obligation to do so) repaid their investors every single dime that was lost during the worst years of the Depression.

When we were discussing her father's career, of all his great accomplishments, Marjorie Graham Janis seemed to be proudest of her father's insistence on repaying Depression-era investor losses:

> When the Depression came in '29, Ben and his company lost a lot of money, and most of the family and friends had been investing there. And then, years after the Depression, he succeeded again and he paid everybody back what they lost. That was really something—I hadn't heard of anyone else who did that. He paid everybody back what they had lost. He had the records and he made sure that everybody who had invested with him regained what they had lost in the Depression. I don't think there were many people on Wall Street who had that kind of a way of returning losses to their clients. He was a very unusual man in that respect.[3]

As Marjorie pointed out, many of the investors were "family and friends" for whose financial welfare Graham felt personally responsible. Moreover, having suffered so deeply and personally from his family's financial troubles as a child, the enormous Depression-era losses sustained under Graham's stewardship weighed on both his conscience and his confidence. However, by the time *Security Analysis* was published in 1934, it was evident that he and coauthor David Dodd had come to realize that they had lived through a wildly anomalous period, "a sort of extreme laboratory test, involving degrees of stress not to be expected in the ordinary experience of the future."[4] Moreover, with the exception of a difficult brother-in-law, his longtime investors were well aware of the widespread financial carnage in the market (and throughout the economy) during that period and maintained their trust in and goodwill toward Graham.

Even Graham's Uncle Maurice, who had lost so much money in Graham's Joint Account that he and his family could no longer afford to live in New York City, did not hold a grudge against his nephew. Dr. Bernie Sarnat, Maurice's son-in-law, told me that "the Gerards did not bear ill will towards Graham about the loss because everyone lost money then."[5] Due to prodding from both the Internal Revenue Service (which challenged the notion that the Joint Account was, in fact, a partnership and not, effectively, a corporation) and investor Fred Greenman (an accountant by profession who, as Graham recalls, "advised us to incorporate our business, saying that otherwise there would always be some doubt about our status under the tax law"[6]), on January 1, 1936, the Benjamin Graham Joint Account was replaced with the Graham-Newman Corporation.

From that point until the corporation's dissolution twenty years later, the partners and their investors would enjoy relatively smooth sailing: improved business conditions coupled with Graham's financial conservatism (which, as evidenced by his post-1929 avoidance of leverage, had hardened somewhat from the sting of his Depression-era losses) ensured that investor funds under Graham's stewardship would appreciate handsomely with markedly less exposure to risk. While he did a far better job of emerging unscathed from Mr. Market's destructive moods, as evidenced by the Graham-Newman Corporation's aggressive purchases of underpriced stocks in the 1937–1938 recession, Graham had lost none of his enthusiasm for capitalizing upon temporary market insanity. However, he had learned to do so more prudently.

The Graham-Newman Corporation's 1946 letter to its investors demonstrates just how successful Graham became in this regard. The letter summarizes the corporation's 1936–1946 performance as follows: "The annual percentage gain to stockholders, based on net asset value at the beginning of each year, averaged 17.6%. This compares with 10.1% in the same period shown by the Standard Statistics—Poor's (S&P) Index of 90 stocks, and 10% shown by the Dow-Jones Industrial Average."[7] Especially when one considers the cumulative year-by-year impact of beating the market by 7.5 percent, Graham's performance (while Newman assisted with administering the corporation, security selection was Graham's domain) during this time was nothing short of stellar. Moreover, having learned from his Depression-era experiences, these superlative results were attained without the use of leverage (e.g., borrowing to purchase stocks) or any other high-risk devices.

Not only would the Depression leave its mark upon Graham's investment approach, but as an intellectual with a strong social conscience (a topic explored in further detail in chapter 14), he felt compelled to grapple with the larger macroeconomic issues. As early as 1931, Graham began attending the New School for Social Research, where he would, in Kahn and Milne's words, "discuss possible solutions to the economic crisis"[8] with such notables in the field as Adolph A. Berle (one of the architects of Franklin Delano Roosevelt's first "New Deal") and William McChesney Martin (a New York Stock Exchange official who, some years later, would gain the dual distinction of becoming both the youngest person appointed to be chairman of the Federal Reserve and the longest-serving official in that extraordinarily powerful post). Martin also helped establish a journal known as the *Economic Forum*, which in 1933 published Graham's first contribution to macroeconomics—an eight-page article titled "Stabilized Reflation," which focused on the need to stabilize commodity prices in order to support a sustained economic recovery.[9]

Although the essential idea of Graham's currency plan was formed in his mind in response to the much milder and shorter-lived economic downturn of 1921–1922, the severity of the Great Depression motivated him to develop it more seriously. Essentially, the currency plan advocated for replacing the gold standard (for backing the value of US currency) with a "basket" of commonly used commodities (Graham's well-detailed macroeconomic prescriptions are the subject of the following chapter). As Graham wrote in his summary: "The increased stability of supply and price that would come with the ever-normal granary is essential."[10] Due to the high standing of Graham's new friends at the New School for Social Research, his economic ideas were discussed at the White House and even received the written endorsement of Agriculture Secretary Henry A. Wallace and the partial agreement of John Maynard Keynes.

Another extraprofessional activity Graham engaged in during this time was playwriting. Due to his exposure to literature and theater as a child, Graham had been an aspiring playwright for decades. During the 1930s, the decade when he solidified his professional standing, he felt settled enough to devote some time to his passion of writing for the stage. This yielded no less than three full-length plays along with a one-act vaudeville sketch. According to Graham, his first play, *China Wedding*, included a partially disguised allusion to alleged adulterous behavior by his then-wife, Hazel. Graham recalls stumbling upon "a number of letters written to my wife by a married artist whom we had known for many years. Some of these letters were fairly incriminating, even though excisions had been made— no doubt of the more lurid passages."[11] However, being a private, nonconfrontational sort of person (who, after all, was having an affair himself with an unmarried woman who was friendly with the Graham family), Graham decided not to confront Hazel about them, at least not initially. He kept two of the letters, which he recalls utilizing for his own protection "once in a very private way, between her lawyer and mine, at the end of our marriage."[12]

Although his first play never made it to Broadway, Graham was pleased that *China Wedding* won second place in Johns Hopkins University's annual contest of "American dramas by new playwrights."[13] Soon thereafter, he completed work on a rather macabre one-act vaudeville sketch, which he titled *The Day of Reckoning*. The plot involves a vengeful barber shaving the man who seduced his wife and stole his money some years previous. As Graham wrote, "The play ends with the villain dying of fright beneath the menacing razor."[14] In retrospect, Graham views this work as a "somewhat-less-than-masterpiece."[15] Somewhat ironically, Graham reached out to a friend of Hazel's to promote *China Wedding* (which Hazel claimed to have liked, without, of course, commenting on the references to letters revealing a wife's infidelity) and the one-act sketch. The friend, Harry Delf, had been a successful vaudevillian who had enjoyed some success as a playwright at the time.

While Delf was not very enthusiastic about either of Graham's works, he was impressed with Graham's "skill in writing dialogue,"[16] which could be applied beneficially to an idea for a three-act comedic play that he was developing. So Delf asked Graham to collaborate with him on the writing project with one important caveat: only Graham's name would appear in the writing credits. Afflicted with Buerger's disease ("a rare inflammatory disease of the arteries and veins in the arms and legs"[17]), Delf was receiving large insurance payments that would continue to come only so long as he was deemed not to be "self-supporting."[18] For this reason, being named as a coauthor of a play that he and Graham hoped to see performed on Broadway (and possibly adapted for the screen) might jeopardize his insurance income.

Aside from his marital infidelities, there were few episodes of dishonest and/or unethical behavior in Graham's personal and professional life. And, as exemplified by his repayment of Depression-era losses at his own expense, Graham was unusually conscientious in financial matters. Nonetheless, as Graham would recognize when reflecting upon this secret collaboration decades later, agreeing to assist Delf with such a scheme was both dishonest *and* unethical.

Since I always had a somewhat holier-than-thou satisfaction in my own financial rectitude, I set down this transgression with as much wonderment as chagrin. Could I have thought, along with nearly everyone else, that it is no crime to outsmart an insurance company? This seems the more incredible to me now since for many years my chief financial gains have come from ownership of shares in insurance concerns. Alas, it matters so much whose ox is gored![19]

The play, originally titled *True to the Marines* before being renamed *Baby Pompadour*, told the story of a prominent newspaper editorial writer, his wife, his amusing mistress ("this apparent ninny has the knack of making spontaneous remarks about current affairs which give the editor great inspiration for his columns"[20]), and the latter's romance with another man. Of course, such a scenario was rife with comedic possibility, which the writers did their best to exploit. Apparently, the script itself was not without its merits, since its pre-Broadway run at Long Island's Red Barn Theatre was, according to Graham, "reasonably successful."[21] Opening night at the Red Barn took place in June 1934, just weeks after the publication of Graham and Dodd's first edition of *Security Analysis* (the "Value Investing Bible," as it has since become known, is now in its sixth [2008] edition[22]). The near-simultaneous release of his first book and his first theatrical production, coupled with increasingly lucrative expert witness assignments, proved highly exhilarating to the forty-year-old investment manager.

Buoyed by success on multiple fronts, Graham, who had already had one extramarital affair, entered (or descended, depending on one's views of marital infidelity) into a more adventurous realm of promiscuity:

> To my own surprise, I found myself gliding, as it were, into a period of romantic attachments of a quite different nature than I had known before. Perhaps my exposure to the atmosphere of the theater as well as the variety of my other activities, exerted an unrealized influence on my erotic life.[23]

Obviously, the passage above is deliberately ambiguous as to what exactly was "different" about his new "romantic attachments." As such, its wording can be interpreted in a number of ways. Since even his recent extramarital affair involved both an emotional and a physical relationship ("I remained faithful to 'Jenny' in my fashion for nearly seven years."[24]), the most likely meaning is that Graham's new "romantic attachments" may have been more casual and less emotionally involved than what he had experienced over the previous twenty years with his wife and mistress.

However, what *is* unambiguously clear is that, by mid-1934, Graham's extramarital activities had extended well beyond a single relationship (which ended "in 1933 or 1934"[25]) that he described as "a combination of sincere friendship with sex."[26] Instead, they included multiple affairs that were probably of a more immediately sexual nature. In other words, it seems that he was no longer merely an unfaithful husband; rather, he had become an active "swinger." Considering that Graham had long known about Hazel's infidelity (which, at least according to the impression conveyed by certain passages in his memoirs, may have involved multiple lovers as well), it is unlikely that the expansion of Graham's own extramarital involvements weighed heavily upon his conscience. However, it established a pattern that, in subsequent decades, would mar relationships with others who were less deserving than Hazel of such deceit. To further complicate matters, another important family event occurred in 1934. In the midst of a complete breakdown of their marriage, the Grahams had another child, Winifred (often referred to as "Winnie"), their third daughter and their fifth, and last, child.

Due in part to the fact that, as a condition of agreeing to bring Graham (and Delf's) play to Broadway, Irving Steinman (the producer brought on board by Delf) had insisted on casting his reportedly untalented fiancé in one of the leading roles, the Broadway production of *Baby Pompadour* proved far less successful than its off-Broadway run. As Graham himself recognized, "the production was a fiasco."[27] The play was roundly panned by almost all theater critics who saw it. As the *New York Times* review reveals, aside from whatever weaknesses the play probably had, it is also likely that "the writer's" active investing, writing, and teaching career in finance and economics did not particularly endear Graham to serious theater critics:

> A biographical note in the program of "Baby Pompadour," which opened last evening at the Vanderbilt Theatre, identifies its author, Benjamin Graham, as "a well-known figure in the financial world" who has connection with the affairs of many important corporations. Mr. Graham is further revealed as the senior author of an authoritative work on "security analysis," a member of the faculty of Columbia University and active in the sphere of economics. In conclusion, playwriting is unblushingly defined as his "hobby."[28]

Moreover, after panning the production in no uncertain terms (e.g., "Alas, the only humor in his [Graham's] comedy comes during those pathetic moments when the unfortunate actors—who are here spared the humiliation of identification—find themselves with nothing more to do than laugh at their own pitiful jokes"), the reviewer takes a parting shot at a Wall Streeter's attempt at playwriting: "Graham had better stick to one thing or the other—or find himself a new hobby."

Nonetheless, Graham never lost his love for the theater, but he no longer wanted to be "a participant."[29] Instead, he redirected his "hobby" time toward more financial writing and macroeconomic research. Regarding the former, he, along with Spencer B. Meredith (then a security-analysis instructor at the New York Stock Exchange), decided to write a book that would assist investors with deciphering financial statements. Of course, understanding financial statements is integral to a successful application of Graham's basic investment principles, so such a book made eminent sense. While portions of *Security Analysis* pertain to this topic, Graham and Meredith's 1937 publication, *The Interpretation of Financial Statements*, addresses this topic exclusively. According to its preface, the purpose of the book is to enable one to read the financial statements of a business "intelligently" so that one is "better equipped to gauge its future possibilities."[30]

The Interpretation of Financial Statements is packed with the discerning analytical wisdom associated with Graham. For example, when discussing the potentially misleading reporting of a company's intangible assets, Graham writes: "In general, it may be said that little if any weight should be given to the figures at which intangible assets appear on the balance sheet. . . . It is the earning power of these intangibles, rather than their balance sheet valuation, that really counts."[31] He also warns against overly simplistic methods of stock selection and encourages a full analysis of all relevant metrics. For example, he warned against those who would use the current-asset-value figure as the deciding factor in their analysis: "When a stock is selling at much less than its current asset value, this fact is always of interest, although it is by no means conclusive proof that the issue is undervalued."[32] That same year, Graham's *Storage and Stability: A Modern Ever-Normal Granary* (the first of two full-length books about macroeconomics) was published. The revolutionary ideas put forth in that seminal work (as well as his related 1944 publication, *World Commodities and World Currencies*) are discussed in the following chapter.

However, at least from a personal perspective, the most momentous event for Graham in 1937 was his acrimonious divorce from his wife of over twenty years. In its later years, their union had disintegrated into a nightmare, not only for them, but also for their children. As Marjorie Graham Janis told me:

> I think that I was a teenager when they would wake me up at night to listen to their arguments—because each one felt that he or she would convince me and that would prove to the other that the other one was wrong. They brought me in to listen but I wasn't supposed to take part. I just listened to these arguments that went on and on and on. They were *awful*. Later, when I was a young adult, I was psychoanalyzed and I spent a lot of time on my parents' arguments to kind of get rid of the upset and anger and anxiety that it provoked in me. I can't recall exactly what the arguments were about. It wasn't so much about the topic at hand but the underlying hostility between them and the fact that they didn't really *love* each other anymore, which was very dismaying for their child, which was me. That was hard and that was *tough*.[33]

I still recall how Marjorie's demeanor changed when she said those words. It's obvious that, some seventy-five years later, the memory of her parents' bitter arguments was still difficult to bear. Unfortunately, the divorce itself would prove even more traumatic for Marjorie; her brother, Newton II; and her sister, Elaine (Winnie was still too young to comprehend such matters). In 1936, Graham and his mother saw Hazel and the kids off as they boarded a ship for California to visit Rhoda Gerard and her mother, who had moved out to Los Angeles with Maurice in 1931 (Maurice had passed away in 1934). Rhoda had spent summers with the Grahams and had grown close to both Ben and Hazel. As Rhoda told me, "Hazel and Ben were like an uncle and aunt to me, when I was a little girl."[34] Spending time with Hazel and the Graham children was supposed to be a happy family reunion of sorts. However, Graham saw this temporary geographical distance between himself and Hazel as an opportune time to divorce his wife with as little face-to-face contact and drama as possible.

As Rhoda's future husband, Bernie Sarnat, told me:

> While Hazel and the girls were here in Los Angeles at one time, she got a telegram from Ben Graham saying, "I'm filing for divorce," and that came as a surprise to Hazel! So Hazel was visiting Rhoda's mother in Beverly Hills when she got the news.[35]

Apparently, Hazel became so distraught by the shocking news that she left her four kids in Marjorie's care at a Los Angeles hotel and wandered around on her own in a state of profound emotional distress. However, she came to her senses once she learned that her kids were about to go hungry for lack of money![36] Initially, Hazel refused to accede to her husband's demands for a divorce, but Graham and his attorney eventually forced her hand.

The details of these negotiations are not entirely clear, but as alluded to earlier in this chapter, Graham's possession of two of his wife's illicit love letters provided him with something of a trump card. As Graham recalls, "I kept only two of these letters—out of a prudence that proved justified by later events."[37] It seems that, aside from inspiring an ill-fated "career as a playwright," those fateful letters helped facilitate a divorce on terms that he found acceptable. Whether Hazel felt that his proposed terms were unfair or she was adopting a "difficult" stance to make the divorce prohibitively expensive for her husband is not entirely clear. However, the latter seems more likely.

In early 1937, the couple filed for divorce in Reno, Nevada. In modern times, when over half of all US marriages end in divorce, it hardly seems like a dramatic event. However, in 1937, when the national divorce rate was just 8.7 percent,[38] the ending of a marriage (particularly in a family of four children) was a strange and almost anomalous occurrence in an America that was significantly more family oriented and religiously observant. As well, it was something of a social taboo that carried a much heavier stigma than it does now (which was probably one of the reasons why Hazel was so unwilling to agree to it). As Marjorie told me, "When he and my mother got divorced, divorce wasn't the common thing that it became later. In fact, it was rather unusual."[39] The relative rarity of divorce made it all the more painful and embarrassing for Graham's kids. Newton II, who had already exhibited signs of mental illness, was particularly vulnerable in this regard. According to some, his mental condition worsened noticeably after his parents' divorce.

Graham may or may not have been aware of these potential consequences, but his difficulties with Hazel had become so acute after twenty years of marriage that he simply could not see a way of resolving their differences. It is fortunate that Graham's memoirs, released to the public twenty years after his death, were never read by Hazel (who was still alive when he died). Aside from the candid reflections on their mutual infidelity, the resentment that Graham still held toward his first wife, many years after the divorce, is palpable. (However, he reportedly had a reconciliation of sorts with Hazel toward the end of his life, a number of years after the bulk of his memoirs had been written.)

Grossbaum residence in Harlem, which was part of the old redbrick building on the left. *Photo by the author.*

Boys High School, Brooklyn, New York, the site of some of Graham's most rigorous academic training. The building has been preserved in its original 1890s form. *Photo by the author.*

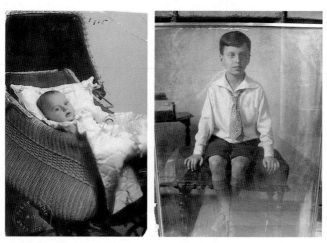

Left: Postcard dated April 12, 1918: "Love to Aunt Nell & Uncle Leon, Baby Newton." *Courtesy of Charlotte Reiter.*
Right: Newton I. *Courtesy of Charlotte Reiter.*

This Riverside residence in Manhattan is where Graham lived with Hazel and their growing family for a number of years in the 1920s. As one of New York's most prestigious addresses, this residence is reflective of his rapid ascendancy on Wall Street. *Photo by the author.*

Dodge Hall, Columbia University, where Graham taught his legendary security-analysis class from 1928 until 1954. *Photo by the author.*

Graham's first wife and first daughter, Hazel Greenwald and Marjorie Janis, in Washington, DC, 1942. *Courtesy of Charlotte Reiter.*

Marjorie, Newton II, Winnie, and Elaine, July 1945. *Courtesy of Pi Heseltine.*

Left: "Graham's Second Family," Mount Kisco, New York, 1947. Graham, Estey, and Buz in the early years of his third marriage and second family. *Courtesy of Benjamin Graham Jr., MD.* **Right:** "Graham in Deep Thought," Mount Kisco, New York, 1947. *Courtesy of Benjamin Graham Jr., MD.*

The Scarsdale residence where Graham lived with his second family (Estey and Buz) during their last couple years in the New York City area (he would commute by train to Graham-Newman in Manhattan). This was a seminal period in his career, highlighted by the publication of *The Intelligent Investor* and his work with a young Warren Buffett. *Photo by the author.*

Chanin Building at 122 East 42nd Street in New York City, where Graham-Newman was located between 1953 and 1957. This is the building that housed the office where Buffett worked under Graham. *Photo by the author.*

Newton II, 1954.
Courtesy of Charlotte Reiter.

Graham and Winnie at her wedding, 1956. *Courtesy of Pi Heseltine.*

Troop 17 --- Beverly Hills
Boy Scouts of America

LEARN THE MORSE CODE IN TEN MINUTES
(By Using the Troop 17 Key Words)

IN THE KEY WORDS: A SYLLABLE CONTAINING **O** STANDS FOR A DASH
A SYLLABLE **NOT** CONTAINING **O** STANDS FOR A DOT

Letter	Key Word(s)	Code Signal	Letter	Key Word(s)	Code Signal
A	A-lone	di-dah	N	No-vice	dah-dit
B	Bro-ther-in-law	dah-di-di-dit	O	O So Good	dah-dah-dah
C	Co-ca-Co-la	dah-di-dah-dit	P	Pa-trol Po-ny	di-dah-dah-dit
D	Doo-lit-tle	dah-di-dit	Q	Quote Quot-a Quote	dah-dah-di-dah
E	Ed	dit	R	Re-volv-er	di-dah-dit
F	F-is-Fool-ish	di-di-dah-dit	S	Since It Is ..	di-di-dit
G	Go Goo-fy	dah-dah-dit	T	Toe	dah
H	Hys-ter-i-cal	di-di-di-dit	U	Un-der Oath	di-di-dah
I	Is It .. ?	di-dit	V	V Is A Vote	di-di-di-dah
J	Je-rome's Old Jokes	di-dah-dah-dah	W	We Won't Work	di-dah-dah
K	Ko-sher Kook	dah-di-dah	X	Ox In A Box	dah-di-di-dah
L	Li-no-le-um	di-dah-di-dit	Y	Yo-del Old Songs	dah-di-dah-dah
M	Morse Code	dah-dah	Z	Zoo Zo-di-ac	dah-dah-di-dit

NUMBERS

1 .----	6 -....	Comma .. .. ..
2 ..---	7 --...	Period .-.-.-
3 ...--	8 ---..	
4 ....-	9 ----.	
5	0 -----	

"The Morse Code Invention" *(left)* and "Slide Rule Patent Application" *(right)* images help underscore Graham's eclectic interest and inventive mind. *Courtesy of Benjamin Graham Jr., MD.*

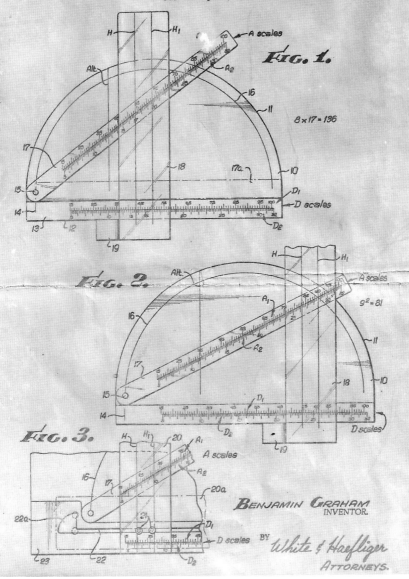

FIG. 1.

$8 \times 17 = 136$

FIG. 2.

$9^2 = 81$

FIG. 3.

BENJAMIN GRAHAM
INVENTOR.

BY

White & Haefliger
ATTORNEYS.

Clockwise from the left: Estey; Winnie; Winnie's first husband, Gary Watkins; Irving Janis; Marjorie (Graham) Janis; Cathy Janis; Graham; Lauren Watkins; Charlotte Janis (now Reiter); and Oliver Watkins, 1961. *Courtesy of Charlotte Reiter.*

Graham and his cat enjoy a playful moment in the backyard of his Beverly Hills home in 1963. During his stay in Los Angeles, the retiree enjoyed passing many quiet days in his backyard study, immersed in a wide variety of books and intellectual pursuits. *Courtesy of Benjamin Graham Jr., MD.*

Swarmed by Spanish birds (Seville, Spain, 1964). Graham spent much of the 1960s and 1970s in Europe. *Courtesy of Benjamin Graham Jr., MD.*

Buz's wedding. *Courtesy of Charlotte Reiter.*

A grandfatherly Graham with Winnie's kids, 1969—Graham, Pi (hiding between his legs), Megan (the baby), Lauren, and Marco. *Courtesy of Pi Heseltine.*

Graham's apartment in La Jolla, California. *Photo by the author.*

Graham with Malou at his eightieth-birthday event. *Courtesy of Pi Heseltine.*

Above: The Heilbrunn Center for Graham & Dodd Investing at Uris Hall, Columbia Business School. *Photo by the author.*

Right: The Benjamin Graham Conference Room at the global headquarters of Brandes Investment Partners in San Diego, California. *Photo by the author.*

THE
BENJAMIN
GRAHAM
ROOM
71

Recommended Books for 2011 Berkshire Shareholders (sixty-two years after its initial publication, *The Intelligent Investor* is displayed on the third row), Omaha Airport, Omaha, Nebraska, April 2011. *Photo by the author.*

Marjorie Graham Janis being interviewed by the author, Palo Alto, California, June 28, 2011. *Photo by the author.*

Benjamin Graham Jr., MD, (Buz) being interviewed by the author, Berkeley, California, June 20, 2011. *Photo by the author.*

It is clear that, as he reflected upon his life in his early seventies, Graham viewed his first marriage with considerable regret:

> Though I liked to oblige and hated to quarrel about anything, I was strongly independent and inwardly resented all forms of domination. If I had known at twenty-three what I know now, our marriage would have gone quite differently. From the very beginning I would have refused to be told what to do, would have insisted that my wishes in all matters carry equal weight with Hazel's, and would even have invented wishes different from hers to make sure that she would not always have things her way. I would have studied more carefully the countless wiles and devices she used to put herself in the right and me in the wrong. I would have devised effective coutermeasures. Instead, I made the great mistake of assuming that each issue that came up was trivial and not worth fighting about.[40]

Yet, as fate would have it, soon after Graham's first divorce, he married another woman who he would also find to be "impossible to live with."[41] Indeed, it seems that Graham had fallen in love with an aspiring actress from Canada whom he had met on a cruise when he was still married. Carol Wade was blond, beautiful, and almost twenty years his junior. These qualities held great appeal for the middle-aged, divorced, yet financially successful "man about town." So, in May 1938, they held a nondenominational wedding (Carol was Protestant) at the Sherry Netherland, a luxurious Fifth Avenue hotel overlooking Central Park. Graham and Wade enjoyed a passionate, illicit affair, but as a married couple, their union was a rocky one almost from the start. It is not entirely clear why the marriage didn't work, although it is probable that the eighteen-year age gap (along with the likely personality differences between an aspiring actress and an avowed intellectual) played a pivotal role in its collapse.

As an illustration of just how poor a match "Ben and Carol" were, Graham recalls how their mutual love of "Sherry," their unusually affectionate Siamese cat, helped keep their troubled relationship from ending even sooner: "Our love for her was one of the few feelings we shared. If it had not been for Sherry, the first year of our marriage might have proved an unmitigated disaster, instead of just a disaster."[42] Despite its humor, Graham's reflection on the pathetic state of his second marriage is not as exaggerated as it may seem, for when Sherry suffered an accidental death and was replaced with another, less affectionate Siamese, it seemed to embody the deterioration of its owners' romantic relationship.

Moreover, as Graham recognized, it bore an eerie resemblance to the loss of Newton I (which proved so detrimental to Ben and Hazel's relationship) and the disappointment surrounding the emotionally troubled son (Newton II), who was supposed to have somehow replaced the Grahams' first child. Graham lamented, "Perhaps the second cat was not affectionate enough; perhaps we expected too much from it; perhaps it sensed our devotion to the memory of Sherry No. 1 and showed her resentment in her behavior. (I write these lines thinking not really of the two Sherries, but rather of my two Newtons)."[43]

Meanwhile, as a native of England (and, presumably, as a Jewish person as well, although he only cites the former in his memoirs), Graham became very troubled by the gathering storm in Europe during the late 1930s. When France fell to the German offensive and the British army escaped so narrowly from certain slaughter at Dunkirk, Graham, typically composed in the face of the usual adversities of life, became uncharacteristically beset by worry. As he recounts in his memoirs:

> I became nervous and depressed—a rare state for me—and less able than before to cope with my domestic problems. This mental degringolade prompted unusual remedies. One of them will sound infantile. I went back to roller-skating, something I had rarely done since childhood. A strange sort of solace was provided by the continuous circling, the rhythmic movements of the body, the soothing music, and even the subdued roar of hundreds of turning wheels. I might begin the session with sad thoughts about the world situation and bitter hostility towards Carol, but eventually I'd find myself

thinking of nothing but my skating maneuvers, and a most welcome peace would descend upon my soul.[44]

Financially, even prior to America's official entry into the war, European demand for US armaments and other goods had provided a massive boost to the national economy that sent the stock market (including, of course, the investments of the Graham-Newman Corporation) soaring. While this was excellent news for Graham as an investment professional, it mattered little relative to "the fall of France and the mortal danger to my native England."[45] A few years later, when America entered World War II directly in 1941, Graham would have the opportunity to translate his concern into meaningful action. To Graham's credit, the war inspired an unprecedented volunteerism from him: he accepted the enormous responsibilities of associate director of the New York State War Finance Committee and, later, chairman of the federal government's War Contracts Price Adjustment Board. Although he could have been paid a much larger sum for these duties, he would accept no more than the minimum $1 for each of these time-intensive posts.

Back in the late 1930s, the escalating conflicts in both Europe and his own home prompted him to spend more time socializing (i.e., with people other than his wife!). Much of this socializing took place at the "Wall Street salon"[46] hosted by Helen Slade and her husband, Henry Sanders. Slade was known to invite only the most illustrious names on Wall Street to her luxuriously catered affairs. Several years later (in 1946), she became what Kahn and Milne described as "the guiding spirit behind the *Analysts Journal* (*Financial Analysts Journal* beginning in 1960),"[47] a periodical to which Graham would make frequent and significant contributions.

Graham remained at the forefront of the profession that he helped found. In fact, it was Graham's idea to conceive of an accreditation system for financial analysts—a standardized system through which one (employer or client) could be assured of a certain level of knowledge and skill from a particular analyst. Graham's brainchild became the CFA (Chartered Financial Analyst) designation, now recognized throughout the world as the ultimate "seal of approval" for financial-analysis skill and ethics. As of 2011, the designation was held by over ninety-five thousand financial professionals across the globe.[48] At a 1947 conference of the Financial Analysts Federation, Graham made a spirited plea for the need for such a designation, and he continued to champion this cause throughout the early 1950s and beyond.

Eventually, even the frequent roller skating and socializing could not withstand the sheer loathing he experienced during the relatively few hours in which Graham could not escape his wife's presence. Realizing the utter absurdity of the situation, Graham insisted on a divorce and, presumably, Carol (who was probably not happy in such a marriage either) did not object. So, a little over a year after their marriage, "Ben and Carol" were no longer an item, and Graham was newly single for the second time in less than three years. As Dr. Sarnat told me in an amused tone, "A year later (after his divorce from Hazel), he married a young actress and, after a year or so of that, he had had enough of her, too!"[49] Understandably, Graham decided to take a hiatus from the search for Mrs. Right and, instead, passed more of his time with three people he had usually gotten along very well with—his two brothers, Leon and Victor, and their mother, Dora. Considering that Dora Graham was robbed and murdered on her way home from a bridge game in 1944, it is fortunate for Graham that he had the opportunity to spend more time with his mother in the early 1940s.

Twice-divorced, grieving for his mother (whom he loved and admired deeply, albeit not uncritically), and feeling painfully alone, it is probably not coincidental that Graham's third and final marriage took place just a few months after his mother's death. At the time, his secretary was an attractive younger woman by the name of Estelle (or "Estey") Messing. Estey's straightforward honesty and natural kindness were the ideal complements to Graham's workaholic lifestyle. One year later, Graham and Estelle had their first and only child, Ben Jr. (or "Buz"). In a situation that is not uncommon today but was highly unusual in 1945, Graham had a child who was younger than his grandchild. In 1939, Graham's daughter Marjorie married; four years later, she gave birth to Cathy, the first of Graham's ten grandchildren.

Notably, Marjorie had married Irving Janis, the acclaimed psychologist who, according to the *New York Times*, became "best known for coining the term 'group think' to describe the sometimes risky way decisions are made in high-powered political and corporate circles."[50] Considering Graham's own intellectualism, it is interesting that Graham's second daughter, the thrice-married Elaine, was also drawn to the intellectual type: her first marriage was to the Harvard sociologist Daniel Bell, the celebrated author of such books as *The End of Ideology*[51] and *The Coming of Post-Industrial Society*.[52] (A 2010 interview of the late academic revealed that Bell's association with his former father-in-law was not only family related: "I worked for Ben, and I made some money with it."[53])

Elaine later moved to her father's native England and married yet another acclaimed sociologist, Cyril Sofer—the noted Cambridge professor and author of such books as *Men in Mid-Career*[54] and *Organizations in Theory and Practice*.[55] Elaine had her only two children with Mr. Sofer prior to the couple's divorce. She would marry (and divorce) a third time before her passing in 2003. Having earned a doctorate in sociology, Elaine was a highly noted Cambridge University academic in her own right and the author or coauthor of such books as *The Psychological Impact of School Experience*[56] and such papers as "Inner-Direction, Other-Direction, and Autonomy: A Study of College Students."[57] Her sister Marjorie, who passed away in 2011, was also a published author. A masters graduate in early childhood education, she worked in that field for many years and wrote a highly regarded book titled *A Two-Year-Old Goes to Nursery School: A Case Study of Separation Reactions*.[58]

Marjorie told me of her mixed feelings regarding her father's marriage to his secretary: "My father remarried later to Estelle, who was very nice, but it was still kind of upsetting for me. And then the fact that he married his secretary was certainly unusual, uncon-ventional."[59] Unconventional though it was, the marriage provided Graham with a measure of domestic tranquility and happiness for some time. However, according to Edythe Safron (later Kenner), a neighbor of the new Graham family, his extramarital proclivities were still active. They were especially problematic for Mrs. Safron, as aside from the fact that she was married herself, she had befriended Graham's new wife. As Janet Lowe wrote in *Benjamin Graham on Value Investing*, "Edythe Kenner also frankly discussed Ben's shame-less sexual advances and how much that annoyed her. . . . Though she rejected his propositions, Edythe sought Ben's guidance in investing a few dollars that she had managed to save from household expenses."[60]

Three years after Buz's birth, the Grahams moved out to the affluent New York suburb of Scarsdale, where they would remain until their departure for California in 1956. When I asked him what kind of father Graham was while he was growing up, his son Buz responded in the following manner:

Well [*pause*], I would say that he was a little preoccupied, there were a lot of things going on in his brain and, you know, I was one of them. But, it was sort of a different time as well, back then. I had more of a classical upbringing. I had a nanny who did most of the stuff, and my mom did some stuff. But he was certainly very approachable and engaging, mostly sort of on an intellectual plane.[61]

There certainly were many things "going on" in Graham's brain. Among the most significant of these were his highly innovative ideas on macroeconomics, the focus of the next chapter.

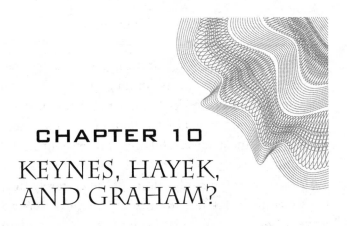

CHAPTER 10

KEYNES, HAYEK, AND GRAHAM?

Due to the extraordinary success of Warren Buffett and his other celebrated value-investing disciples, in the early twenty-first century, Benjamin Graham is associated almost entirely with the field of investing, not economics. However, Graham himself considered his proposals for what he believed to be a more stable form of currency to be the most seminal contribution of his life's work. As he wrote in 1965, "If my name has any chance of being remembered by future generations—assuming that there will be future generations—it will be as inventor of the commodity reserve currency plan."[1] Considering that, some thirty-five years after his passing, his book *The Intelligent Investor* is consistently ranked in the top two or three hundred of Amazon.com's more than seven million books, Graham's speculation that his name might be forgotten seems misplaced. However, from a modern perspective, his prediction regarding posterity's greater acclaim for his economic treatises relative to his far more voluminous investment writings seems equally misguided.

After all, even among those who appreciate the revolutionary implications and impact of Graham's seminal contributions to finance, relatively few are even aware of his economic ideas. After all, he spent the whole of his forty-two-year full-time career working on Wall Street, of which thirty-three years were spent managing or comanaging his own successful fund utilizing his own methods. This track record speaks for itself and lends credibility to any investment-related material penned by Graham. (Of course, the fact that Warren Buffett, the most successful investor in human history, identifies Graham as his primary mentor in the field enhances this credibility even further.) Conversely, although he certainly devoted some time to discussing, thinking, and reading about the macroeconomic challenges of his day, Graham's "trade" was investing, not implementing large-scale transformations of the monetary system.

This dynamic accounts for some but not all of the discrepancy between Graham's iconic status in investment finance relative to his less prominent standing in economics. Another important reason is that, while Graham's currency proposal was considered (with varying degrees of thoroughness) by some of the most prominent economists of his time, Graham's value-investment paradigm has not only been thoroughly examined, parsed, and discussed within the financial-analyst community, but most importantly, it has been *implemented successfully.* As I write, Graham's investment principles are being applied actively to the allocation of literally hundreds of billions of dollars throughout the United States and, indeed, the world. Yet, in the sphere of macroeconomics, eighty years after it was first proposed, his exhaustively detailed proposal for an alternate basis of currency has yet to be implemented in any substantive manner.

Consequently, unlike the labyrinth of performance statistics accumulated over eight decades of applied value investing, there is a dearth of empirical data with which to support (or, for that matter, refute) Graham's economic views. Nonetheless, they were certainly meritorious enough to generate considerable discussion and, in some cases, praise among some of the most notable economists and government officials of Graham's time. They have since faded mostly into obscurity, although, as will be discussed below, they still resurface in interesting ways from time to time. Overall, were he alive today, Graham would have felt disappointed about the general neglect of what he considered to be the most significant piece of his intellectual legacy. His close friend and former teaching assistant Irving Kahn certainly harbors that feeling. As Mr. Kahn told me in September 2011, "Ben's best book is not the book he's known best for [*The Intelligent Investor*]. His best book, his most important book, was *Storage and Stability*."[2]

Although I'm not as certain that it was Graham's *best* book (however one chooses to define that), I was surprised at how deeply a book on such a "dry" topic as currency stabilization held my interest throughout. As usual, Graham's writing style in *Storage and Stability* is engaging and persuasive. The book represents a cogent and thorough analysis of a large body of economic data peppered with fascinating historical references and insights. At least from a biographical perspective, it is also, as Kahn characterized it, an *important* book. Aside from what they reveal about Graham as a theoretician and a socially conscious human being, the essential principles from *Storage and Stability* as well as his later work, *World Commodities and World Currencies*, present a fascinatingly novel conception of not only currency, but also production, employment, and even international relations. In order to understand these principles, it is instructive to gain an understanding of the challenges that motivated Graham to formulate them.

"MR. MONEY"

Chapter 8 discussed Graham's unorthodox view of the stock market as a system that, contrary to the prevailing wisdom of his day and ours, is *not* inherently and unquestionably rational. Rather, it is prone to frequent bouts of wildly irrational/inefficient behavior, which Graham encapsulated in the fictitious character of "Mr. Market." Similarly, beginning as early as 1921, toward the end of what is now known as the 1920–1921 Depression (one definition of *depression* is a drop in gross domestic product of greater than 10 percent[3]) or the 1920–1921 Deflation (defined as "a negative average inflation rate"[4]), Graham began to recognize the inherent inefficiencies of the allegedly "rational" US monetary system. Recalling what he (slightly inaccurately) refers to as the "Depression of 1921 to 1922"[5] in his memoirs, Graham describes this period as being "when the world had perhaps its first real exposure to poverty in the midst of plenty."[6]

Ever the logician, upon examining this state of affairs in greater detail, he came to see it as a gross and indefensible failure of common sense on the part of policymakers. As he wrote in his memoirs,

> If a nation lacks the means of production—in fertile land, manufacturing capacity, technical knowledge—then its standard of living must necessarily be low. But it seems logically absurd for a country like ours, blessed with so many resources, to find itself unable to buy it own products, suffering at once from an excess of goods in the warehouses and too few on the shelves of its families.[7]

During this severe (albeit relatively brief) downturn of the early 1920s, Graham noticed that gold producers were "exempt from the difficulties that bedeviled the rest of us."[8]

This perplexing situation was a direct consequence of the gold standard: American dollars had long been "backed" by gold (and, to a lesser extent, silver) in the sense that each dollar represented a defined quantity of the metal. This dynamic was enshrined in federal law with the 1900 passage of the Gold Standard Act.[9] So, while prices of essential commodities plummeted calamitously during the 1920–1921 period, the price of gold was an oasis of stability amid economic chaos. As Graham recognized, "No matter how large their output, they [gold producers] could sell it immediately at an assured price—then $20 an ounce."[10] Clearly, something was fundamentally wrong with a monetary system that, in times of economic crisis, wreaked havoc upon so much of the economy while sparing (even benefiting) those who produce the only tangible item with which its paper money is linked.

A twenty-seven-year-old employee of Newburger, Henderson, and Loeb at the time, Graham witnessed the economic carnage of falling prices (and their domino effect from one industry to another) reflected in the corporate financial information that he pored over each day. He was both dismayed and intrigued by the glaring irrationality of a monetary system that seemed to exacerbate, instead of contain (let alone reverse), the damage. Ideally, a monetary system should serve to help revive a troubled economy through the stimulus of additional liquidity (i.e., stimulating demand and stemming further price drops by injecting more money into the economy). Although Graham had no economic training (as mentioned earlier, he had dropped out of the only economics course he had ever registered in at Columbia), he had the same combination of rigorous mathematical training and natural facility with logical thinking that he applied so fruitfully to the realm of investment finance (in which he also had no formal education). Undaunted by the novelty of the field, Graham set his mind to considering this problem.

As one would expect, considering the distinctive nature of his contributions to investment finance, the results of Graham's consideration of macroeconomic issues were very interesting. While prominent economic theorists of the time were addressing the glaring weaknesses of the system with adjustments to the relationship between dollars and gold,[11] in characteristic Graham fashion, he considered an entirely different solution, one that was more mindful of the plight of raw-material suppliers and its impact upon the wider economy. As Graham recalls of his initial flash of inspiration (ca. 1921) regarding this matter, "A better standard, I felt, was to give a designated bundle or 'market basket' of basic raw materials a monetary status equivalent to that which had always been accorded to gold."[12]

Specifically, Graham advocated for a "commodity-unit" currency representing a basket of twenty-three commonly used commodities[13]—"the former 23 gr. of gold in the dollar are to be replaced by 23 small quantities of different basic raw materials."[14] In this manner, some of the stability enjoyed by gold producers during the 1920–1921 Depression could be experienced by those who supply/ produce what Graham describes as the "tangible, basic goods that we use and need, in their proper relative amounts."[15] This would be a monetary system that would provide greater stability to the prices of basic foodstuffs (wheat, sugar, etc.), textiles (e.g., cotton), metals (e.g., copper), and other vital tangible elements of American production and consumption, such as rubber. In other words, just as gold had enjoyed greater stability by being *the* constituent element of the monetary unit (the dollar), by being elevated to constituent elements of the dollar, the price stability of the primary inputs of production would be enhanced considerably. The improved stability of these primary "inputs" would, in Graham's view, then ripple throughout the economy, leading to greater overall stability in pricing, production, consumption, profitability, and employment.

During downturns, the government would purchase a reserve of this basket of goods (on an established proportional basis set by the government) from its suppliers to absorb excess capacity. Then, when the economic cycle turned yet again, these reserves would be sold off in exchange for money. Of course, during the lean years, the reserves would also have the added benefit of providing an emergency supply of essential goods. According to his memoirs, as early as 1921, Graham was of the opinion that "the chief cause of depressions in the modern world, I felt, was the public's lack of purchasing power to absorb the increased production resulting from previous economic booms."[16] This lack of adequate consumer spending forced factories (and other businesses) to adjust to lower consumer demand by producing at lower levels. This, in turn, led to lay-offs that depressed the economy even further.

Graham's reflection regarding the public's purchasing power is significant, as it was arrived at many years prior to the publication of John Maynard Keynes's major works in this regard (most notably, Keynes's 1936 classic *General Theory of Employment, Interest, and Money*[17]). Graham does acknowledge reading John A. Hobson's 1922 work *The Economics of Unemployment*,[18] which espouses similar ideas. However, he claims to have arrived at a similar conclusion prior to reading Hobson, just as he claims to have considered a commodity-based currency prior to learning of a similar, though less elaborate, scheme proposed by none other than Thomas Edison. Considering the number of instances in which he criticizes himself and even his work (e.g., regarding *Baby Pompadour*, the poorly received play he cowrote: "The probabilities are that it wasn't good enough for Broadway and that it deserved to fail."[19]) Graham's memoirs, intended only for posthumous publication, are among the most candid that I have read. Consequently, I am inclined to believe Graham's contention that he had formulated his own conceptions on these matters independently of Hobson, Keynes, and Edison.

In any case, conscious of the scourge of insufficient demand during business-cycle downturns, Graham believed that his commodity-reserve system would help smooth out the business cycle by ensuring a consistent minimum level of demand for his basket of "basic durable raw materials."[20] Unfortunately (or not, depending on one's opinion of the merits of Graham's economic prescriptions), Graham was too focused on his work at Newburger in 1921 to do much about his plan other than discuss it with his uncle, Maurice Gerard, who found it very intriguing. Moreover, the downturn during the early 1920s, severe as it was, became an obscure footnote in American history as the 1920s "roared" on to unprecedented prosperity. Graham, supporting a growing family during this time, recalls how his reserve plan faded into irrelevance for the remainder of that decade: "I put the plan aside during the ensuing boom years: I was too busy making money on Wall Street. (These years, by the way, were marked by unusual stability in the price index.)"[21]

A PRESCRIPTION FOR "MR. MONEY'S" PARALYSIS

While monetary stability may have seemed like an academic, even trivial, matter in 1923 or 1928, by 1932 it was anything but. According to Milton Friedman and Anna Schwartz's *A Monetary History of the United States, 1867–1960*, the US money supply had contracted by over one-third during the period between 1929 and 1933, "more than triple the largest preceding declines recorded in our series"[22] of US monetary contractions that "seized up" the entire economy: "U.S. net national product in current prices fell by more than one-half from 1929 to 1933; net national product in constant prices, by more than one-third; implicit prices, by more than one-quarter; and monthly wholesale prices, by more than one-third."[23] Of course, plummeting prices impacted production, which, in turn, led to a 24.1 percent unemployment rate in 1932.[24] In Friedman and Schwartz's view, the monetary contraction was the primary reason that an otherwise ordinary recession descended into the worst economic crisis in American and, ultimately, *world* history.

Friedman and Schwartz were reflecting on the calamity of 1930s monetary dynamics in 1963. However, as evidenced by the superlative work of John Maynard Keynes and others, the role of monetary policy in the crisis did not go unnoticed by macroeconomic thinkers of the Depression era itself. By then, the quest for monetary stability had become a matter of the utmost importance to anyone with a stake in the US economy and a social conscience about its less fortunate participants. Graham had both. By then, he was an active participant in Alvin Johnson's group, the Economic Forum, whose stated objective was "to exchange ideas about how to improve 'the sorry scheme of things.'"[25] Johnson' group was a kind of informal think tank, with a number of great intellects but only limited political influence. At a 1932 session of the Economic Forum, Graham presented several economic plans to the group, of which the commodity-reserve currency plan was best received.

By coincidence, and entirely unbeknownst to the New York resident, a currency modification plan along related (but far from identical) lines had been developed during the same year by the Dutch academic Jan Goudriaan at the University of Rotterdam and published in an obscure thirty-two-page pamphlet titled *How to Stop Deflation*.[26] While Goudriaan advocated for the replacement of the gold standard with a commodities-backed currency, the government-run reserve, which, for better or worse, was the central element of Graham's plan, was not part of Goudriaan's vision. As Kahn and Milne recount, "This pamphlet was little known and Ben did not hear of it for several years. In time, Ben became friends with Professor Goudriaan."[27] Another European thinker who had briefly posited some incomplete aspects of a commodity-related currency (only to dismiss them as "most inconvenient"[28]) was the nineteenth-century British economist William Jevons (whom Graham was not familiar with until some years later). Of course, prior to our current "information age," the discovery of such transatlantic academic synchronicities after the fact was not uncommon.

According to Graham, the purpose of the group's self-named periodical, edited by Joseph Mead and William McChesney Martin (the future Federal Reserve chairman), was to "publish as many of the new proposals as the editors deemed worthy of attention."[29] Apparently, Mead and Martin considered Graham's commodity-reserve currency plan to be sufficiently "worthy of attention" for publication in the Spring 1933 issue of the *Economic Forum* as an eight-page article titled "Stabilized Reflation."[30] As Graham explains, the since-discarded term *reflation* was then "a popular term to describe a return of conditions from deflation to normal without bringing on the counterevils of inflation."[31] That same spring, Franklin Delano Roosevelt (FDR) took the reins of the executive branch in Washington, where he would soon embark upon ambitious reforms and programs, unprecedented in their scope, to attempt to address the near paralysis of the country's economic condition.

Somewhat surprisingly (considering his immigrant background and his lack of social connections to the "blue blood" circles of the Roosevelt family), Graham actually had multiple entrées into the heart of the new administration—including a friend who was once a classmate of the new president. Indeed, FDR himself reportedly considered the plan seriously on more than one occasion, and his agriculture secretary (and later, vice president) Henry Wallace invited Graham to meet with him in Washington regarding his plan. Encouraged by this positive (albeit noncommittal) feedback from the very highest echelons of the US government, Graham worked extensively on further developing and formalizing the commodity-reserve currency plan. This work culminated in a 235-page presentation of the plan, published in 1937 as *Storage and Stability*.

Regardless of one's opinion of his ideas (with respect to investment finance, macroeconomics, or any other issue on which he posited a novel/alternate hypothesis), Graham's views were almost always thoroughly researched and well presented. A tour de force of agricultural and monetary history and policy, *Storage and Stability* is no exception. Graham commences with the vexing problem of agricultural surplus and the absurd "solutions" to the problem that a poorly conceived monetary system has led to: "That surplus stocks of goods have played an overshadowing part in the depression of the 1930s can scarcely be gainsaid. The point was brought home in a spectacular manner by the government-sponsored plowing under of cotton and slaughter of pigs in 1933."[32] Graham then explains that such gross inefficiency is a direct consequence of paper money's near-complete divorce from tangible items of direct relevance to human welfare: "Wealth, in short, became not so much the actual ownership of things as the ability to purchase them."[33]

THE HISTORICAL BASIS OF STORAGE

Charles Brandes, Graham's preeminent West Coast disciple, told me something very insightful about his mentor's outlook on the world: "I think that this knowledge of his history gave him the perspective of eternity, which can be a great advantage in investing."[34] Not only did his historical knowledge help shape his approach to investing but, as evidenced by Graham's reflections on various other topics in his memoirs (theology, friendship, and so forth), the rare breadth and depth of his historical understanding informed his view on every aspect of life to which he turned his attention. Collectively, Graham's works on macroeconomics exemplify his "eternal" perspective on current problems. In fact, the essential premise of the commodity-reserve currency plan is a historical one.

In *Storage and Stability*, Graham explains how, due to the advent of commercial and investment banking, liquidity (i.e., the speed with which an asset can be converted into cash) has trumped all else, much to the detriment of many important groups of producers. "The relegation of merchandise inventories to their present inferior and even dubious state as regards liquidity has been a gradual process of long duration."[35] The unfortunate series of historical developments that led to this situation, according to Graham, account for why inventories of entirely useful and needed (albeit not always immediately) products such as basic foodstuffs, textiles, and essential (but non-precious) metals have become "looked upon either as a means of making money or as an obstacle to making money, depending upon market conditions."[36] The latter leads to the rather perverse scenario of "both the business man and the farmer"[37] identifying surplus inventory as the culprit to the extent that crop burning and the like are seen as wholly rational, even necessary, countermeasures against falling prices.

Along with the businessman and the farmer, the policymaker played a central role as well, particularly in the years immediately preceding the publication of *Storage and Stability*. FDR's Agricultural Adjustment Act (AAA), a central element of the new president's New Deal, was designed to impose a "floor" under crop and livestock pricing through production restrictions. To this end, it necessitated payment to farmers for *not farming* portions of their land and led to significant crop burning and livestock slaughter. However, the act did serve Roosevelt's primary aim of supporting (some) farmers through raising prices for agricultural products. "Although quite controversial when introduced—especially because it required the destruction of newly planted fields at a time when many Americans were going hungry—the AAA program gradually succeeded in raising farmers' incomes."[38] However, due to a number of unintended consequences of the act (which was declared unconstitutional by the Supreme Court in 1936 due to states' rights issues[39] but was soon replaced with a similar piece of legislation), it proved to be a boon for large farming businesses but struck the final death knell for tenant farming,[40] long an important element of the US economy, particularly in the South.

Graham believed that such restrictions on agricultural (and other raw-materials) production "can be defended neither by theory, by practical result, nor by the law of necessity."[41] He believed that a government-run system of storing surplus production in a reserve was far more efficient and conducive to long-term economic well-being than the destruction and distortions wrought by production restrictions. In a fascinating series of historical (and quasi-historical) examples, Graham makes a convincing case that "throughout the ages prior to the twentieth century the primary concern of the State with agricultural surplus was first to promote it, and secondly to *conserve* it for later needs by storage."[42] Going as far back as the biblical account of Joseph storing provisions in advance of Egypt's famine and the well-documented storage systems employed by the Peruvian Incas and ancient Chinese, all the way through the practices of the dominant European nations of the sixteenth through the nineteenth centuries, Graham provides ample historical precedent for his thesis.

He also illustrates instances of severe production restrictions throughout the world in the twentieth century, such as coffee destruction in Brazil, tobacco destruction in Greece, and "plowing under of cotton in the United States."[43] Moreover, as Graham highlights, even in the twentieth century, storage schemes have been employed successfully by such countries as Canada and Argentina. So, according to him, government imposition of production restrictions in 1937 was representative of a recent phenomenon entirely out of sync with human history and sound economic policy. However, Graham was hardly an Austrian noninterventionist (in economics, the term "Austrian" is meant to connote the laissez-fare approach to economic problems advocated by Austrian economists including Carl Menger, Ludwig von Mises and, to a lesser extent, Friedrich Hayek). Instead of promoting a more passive response to calamitous price drops, Graham had developed a fairly involved and elaborate system that, due to its proposed scope and powers, could only be established and administered by a strong central government.

DEVILISH DETAILS: THE MECHANICS OF THE COMMODITY-RESERVE CURRENCY

In *Storage and Stability*, Graham writes: "The idea that the State should accumulate commodities when they are in oversupply, and send them out into consumption when they are needed, sounds reasonable enough in principle. The difficulties are those of application."[44] As for the currency aspect of the plan, Graham's contention that "the *modernized* gold standard"[45] could be preserved "alongside" his plan would also necessitate some logistical maneuvering. (The 1934 passage of the Gold Reserve Act granted the president the authority to devalue the gold value of the dollar; FDR proceeded to devalue the dollar by 40 percent.[46]) Certainly, logistical simplicity is not one of the strengths of Graham's macroeconomic prescriptions. Nonetheless, he was of the mind that complex problems do not always have simple solutions and that relatively complex systems, if constructed thoughtfully, could yield important, albeit imperfect, socioeconomic benefits relative to the status quo. Considering that *Storage and Stability* was published in 1937 (when the US economy had slipped back into a sharp recession after recovering somewhat from the worst of the 1929–1933 period[47]), it would have been difficult for one to argue that the status quo was a desirable state of affairs.

The basket would consist of twenty-three items from four distinct categories: foods (corn, wheat, sugar, oats, coffee, barley, rye, cocoa, and cottonseed oil), textiles (cotton, wool, and silk), metals (copper, lead, tin, and zinc), and a number of goods Graham categorized under the term "miscellaneous" (petroleum, animal hides, rubber, cottonseed meal, flaxseed, tobacco, and tallow—a form of livestock animal fat that can be preserved without refrigeration). In *Storage and Stability*, Graham called for a new governmental body to administer both the storage and the currency dimensions of his plan:

> A monetary agency—presumably in the Treasury Department—would be prepared to issue currency upon delivery to it of warehouse receipts calling for any quantity of *complete* commodity units. Conversely it would be prepared to deliver warehouse receipts for the correct amount of complete commodity units in exchange for, *i.e.*, in redemption of, any amount of currency that might be tendered for this purpose.[48]

Although far more detail is provided in *Storage and Stability*, the passage above is an apt outline of how a central element of the storage mechanism would work. With respect to the "stability" element of his proposal, Graham was an advocate of government purchases and sales of commodities on the "open market" (not unlike the Federal Reserve's purchase and sale of various government securities to "re-balance" the economy in one direction or another):

> The general price level for basic raw materials in the open market would be held close to the standard level by the most direct method possible, viz., the purchase of these commodities in the open market whenever the price level tended to decline, and their sale in the open market whenever it tended to advance above the standard level. . . . The stabilizing mechanism would therefore operate on two fronts at the same time. It would increase or decrease the money supply, and it would decrease or increase the (open-market) supply of commodities, to countervail any general tendency of raw materials prices to decline or advance.[49]

Considering that, as Graham himself concedes, such a stabilization mechanism "bears a close analogy to the orthodox method of stabilizing the foreign exchanges under the gold standard,"[50] it is not as far-fetched as it may seem at first glance. Moreover, Graham argues persuasively for the benefits of stabilizing commodity prices (instead of a single precious metal), concluding that a US dollar backed by a basket of essential commodities will be "essentially sounder than a gold dollar. It will be more closely related to the things people want and use."[51]

Another fascinating aspect of his plan, particularly in the wake of the enormous credit boom and bust of the previous decade (the 2000s), is how it could, in Graham's view, help minimize the need for unsound expansions of credit. Establishing that "ordinary consumption tends to fall short of production during a period of business expansion,"[52] Graham observes that "credit extension"[53] then becomes the most obvious (but hardly the most farsighted) means to "make up the difference."[54] Having witnessed both the heights of the 1920s credit boom and the depths of the 1930s Depression (during which he initially lost over two-thirds of his money), Graham was wary of a business cycle in which "each period of prosperity has been said to bear within itself the seeds of its own collapse."[55] Through government purchases/sales and storage/delivery, his proposed system was designed to necessitate stable pricing and demand for the fundamental inputs of production (raw materials). As such, in Graham's view, it had the potential to take the place of "speculative credit expansion (or of government deficits) as the marginal or effective factor in maintaining prosperity."[56]

STORAGE AND *GLOBAL* STABILITY

In the early 1930s, when Graham revisited the commodity-backed-currency idea (the general contours of which he had already conceptualized ten or eleven years earlier), and in the mid-1930s, when he wrote a full-length work on the subject, he was motivated by the unprecedented paralysis of the US economy. In the early 1940s, when he wrote *World Commodities and World Currencies* (published in 1944), he was, of course, motivated primarily by how the global economic instability and protectionism (i.e., various countries' imposition of tariffs and other trade barriers) of the previous decade had been a primary cause of the disastrous breakdown of international relations that culminated in the horrors of World War II. It was Graham's contention that an internationalized implementation of his commodity-reserve currency plan (in a somewhat modified form) could help serve "the task of the postwar world to resolve this conflict between stability and abundance."[57]

The central premise of *World Commodities and World Currencies* is that a subsidiary agency of the still-nascent International Monetary Fund (IMF—established officially in 1944) be formed to "purchase, hold, and sell primary commodities on a composite or unit basis."[58] This prospective global agency, for which Graham suggested the name International Commodity Corporation (ICC), would manage an internationally honored currency based on a basket of the following fifteen commodities (presumably, these would be easier to manage for a global currency than the twenty-three suggested for the US dollar in *Storage and Stability*), classified under two categories: The agricultural category would include wheat, corn, cotton, wool, rubber, coffee, tea, sugar, and tobacco.[59] Graham classified the remaining six commodities—petroleum, coal, wood pulp, pig iron, copper, and tin—as nonagricultural commodities.[60]

In a mechanism modeled after his conception of support for a commodity-backed US dollar, Graham suggested that the proposed ICC would maintain stable pricing through purchases and sales on the market:

> When the composite price falls to 95 per cent of the base, ICC will buy appropriate amounts of all 15 commodities in the world export markets. . . . Whenever the composite price of the unit commodities advances to 105 per cent of the base, the corporation will sell out complete commodity units. . . . Both purchase and sale policy will thus be entirely automatic.[61]

According to Graham, this would help stabilize both prices and the value of money throughout the world, thereby helping to avoid the nightmarish "wheelbarrow Deutschemark" hyperinflation scenario of Weimar Germany that helped facilitate Hitler's ascent to power.[62]

The most obvious objection to such an international currency scheme is the difficulty of imposing it upon a world in which economic sovereignty is held sacrosanct by almost all nations. Graham counters this objection in the latter part of *World Commodities and World Currencies*:

> An international commodity-reserve currency does not bind any nation to do or not to do anything within its borders. It is solely a buying and selling system applicable to a limited group of commodities, under which the products are at times bought and stored and at other times disposed of in the world's markets.[63]

In fact, he even presents a case for why such a currency would facilitate, instead of hinder, the management of national economic policy, arguing that, "generally speaking, national economic objectives can be more readily attained against a background of stable than of widely changing world prices."[64]

TWENTIETH-CENTURY TITANS

In the realm of twentieth-century macroeconomics, two names hover above all others: John Maynard Keynes and Friedrich August Hayek. The latter is a Nobel Prize–winning economist who, according to the Von Mises Institute (an organization of the Austrian school of economics defined above), is "undoubtedly the most eminent of the modern Austrian economists"[65] and the economist who has been "more successful than anyone else in spreading Austrian ideas throughout the English-speaking world."[66] In 1967, recalling the "drama" of the great economic debate of the 1930s, the British economist John Hicks wrote that "the new theories of Hayek were the principal rival of the new theories of Keynes."[67]

As for Keynes, a recent biography of the man states that "along with Marx, Darwin, Freud, and Einstein,"[68] John Maynard Keynes "belongs in the pantheon of seminal thinkers who triggered modern intellectual revolutions."[69] More so than any other economist of the past one hundred years, Keynes has determined the thrust of postwar economic policy. Due in part to the stature of modern Keynesians such as Paul Krugman, Keynes's ideas continue to figure prominently in the current economic debate. Although this debate is often characterized as Keynesian versus Austrian, Keynes and Hayek were great admirers of each other's work. Certainly, both men are widely esteemed as members of the highest echelon of Western economic thinkers. Something else remarkable about the two eminent economists is that they both took the time to respond to Graham's commodity-reserve currency plan!

Certainly, Graham's plan was an interventionist one. The ideas put forth in *Storage and Stability* (1937) would require the active participation of the United States Treasury Department, the Department of Agriculture, and other "vital organs" of the federal government. As for the ideas put forth in *World Commodities and World Currencies*, they would require the consent of all major economic powers as well as the creation of a new global agency that would be empowered with significant influence upon the global economy. These are some of the reasons why it is somewhat surprising that, of the two economists, it was Hayek, of the less interventionist Austrian school, who gave Graham "strong support of the plan in its international application."[70] In fact, Hayek wrote a full-length article endorsing the plan titled "A Commodity Reserve Currency,"[71] which was published in the June–September 1943 issue of the *Economic Journal*.

As for Keynes, his support was more equivocal, as he considered rising prices to be more conducive to full employment than Graham's objective of price stabilization. Nonetheless, he did recognize the merit of other aspects of Graham's plans. As Keynes wrote in a personal letter to Graham, "On the use of buffer stocks as a means of stabilizing short-term commodity prices, you and I are ardent crusaders on the same side."[72] According to Kahn and Milne, "Ben exchanged a number of letters with John Maynard Keynes on this and other economic topics."[73] Whatever one's opinion of his plan may be, it is a testament to his extraordinary intellect and writing skills that Graham, with no formal economic training, could conceive, develop, and present his plan in such a way as to elicit considered (and, on balance, positive) responses from two of the greatest economists of the era (and, indeed, of modern history).

Moreover, as mentioned above, the Roosevelt White House recognized the merits (and seriously considered the implementation) of various aspects of the commodity-reserve currency plan. As well, a summarized proposal of Graham's international conception of the plan was submitted to the fabled Bretton Woods conference of 1944,[74] the effective birthplace of the IMF and the precursor to the World Bank.[75] Nonetheless, to his great disappointment, Graham would never witness the implementation of his currency plan on either the national or the global scale. However, as late as 1965 (eleven years prior to his death), Graham remained convinced that his plan was still preferable to the status quo or any of the other currency schemes that had been proposed since: "If ever expert world opinion should become ready for a new and improved formulation of sound money, my idea might be accepted as the best of its kind."[76] While "expert world opinion" has yet to accept Graham's plan as "the best of its kind," it has resurfaced in some interesting places since his passing in 1976.

COMMODITY-RESERVE CURRENCY: AN IDEA AHEAD OF ITS TIME?

In a 1989 *New York Times* piece titled "The Volatile Dollar: The Floating Dollar Needs an Anchor," the Boston-based economist David Ranson makes a strong argument for Graham's commodity-reserve currency in the face of the "high price"[77] that the United States has paid for "the instability of the dollar."[78] However, Ranson makes no mention of Graham or either of the late writer's books on the subject. If Ranson had just referred to a commodity-backed currency in general terms, one could argue that he may have arrived at such a conclusion independently of reading Graham. However, the fact that Ranson mentions "a set basket of commodities"[79] in his piece makes it fairly likely that he had read of Graham's commodity-reserve currency plan. Certainly, Graham's friend, client, and student Robert Heilbrunn saw it that way. Just a few weeks after Ranson's piece was printed, a letter to the editor from Heilbrunn titled "Fixing the Dollar" appeared in the *New York Times*. After stating his agreement with Ranson's central premise, Heilbrunn made sure that readers knew that Graham had devised such an idea many years before:

> As far back as 1937, no less an expert than Benjamin Graham, one of America's most highly respected authorities in the field of investing, advocated securing the currency with approximately 20 basic commodities. . . . Now is the time for this proposition to be submitted to the legislators anew.[80]

In 2002, an overview of the history of currency reform by the British writer (and fellow of the London-based New Economics Foundation) David Boyle was published. The 274-page book, titled *The Money Changers: Currency Reform from Aristotle to E-cash*, included only the currency reform contributors/topics that Boyle considered worthy of discussion in a twenty-first-century context. Interestingly, while *Storage and Stability* was ignored, there was a "Benjamin Graham" entry for the international commodity-backed currency plan detailed in *World Commodities and World Currencies*. Boyle believed that then-recent events were proof of the prescience of Graham's 1944 book: "Floating currencies—as we have them now—are thoroughly dangerous, he [Graham] warned, because they are not based on anything. The Asian currency crisis—and all the other sharpening currency crises over the past half century—seems to have proved his point."[81] It is certainly remarkable to see a "Benjamin Graham" entry following an entry for the renowned economist Irving Fisher in a twenty-first-century work on macroeconomics.

Even more recently, in January 2011, a New York–based US-Chinese trade specialist gave a speech at the London School of Economics (LSE) endorsing Graham's international currency plan. In it, John W. Allen, a Harvard MBA graduate who once worked with Sir James Wolfensohn (chairman of the World Bank from 1995 to 2005), actually described Benjamin Graham as one of "history's most eminent economists."[82] Citing the governor of the Central Bank of China's recent advocacy of a new reserve currency "disconnected from individual nations"[83] and "able to remain stable in the long run,"[84] Allen told his illustrious LSE audience that "these were the same thoughts put forth by Benjamin Graham in his book *World Commodities and World Currencies* in 1944."[85] Certainly, if such an international currency is ever implemented (due to China's insistence or any other reason) and modeled after the ideas detailed in his writings, Graham's 1965 prediction that future generations would remember him best for his commodity-reserve currency plan may be proven correct after all.

CHAPTER 11

AN EAGER YOUNG STUDENT FROM OMAHA

It is curious that Graham seems to have chosen 1940 as the cutoff point for relating his personal history to readers of the first fourteen chapters of his memoirs. There are two additional chapters beyond that point, each of which focuses exclusively on an important aspect of his noninvestment work: "My 'Career' as a Playwright" and "The Commodity Reserve Currency Plan." However, neither of these relatively brief chapters extend his life story much beyond 1940, particularly with respect to personal/romantic events. The nonchronological structure of the final two chapters is particularly interesting when one considers that, as can be inferred from contemporaneous references here and there, Graham probably stopped working on "Things I Remember" (as he initially named his memoirs) eight or nine years before he died. As well, some of the contributions to earlier chapters about his public-school days seem to have been made much later than some of the contributions to chapters pertaining to his career at Newburger and beyond. This indicates that, instead of being an incomplete memoir in the traditional sense, Graham's may have been cut short intentionally at 1940.

Although his greatest professional triumphs occurred beyond that point (as he well knew, writing his memoirs from around 1957 to 1967), so did some of the most painful and controversial (even scandalous) events of Graham's personal life. While he was obviously eager to provide his account of his marriage to Hazel, the loss of his first son, and other disagreeable aspects of the first forty-six years of his life, Graham may not have felt as comfortable expressing his feelings about what had since transpired in his personal life. It is probable that Graham had yet to "come to terms" with some of his more recent memories. As he wrote in his memoirs, "I have the most selective memory imaginable, the principle of selectivity being to forget as quickly and as completely as possible all disagreeable events."[1]

In any case, the fact remains that Graham's personal chronological memoirs end after the dissolution of his second marriage. Nonetheless, since they were written in the 1950s and 1960s, Graham's memoirs still offer some subtle (and, occasionally, revealing) glimpses into his later life. Fortunately, my interviews with Benjamin Graham Jr. (his only child from his third marriage), Warren Buffett, Dr. Bernie Sarnat and his wife Rhoda (Graham's neighbors from 1956 to 1965 and close personal friends of his third wife), Dr. Robert Hamburger and his wife Sonia (friends of Graham and his lover, Marie-Louise Amingues, during the final stage of his life), and various secondary sources help complete the story of Graham's latter years, beginning in the late 1940s.

BRINGING "VALUE" TO THE MASSES: *THE INTELLIGENT INVESTOR*

Among the most noteworthy quotes from my interview with Irving Kahn was the following statement from the 106-year-old devoted friend, associate, and (along with Warren Buffett) lifelong "champion" of Graham: "Benjamin Graham remains the father of investment analysis for both elementary and advanced pupils."[2] Advanced students of Graham's financial-analysis methods who were not fortunate enough to attend his lectures in person generally chose to learn the "father's" wisdom from the exhaustive analyses found in *Security Analysis*, the original value "Bible" that Graham coauthored with David Dodd in 1934. However, both the level of detail and the tone of that classic work were poorly suited to the "elementary pupil," the person who was not training to become a full-time investment professional but who had sufficient disposable income and spare time to benefit from some independent application of Graham's principles.

As Kahn and Milne wrote in their 1977 tribute to Graham, "Recognizing the need to bring his approach to the attention of the astute layman, Ben in 1949 wrote *The Intelligent Investor*."[3] Or, as Warren Buffett described its intent to me, "Certainly, when he wrote *The Intelligent Investor*, Ben wanted to write something that would be useful for the masses and not just for the few. He was trying to make his investment approach useful for a dentist in Pocatello, Idaho, or a lawyer in Austin, Texas."[4] Published by Harper & Row in 1949, *The Intelligent Investor* has since become (along with *Security Analysis*) one of Graham's two perennial classics and the most successful of the five full-length works he wrote (or cowrote) that were published during his lifetime. Currently in its fifth edition, the book has sold well over one million copies since its initial publication over sixty years ago. As of this writing (in late 2011), its latest (2003) edition is number 262 on Amazon.com's bestseller list[5]—not just of business books, but of *all* Amazon.com's more than seven million titles!

The ongoing success of *The Intelligent Investor* is not difficult to fathom. Written for the "lay investor" instead of the finance community, the book imparts Graham's sound security-selection principles in a manner that is less technical and more conversational than Graham and Dodd's *Security Analysis*. Moreover, in order to maximize its usefulness to the general public, *The Intelligent Investor* makes an important distinction between two categories of lay investors: the enterprising investor (defined as one who is willing "to devote time and care to the selection of sound and attractive investments"[6]) and the defensive investor ("one interested chiefly in safety plus freedom from bother"[7]). As detailed in chapter 4 of the present volume, Graham provides two sets of security screening criteria that are tailored specifically for each category.

Moreover, well aware of the behavioral traps to which lay investors are especially vulnerable, as the following passage from the 1949 edition demonstrates, the book highlights the critical (but frequently overlooked) psychological dimension of investing. The following passage from the original (1949) edition is an apt example: "It is becoming increasingly difficult to attain that peculiar combination of alertness and detachment which characterizes the successful investor as distinguished from the speculator. Intelligent investment is more a matter of mental approach than it is of technique."[8] In other words, the proper psychological framework (the "combination of alertness and detachment") supersedes the more technical aspects of value investing. Similarly, *The Intelligent Investor*'s "Mr. Market" (Graham's clever personification of market behavior, discussed in chapter 8) underscores an important psychological dynamic in a way that can be readily understood by the nonprofessional investor.

As Warren Buffett wrote, several decades after the first publication of *The Intelligent Investor*, "I read the first edition of this book early in 1950, when I was nineteen. I thought then that it was by far the best book about investing ever written. I still think it is."[9] Considering that *The Intelligent Investor* was, at least in an intellectual sense, Buffett's first proper introduction to Graham, I asked Buffett about both his initial reaction to the book and its long-term impact upon the course of his fabled investing career:

> It just made sense. I mean, I read every book in the Omaha Public Library on investments by the time I was eleven and I reread most of them; and, you know, my Dad was in Congress, so I had access to the Library of Congress. So my Dad got me all the books—they were all interesting to me and I tried various theories of investing. But then, when I read *The Intelligent Investor*, it just made clear sense to me as a book about investing, and I've been following it ever since. My life would have been entirely different had I not

encountered that book. Who knows where it would have gone exactly? However, I can absolutely assure you that it would have been entirely different . . . probably would have taken a couple of zeros off my net worth![10]

VALUE HEIR FROM THE HEARTLAND

Of course, Buffett's reading of *The Intelligent Investor* was not only a defining moment in *his* life but, as subsequent events would demonstrate, it was a pivotal moment in the life and legacy of the book's author as well. When examining the two men's life stories together, there are a number of striking similarities that, collectively, make their eventual "crossing of paths" seem all but inevitable. On the surface, the Midwestern "born and bred" Protestant son of a Republican congressman and the immigrant great-grandson of the Chief Rabbi of Warsaw, born over thirty-five years apart, would seem to have emerged from entirely different worlds. However, on a deeper level, there are some remarkable parallels between the origins and formative experiences of the two "titans" of value investing.

Buffett's Huguenot (French Protestant) ancestors were known for their thrift and entrepreneurial skill, traits ascribed to some Jews as well (and certainly applicable to some of Graham's forebears). In 1869, Buffett's great-grandfather established the S. H. Buffett Grocery Store in Omaha, Nebraska, which later evolved into the highly successful Buffett & Son grocery enterprise managed by Buffett's grandfather. While Howard Buffett, Warren's father, had, according to Buffett biographer Roger Lowenstein, "no interest in becoming a third-generation grocer,"[11] he did become a very successful entrepreneur in other industries (prior to his political career). Of course, Graham's father and grandfather (of "Grossbaum & Sons") were also successful entrepreneurs. Moreover, Howard Buffett was known to be a deeply religious (Presbyterian) man; in *The Money Masters*, John Train describes the elder Buffett as "a hyperconservative of messianic zeal."[12] Graham's father, Isaac, a deeply pious man, was known for his strong religious convictions as well.

Another interesting parallel is the misfortune that befell the two families when both Buffett and Graham were still children. Whereas the Graham (then Grossbaum) family's 1903 descent into poverty was due to Isaac's death, the Buffett family's financial ruin in 1931 was a direct consequence of the Great Depression. A securities salesman for a bank that went under, Howard Buffett lost both his job and the family savings (prior to the establishment of the Federal Deposit Insurance Corporation [FDIC] in 1933, depositors were personally vulnerable to bank failures) on the same fateful day. Fortunately, Howard would go on to establish a brokerage firm as well as a livestock-feed company, and within a few years, the family's severe economic hardships would *seem* like a distant memory, but, as Lowenstein recounts, they had already left a deep and permanent impression upon a young Warren Buffett: "He emerged from those first hard years with an absolute drive to become very, very rich. He thought about it before he was five years old. And from that time on, he scarcely stopped thinking of it."[13]

As with Graham's childhood experiences, Buffett's firsthand brush with destitution during his formative years strengthened two defining traits that would shape the rest of his life: a steely (but principled) determination to attain financial success and the kind of visceral appreciation for *value* that only those who have experienced the pain of poverty can understand fully. An Omaha taxicab driver who was working at a local GM dealership in the late 1980s and early 1990s (long after Buffett had become a billionaire) told me that when the dealership advertised large discounts on their cars due to surface damage from a hailstorm (none of which were luxury vehicles), Omaha bargain-seekers snapped them up, including Buffett himself![14] (Buffett confirmed the veracity of this story for me, although he clarified that it was his daughter who actually went to the dealership and purchased the car on his behalf.)

With respect to determination, just as "Benny Grossbaum" earned substantial sums of money as a youth, so too did Buffett, albeit with a more entrepreneurial bent. Through unusual industry and creativity, Buffett had transformed what others would have regarded as merely a regular Washington, DC, paper route (his father was serving as a congressman at the time) into a surprisingly lucrative enterprise. As Lowenstein recounts, when Buffett was only fourteen years old, "he was earning $175 a month—what many a young man was earning as a full-time wage—and saving every dime."[15] That same year, Buffett had also commenced an investing career of sorts by purchasing forty acres of farmland back in his home state of Nebraska.

This combination of determination and instinctual value-seeking (what Lowenstein described as "an ambitious but prudent capitalist zeal"[16]) is why Buffett was so receptive to the "margin of safety," "intrinsic value," and other aspects of the inherently cautious Graham "gospel" put forth in *The Intelligent Investor* and *Security Analysis* (which Buffett read soon after). However, what made Buffett unusually successful in applying (and later, modifying) Graham's principles was a superior intellect, another defining characteristic shared with his mentor. In fact, Lowenstein's description of Buffett as a youth applies equally well to Graham: "Warren was known as a bookworm, and was certified in the neighborhood lore as having a 'photographic memory.'"[17] Similarly, Graham's son Buz told me of the first time he realized just how extraordinary his father's memory was: "One thing that blew me away is when I was a high-school student and I took Latin and my father asked 'what are you studying?' I told him that I was studying Cicero's first oration against Cataline, whereupon he recited it verbatim in Latin, from memory, and it was about three pages, the whole thing."[18]

Another essential similarity is that, like Graham (who majored in mathematics), Buffett is blessed with a remarkable facility with numbers. As Andrew Kilpatrick recounts in *Of Permanent Value: The Story of Warren Buffett*: "In church he [a teenage Buffett] calculated the life span of the composers of hymns, checking to see if their religious calling rewarded them with extra longevity. His conclusion: no."[19] Aside from their shared fascination with numbers, Kilpatrick's amusing anecdote also illustrates another intriguing similarity between Buffett and Graham: both men were fiercely independent thinkers who, despite being born into conservative religious families, became politically liberal (generally) and religiously nonobservant. As discussed in previous chapters, this intellectual and emotional capacity for independent and frequently *contrarian* decision making is a central element of successful value investing.

However, unlike Graham and his Renaissance-like fascination with a wide array of disciplines, languages, and the like, Buffett focused the bulk of his formidable intellectual energy on investing from a very young age. He began reading investment books as an eight-year-old and, as mentioned above, Buffett had already read through the Omaha Public Library's full selection of investment titles by his eleventh birthday (according to Buffett biographer Alice Schroeder, Buffett was only ten years old when he read of the Northern Pipeline story of the late 1920s [discussed in chapter 7], "well before he understood who Benjamin Graham was in the investing world"[20]). He then proceeded to read through the much larger collection of the Library of Congress. Moreover, throughout his adolescence, he was also an avid reader of the *Wall Street Journal*, among other financial publications. By 1950, Buffett had also acquired a respectable formal education in the field, completing a bachelor's degree at the University of Nebraska that he had originally commenced at the University of Pennsylvania's Wharton School of Finance and Commerce (as it was then known). So, although he was only nineteen when he read *The Intelligent Investor*, Buffett was probably as well-read in the field of investment finance as many Wall Street veterans of that era.

"THE BEST TEACHER
I EVER ENCOUNTERED"

As Buffett recounts in Alice Schroeder's *The Snowball: Warren Buffett and the Business of Life*, the content of his application to the Columbia Graduate School of Business (where *Security Analysis* coauthor David Dodd was associate dean and admissions "gate-keeper") was somewhat unusual. However, it was a telling reflection of the awe in which he held Graham (and Dodd) after reading *The Intelligent Investor* and, soon thereafter, *Security Analysis*: "I probably wrote that I just found this catalog at the University of Omaha, and it said that you and Ben Graham taught, whereas I thought you guys were on Mount Olympus someplace just smiling down on the rest of us. And if I can get in, I'd love to come."[21] Certainly, Buffett idealized Graham from afar before he met him in person (in the mid-1980s he told an Omaha reporter that the revelatory feeling he had when reading Graham for the first time was "like Paul on the Road to Damascus"[22]). Then, as a student of Graham's at Columbia, Buffett soon realized that Graham was not only a great writer/theoretician and investor but an outstanding communicator of ideas, too. Indeed, in 1995, Buffett wrote to Berkshire Hathaway shareholders that "the time I spent in Ben's classes was a personal high."[23]

When I asked what was so special and enjoyable about Graham's teaching methods, Buffett told me:

In [Graham's] class, he was always using something that was right in front of you that day in terms of a possible investment. And the other thing is that he was very imaginative in terms of concocting situations to illustrate points. Sometimes he would use Company A and Company B, which looked like two dramatically different investment opportunities, and then later he would reveal that Company A and Company B were the same company at different points in history, and that sort of thing. He had ways of engaging you that were terrific. He was the best teacher I ever encountered. He was a very likable person, too, so that always helped [him] as a teacher. So, you felt that he was empathetic to you. So, I learned a lot about teaching from him as well as investing.[24]

Considering that Buffett was the only student to receive an A+ grade from Graham, the admiration was mutual. Bill Ruane, a now-deceased classmate of Buffett's at Columbia, described the chemistry between Graham and his star student to Andrew Kilpatrick: "'Sparks were flying,' recalls Ruane. 'You could tell then he [Buffett] was someone who was very unusual.'"[25] Both inside and outside Graham's classroom, Buffett was eager to learn everything he could, not only about his professor's investment methods but about the professor himself. As Janet Lowe observed, "It was not just an analytical approach to investments that intrigued Buffett. He was also captivated by Graham's personality."[26] The young Buffett's fascination with his new professor is best exemplified by what he did upon reading that Graham was chairman of the insurance company GEICO: Instead of merely reading more about GEICO (which was not a high-profile enterprise at the time), Buffett took the train from New York down to the company's Washington, DC, headquarters.

Dr. Bernie Sarnat, who would befriend Buffett just a couple years later, told me in an amused tone, what transpired next:

> There's a story about Warren going down to GEICO in Washington, DC. It was a Saturday and he didn't expect anyone there and he knocked on the door. . . . Finally, a janitor opens the door and says, "What do you want?" So Warren says, "I just want to talk to someone here," and so, the janitor answers that "the only one here is Davidson," and Davidson was the president or vice president [at the time, Lorimer Davidson was financial vice president but he later became CEO] of the company. So Warren said "OK," and he had a wonderful afternoon talking with Davidson.[27]

As Davidson told Lowenstein, he was very impressed by the inquisitive college student in front of him: "After we talked for fifteen minutes I knew I was talking to an extraordinary man. He asked searching and highly intelligent questions."[28] (However, it is doubtful that even Davidson expected to see this impressive young man later attain full control of GEICO!)

Similarly, upon learning of Graham's investment in Marshall Wells (distributors of air-conditioning and ventilation equipment), Buffett attended its annual meeting with fellow young "Grahamites" Fred Stanback (his classmate) and Walter Schloss (a young Graham-Newman employee). These men, along with such men of finance as Bill Ruane, Tom Knapp, Marshall Weinberg, and others, would form a strong social circle around their mutual admiration of Graham and his highly effective security-selection methods. As Lowenstein wrote, this budding group of Graham devotees "had the beginnings of a tribe, and they gravitated to Buffett, who was witty, likable, and—they knew—a step ahead of themselves."[29] Some of the friendships among this most successful "crop" of value disciples would prove enduring, and although various differences in approach would emerge between some of these men, they would always agree on how fortunate they were to have encountered Graham.

Upon graduating from Columbia, Buffett (who, according to John Train, "believed in going to work for the smartest person available"[30]) did his best to convince his favorite professor to hire him at Graham-Newman, even offering to work for free. Considering Buffett's superlative academic performance and his natural rapport with Graham, he must have been both dismayed and surprised by his mentor's refusal to hire him. As Irving Kahn explained to me,

> Warren Buffett wanted a job with Ben but Ben wouldn't give him a job, and he said that it wasn't because of a lack of experience but that he tended to favor boys that were Jewish because they were so often discriminated against. But later, he changed his mind about that and gave a job to Warren anyway.[31]

From a twenty-first-century perspective, Graham's initial refusal to hire the young Nebraskan due to the fact that Buffett was not Jewish might seem odd. There's no question that it was blatantly discriminatory, but before judging Graham's decision as inherently wrong or indefensible, it is important to be cognizant of the relatively tense ethnic dynamics of early 1950s Wall Street. In *King of Capital*, a biography of former Citigroup chairman Sanford ("Sandy") Weil, authors Amey Stone and Mike Brewster explain that Weill established his first company (Carter, Berlind, Potoma & Weill) due largely to the fact that Jews (particularly those of Eastern European, as opposed to German, extraction) were being shunned by some of the "blue-blooded" Wall Street firms:

> When Weil made the rounds of Wall Street after college in 1955, the older firms were clinging to power, and still weren't a place of opportunity for outsiders. Even as late as 1961, a year after Weil started his own firm, the young economist Henry Kaufman declined to pursue a coveted position at Smith Barney because he was warned by a mentor that he would never be able to climb to senior management because of his religious affiliation.[32]

Although Graham explained the context of his decision to his star student, it is likely (and understandable) that Buffett felt stung by it anyway. As Schroeder notes, although Graham's decision "must have been incredibly disappointing"[33] for her subject, "Buffett found it impossible to say anything that could be interpreted as critical of Graham, even decades later."[34] Moreover, not one to brood over his setbacks, Buffett chose to see Graham's initial rejection as a temporary obstacle, and he did his best to overcome it. Back in Omaha, the newly minted Columbia graduate maintained a correspondence with Graham and even sent him suggestions regarding specific investment opportunities. Eventually, this correspondence had the desired effect. In 1954, impressed by his former student's extraordinary analytical abilities (and, most likely, his polite tenacity as well), Graham finally relented. Buffett returned to New York yet again to become a full-time employee of the Graham-Newman Corporation. Eventually, he became what Schroeder described as the "golden boy"[35] of Graham-Newman.

By the time Buffett joined Graham-Newman, he was married to Susan (or "Susie"). Toward the end of that year, the young couple gave birth to their first son, Howard *Graham* Buffett. The child's first name was a tribute to Buffett's father and the middle name, of course, was a tribute to "Ben"—a man Buffett had come to admire not only as an investor but also as a person. I asked Buffett about a fairly recent (2009) video in which, recalling his time at Graham-Newman and Graham's generosity, he spoke about how, in personal dealings with Graham, one never could "balance the books"[36] with him:

> Well, you just always felt that he was always doing things for you and it was always hard to figure anything to do for him. When my first son was born, he gave us a variety of presents. When he found out that my wife liked dancing and I wasn't doing much the next day, I found a gift certificate to take dancing lessons at Arthur Murray sitting on my desk. When he gave you something, whether intellectually or physically, he just had no expectation of anything in return. It was very hard to think of anything to do in return. So, you never *could* balance the books with Ben.[37]

At the same time, according to Dr. Sarnat, a friendship was developing between Susie Buffett, whom he describes as "quite a delightful person,"[38] and Graham's wife Estelle: "When Warren was working for Ben—and remember that Warren was a 'nobody' at the time—Estey went out of her way to help the Buffetts, who had one son at the time. Estey was a very giving person and she became very friendly with Susie."[39] According to Buffett, although he was on very good terms with Graham (as he told me, "Ben couldn't have been nicer to me"[40]), their personal friendship really began to flourish some years later when the Buffetts would come out to visit the Grahams in California.

HAPPY DAYS ARE HERE AGAIN?

On the surface, the late 1940s and early 1950s would seem to be among the happiest and most successful times in Graham's life. With respect to his family life, he was now married to a loving and devoted woman with whom he had a happy and healthy young child, and his two eldest daughters were happily married (his youngest daughter, Winnie, would marry in 1956). He seemed to enjoy being both a father and a grandfather. Professionally, he had written and published his most successful book (the second edition of which was already in print by 1954) and Graham-Newman continued to prosper. According to Graham-Newman shareholder letters from that era, from January 31, 1946,[41] to January 31, 1954,[42] the company's net asset value grew by over 75 percent. It is important to clarify that this growth was primarily from assets under management. As Graham said in 1955, "We have paid back to our stockholders virtually all the earnings that have been made, so that in a sense our present value is very similar to the amount of money paid in."[43]

As well, in 1949, at the behest of existing and prospective investors, Graham and Jerry Newman expanded operations by establishing a separate partnership. Despite the fact that Newman and Graham LP (limited partnership) required a steep $50,000 minimum investment, its initial capitalization was well over $2.5 million. Moreover, the two partners' greatest coup, their 50 percent purchase of GEICO (detailed in chapter 6), also occurred during this period. These developments were all highly lucrative for Graham personally: in 1954, he earned approximately $87,000 (roughly $710,000 in 2011 dollars) from the Graham-Newman Corporation alone[44] (i.e., not including compensation from the limited partnership). Additionally, Graham was still earning considerable sums from his work as an expert witness and, increasingly, from book royalties.

Like a proud parent, he was also enjoying witnessing the growth of the new profession and accreditation system that he played an indispensable role in creating. This is best exemplified in "Toward a Science of Security Analysis,"[45] his speech to the recently formed National Federation of Financial Analysts Societies. The speech was classic Graham, prescient ("it is virtually certain that this movement will develop ultimately into full-fledged professional status for our calling"[46]), erudite ("the words that Goethe put in the mouth of Orestes"[47]), and thorough. He concluded with a hopeful statement to the attendees of the federation's fifth annual convention that "security analysis may begin—modestly, but hopefully—to refer to itself as a scientific discipline."[48]

Philanthropy also began to figure more prominently in his life. Certainly, charitable giving was a lifelong endeavor for Graham: a *New York Times* article from May 1926 regarding a fundraising drive for "Polish Jews in desperate need"[49] lists "Benjamin Graham" as a contributor. Moreover, many years later (in 1965), Graham and his two brothers put up the money to rebuild an African American Baptist church in Connecticut[50] that had been destroyed in a fire.[51] However, in the early 1950s, feeling more settled professionally than ever before, Graham also began to devote more of his *time* to philanthropic activities: from 1951 to 1953, Graham served as president of the Jewish Guild for the Blind (a bit of a misnomer, since the guild helped all blind people who sought its assistance, regardless of religious affiliation). Graham would stay on the board of this organization for the remainder of his life. Unfortunately, in the midst of all these positive and productive developments, Graham was about to be struck by a terrible tragedy.

THE WAYWARD SON

Only nine years old when his parents divorced, Newton II was somewhat awkward and emotionally troubled when his parents were still together. However, the divorce seemed to further exacerbate his emotional distress, and he seemed to slide into a kind of semidetached state that further complicated his relationships with his parents.

His lifelong difficulties relating to Graham and Hazel were likely worsened when his parents subsequently married other spouses (and, in Graham's case, began a new family). As Marjorie Graham told biographer Janet Lowe: "After Ben and Hazel divorced, Newton had a lot of difficulties. He went to live with Ben and Estey. . . . They were not able to keep him. They sent him to boarding school."[52] As Lowe observed after speaking with Marjorie about Newton II, "Marjorie felt that Newton never had a real family life, and in fact, despite Hazel and Ben's attempts to help, there was an emotional distance between the young man and his parents."[53]

Marjorie's assessment seems to be corroborated by her father's own recollections of Newton II (from his memoirs): "He did not seem really at home with us; he was extremely difficult to get along with; it was soon evident that he was highly neurotic."[54] Similarly, as Lowe wrote regarding Newton II's time with Graham's second family in Scarsdale, "Newton found it painful to relate to people and spent hours reclusively in the attic playing his cello."[55] However, there is hardly a unanimous consensus on this matter: Charlotte Reiter is a retired registered nurse/family nurse practitioner with considerable knowledge of mental-health issues. She recalls pleasant interactions with "Uncle Newton" as a very young girl, and she disagrees with her grandfather's assessment of the severity of Newton II's mental condition: "He might have been neurotic to some extent—sure, who among us isn't? As far as I can tell, Newton did not display the symptoms of schizophrenia or any other psychosis. Obviously, he was troubled and depressed or despairing, but he was socially functional right to the end."[56]

In early 1953, during the final stages of the Korean War, Newton II was drafted into the US military. The timeline of Graham's life and legacy (e.g., his posthumous election to the US Business Hall of Fame) that is appended to the 1996 publication of his memoirs (which, of course, were not written by Graham himself) describes Graham's second son as a "Korean War veteran,"[57] but various other sources (including Dr. Sarnat) recall the more likely scenario that Newton II was sent first to serve at a US Army base in West Germany (as it was then known) prior to serving in France. Given the fact that the military may not have considered "Private Newton Graham" of sound enough mind for a combat role, it might have deliberately stationed him in a noncombat role and/or region. Or, even if he *was* intended to fight "on the Peninsula," it is probable that, by the time he completed whatever assignment or training he had in West Germany, the Korean War was already over. In any event, to Graham's credit, he was uneasy about his son's military service from the outset. Well aware of Newton II's history of recurrent emotional problems, whether or not live combat would be involved, Graham was concerned about how his son would respond to the social and disciplinary stresses of military life.

However, "orders were orders," and it seems that Newton II himself did not object too strenuously to military service. So, in 1953, as a show of moral support to their recently enlisted son and brother, Newton II's family held a farewell dinner for him at Manhattan's luxurious Waldorf-Astoria Hotel. The affair was attended by everyone in the new serviceman's immediate family (i.e., his parents and sisters), along with Estelle; Hazel's second husband, Arthur Greenwald; Marjorie and Elaine's husbands, and several others. Unfortunately, that dinner proved to be more of a farewell occasion than it seemed at the time. As his father feared, Newton II, the socially awkward and highly sensitive "black sheep" of the family, did not take well to military life. Presumably, through letters and phone calls, Graham became aware of his son's lapse into severe emotional instability. At that point, he must have been concerned about the possibility of suicide. According to Lowe, "Ben became alarmed. He wrote letters to government officials and did what he could to get Newton discharged."[58]

Tragically, Graham's worst fears were realized when he received word of Newton II's suicide in 1954. Upon hearing of his son's death, Graham left for France immediately. While sorting through Newton II's life in that country, he met Marie Louise, his late son's former lover who was in her forties at the time. It is probable that the first meeting with "Malou" prompted a correspondence that *then* developed into something rather unexpected (at least for Graham's family)! However, one of the people I interviewed who was quite familiar with the circumstances behind that relationship claims that it probably "started" during Graham's 1954 trip to France. In either case, this relationship and its impact upon various aspects of Graham's life and thinking will be detailed further in subsequent chapters.

Perhaps due to the severe pain and embarrassment that his second son's suicide must have caused him, Graham, in his memoirs, is uncharacteristically defensive about Newton II's unhappiness (curiously, his *suicide* is not mentioned at all). After presenting a number of possible reasons for Newton's difficulties ("At times we have blamed ourselves because we gave this child our first Newton's name and endeavored from the start to consider him our first-born returned to us."[59]), Graham dismisses them with his assertion that "it was simply Newton's misfortune and our own that he was born to be what he was."[60] However, as with portions of many memoirs, one sometimes gets the impression that, when Graham reflects on specific people or issues, these reflections reveal his conscious or surface-level feelings (i.e., what he believes he "should" feel). Consequently, these may not always be indicative of his most deeply held beliefs.

For example, he wrote, "I feel little emotional loyalty to the Jewish people from whom I sprung"[61] despite the fact that, by his own admission, he initially excluded his only A+ student from his firm out of a strong sense of loyalty to fellow Jews. There are a number of other examples from his life that seem to contradict this statement as well. However, I do not believe that Graham was consciously lying when he wrote those (or any other) words in his memoirs. Rather, I believe that those words reflect the possibility that the former "Benny Grossbaum" may have felt somewhat conflicted about his Jewish identity on a subconscious level. Similarly, I believe that Graham's more abstract reflections on what he considered to be the weaknesses of his personality, written only three years after Newton II's suicide, may reveal at least as much about his emotional response to that loss as his comments about Newton II quoted above.

Writing of himself in the third person and in the past tense (which is hardly indicative of someone who is comfortable with "owning" his feelings) in an essay titled "Benjamin Graham's Self-Portrait at Sixty-Three—May 1957,"[62] Graham laments that "he lacked genuine sympathy, a true sharing of the joys and sorrows of others"[63] and that "his first nature was remote and inaccessible to others. B. [which is how Graham refers to himself in this essay] saw this all at last. He felt the need for less superiority and more humanity."[64] Considering that this was written only three years after the suicide of a son who, justifiably or not, *felt* neglected by his parents, it seems all but certain that at least some of those revealing words betray Graham's true feelings on the tragedy. However, since such expressions of heartfelt remorse were not consistent with his stoic exterior, he could only express them in an "arm's length" manner.

END OF AN ERA

The following year, 1955, was an important transitory period in Graham's life. His son Buz told me of his family's relocation to California: "I know that we moved out here [California] for a few months to kind of try it out. We lived in Beverly Hills for half a school year and then, the following year [1956], we moved for good."[65] So Graham must have spent at least a couple months (half of a middle-school year) in Los Angeles in 1955 preparing for his semiretirement in California. The other notable occurrence in Graham's life during that year also took place outside of New York City. On March 11, Graham was invited to Washington, DC, to testify before the US Senate's Committee on Banking and Currency.

According to government archives pertaining to this committee's work during the period described as "January–May 1955,"[66] the committee was led by Senator James William Fulbright (Democrat, Arkansas), and its purpose was described as follows: "The committee was concerned, in particular, with margin buying, speculation, proxy voting, investment advisors, large institutional investors such as pension funds, and with applying existing regulations to dealing in over-the-counter stocks."[67] Graham would be called back to Congress three years later for further expert testimony pertaining to the securities industry. The fact that Graham was a congressional expert of choice for such matters is an apt reflection of just how far his profile had risen (due, in large part, to his widely read publications in the field). It was also a testament to the unfailingly ethical and law-abiding manner with which he and Jerry Newman had managed their investment business since its inception. Graham had operated successfully on Wall Street for over four decades without the smallest blemish on his name.

However, by 1956, Graham had decided that it was time to retire from the securities business and move out to Los Angeles, where both of his brothers had taken up residence. It is telling that when Graham and Jerry Newman decided to retire from managing their fund, their first choice for a replacement management team consisted of Mickey Newman and Warren Buffett, the former to take his father's place as administrative manager and the latter to take Graham's place as the firm's chief analyst. However, Buffett's primary motivation for taking a position at Graham-Newman in the first place was the opportunity to work closely with Graham. With "Ben" (as he called him) gone, he saw little reason to stay, even as a manager. Moreover, by that time he had already grown homesick for Omaha. As highlighted in the following chapter, it is notable that Buffett and a number of others steeped in the application of Graham's principles became some of the "brightest lights" of the investment world.

CHAPTER 12
DISCIPLES OF VALUE

The great advances in applied science that have transpired in recent centuries (e.g., electricity, aeronautics, etc.) have elevated the quality of life in Western (and, increasingly, non-Western) civilization immeasurably. At least some of the impetus behind this remarkable series of tangible scientific advances stems from the great English thinker cum statesman Sir Francis Bacon and others of his era who gave us the modern scientific method.[1] Prior to adoption of this method, ideas would often be accepted because they seemed to follow logically from other ideas that, in turn, also *seemed* to be logical. Bacon recognized the degree of subjectivity behind such dubious conclusions ("for what a man had rather were true he readily believes"[2]) and instead insisted that the only objective "authority" in determining the validity of an idea is whether or not it conforms to empirical evidence. If it does not, the idea must be modified until it does. This is the premise behind experimental science, a term that has since become synonymous with *modern* science.[3]

Unlike some other investing "hypotheses," the validity of the value-investing approach can be demonstrated scientifically without resorting to what Bacon called "sciences as one would wish."[4] Although investing is not a physical science per se, it is not an abstract one either. Results can be measured in very tangible terms and there is little disagreement that overall return relative to "average" market performance (usually represented by the S&P 500 and/or Dow Jones Industrial Average [DJIA] indices) is the most relevant measure for the observer. As Graham (who sought to elevate his profession to "a scientific discipline"[5]) would have hoped, the value school's decades of "empirical evidence" (i.e., performance data) demonstrate that his methods (and reasonably similar variations thereof) have withstood the rigors of the modern scientific method.

Bruce Greenwald, PhD, is a finance professor at Columbia University and the director of its Heilbrunn Center for Graham and Dodd Investing. Along with his coauthors Judd Kahn, Paul Sonkin, and Michael Van Biema, Greenwald wrote the following in the 2001 book *Value Investing: From Graham to Buffett and Beyond*: "The best proof of the theory is in the results. The historical record confirms that value investing strategies have worked; over extended periods, they have produced better returns than have both the leading [investing] alternatives and the market as a whole."[6] It's important to focus on the words "over extended periods" because, as will be demonstrated below, one can find a number of periods when even some of the most successful and highly regarded value-fund managers have underperformed the market.

This is due to the critical fact that the wider (i.e., non-value-oriented) portfolio-management industry is driven (in terms of management compensation incentives and client expectations) by near-term performance. As investment advisor and broadcaster Gabriel Wisdom wrote in his cleverly titled *Wisdom on Value Investing*, "The intense focus on short-term results puts pressure on portfolio managers to disregard the long-term economics of a business in favor of market action."[7] Not surprisingly, such a focus often succeeds in generating superior short-term results. However, just as a sprinter can easily outperform the marathon runner over a small segment of the race, only to impair him- or herself for the duration of the contest, so, too, does the short-term fund manager often sacrifice "tomorrow" to beat out his peers "today" through riding short-term "waves." A study published by the London School of Economics and

Political Science concluded that "those who are impatient for results or who have no ability or desire to undertake the hard work of fundamental analysis to find cheap stocks, will use momentum. In fact, over the short-run, momentum is usually the best bet."[8]

Of course, there are also those who, responding to conflicting pressures and beliefs, veer between the two approaches. Such a hybrid approach, involving a sizable number of "investments" that Graham would define as "speculations," is *not* value investing. As described in a previous chapter, a young Graham succumbed to temptation and decided to forego his own prudent investment principles to invest in the "hot stock" of Pennsylvania Savold. Despite being the father of value-investing theory and among its most consistent practitioners, he later realized that his apparent "investment" was wholly speculative (with typically speculative, that is, disastrous, results). For Graham, that was the exception that proved the rule. However, once one engages in such "investment" more habitually, the benefits of previous fundamentals-oriented value investing can evaporate quickly.

The same dynamic was highlighted in "How Omaha Beats Wall Street,"[9] a fascinating *Forbes* article that, in 1969, introduced the phenomenon of Graham's star disciple to a national readership. The article notes that, unlike Warren Buffett, there were putative value investors who conveniently strayed from their principles during the technology-driven "boom" decade of the 1960s (which, from an investment perspective, was remarkably similar to the more recent "dot-com" era—startups with great "sizzle" but little substance, outrageous P/E multiples, and, ultimately, enormous losses for imprudent investors):

> A lot of young money men who now are turning in miserable performances began with the same investment ideas [as Buffett] in the early Sixties but then forgot them in the Great Chase of the Hot Stock. Buffett, however, stayed with his principles. He doesn't talk about concept companies or story stocks. He has never traded for a fast turn on an earnings report or bought little unknown companies.[10]

DIRECT DISCIPLES

Along with Buffett, there are a number of other *consistent* value investors who were taught, to one extent or another, by Graham directly. This is a select group comprised of those who worked with or under Graham in one capacity or another (among them Warren Buffett, Tom Knapp, Walter Schloss, Irving Kahn, and Irving's son Thomas, who assisted Graham with the 1973 edition of *The Intelligent Investor*) and/or took his class at Columbia or the New York Institute of Finance (Bill Ruane), or were tutored by him personally (Charles Brandes). Another "first generation" investor who had some (albeit comparatively limited) personal contact with Graham was Ed Anderson. Considering that the superlative value-investing skill of both Anderson and his partner Tom Knapp (who, as a Graham-Newman employee, had *extensive* direct contact with Graham) is reflected in the performance of the Tweedy, Browne investment fund. Anderson's work has not been excluded from this survey.

It is important to clarify that while these legendary investors all emerged, intellectually, from "Graham and Doddsville," they each developed their own unique approaches. For example, Buffett and Munger practice what noted value guru Robert Hagstrom describes as "focus investing"[11] (i.e., holding positions in a concentrated group of securities). The selection criteria involved in what Buffett describes as "a few outstanding companies" are not wholly quantitative. When I asked him about this apparent divergence from Graham, Buffett responded that

> Ben felt that what I do now makes sense for my situation. It still has its founding in Graham, but it does have more of a qualitative dimension to it because, for one thing, we manage such large sums of money that you can't go around and find these relatively small price-value discrepancies anymore. Instead, we have to place larger bets, and that involves looking at more criteria, not all of them quantitative. But, Ben would say that what I do now makes sense, but he would say that it's much harder for most people to do.[12]

As highlighted in chapter 6, Buffett's friend and former Graham-Newman colleague, the late Walter Schloss, held a portfolio with a large and well-diversified set of securities, in stark contrast with Buffett's "focus investing." Yet, despite adopting different tactics, they adhered to the same fundamental security-selection paradigm common to all intellectual "natives" of "Graham and Doddsville." As Greenwald and his colleagues observed,

> Over the many years that the Schlosses have managed money, they have found themselves investing in different industries, in large, medium, and small companies, in companies with shares that have plummeted in price, and in those that have slid downward gradually but persistently. The unifying theme is that the stuff they buy is on sale.[13]

In other words, for Walter Schloss (along with, from 1973 onward, his son, Edwin), the essential criterion was an advantageous price-value discrepancy, regardless of a company's size, industry, management, and so forth.

As Buffett observed in 1984, when he gave his "Superinvestors of Graham and Doddsville" address at Columbia, "He [Schloss] owns many more stocks than I do—and is far less interested in the underlying nature of the business."[14] In fact, when Buffett extolled the virtues of "superinvestor" Walter Schloss (actually he is the first of the Graham disciples that Buffett highlighted in that 1984 speech), Schloss held over one hundred stocks of all sorts.

Clearly, despite this difference, Buffett considered his former Graham-Newman colleague to be a fellow practitioner of the "Graham and Dodd" investment approach. After all, the fundamental principle underlying both men's work is the same. Although they each have their own preferences regarding certain aspects of investing, Buffett clarified that the common thread running among his nine featured superinvestors is that they all "search for discrepancies between the value of a business and the price of small pieces of that business in the market."[15]

Somewhat tentatively, I am also including Charlie Munger's pre-Berkshire-Hathaway performance in this group since, through Buffett, Munger did have some personal interaction with Graham in the period (1962–1975) during which he managed his own investment partnership. The tentativeness with which Munger's investment partnership is included in this survey is certainly not due to its performance (which was exemplary). Rather, it is due to the fact that Munger is considered to be far more influenced by Phil Fisher than Graham. Morningstar, an acclaimed investment-research entity, provided the following single-sentence summary of Fisher's investment approach: "Purchase and hold for the long term a concentrated portfolio of outstanding companies with compelling growth prospects that you understand very well."[16] Although Munger did adhere to Graham's "discount-to-value" approach, as a Fisher aficionado, he placed a much greater premium on the long-term competitive position of the business than Graham ever did.

However, considering that Buffett described Berkshire's vice chairman as one of the "Superinvestors of Graham and Doddsville"[17] and that, in Munger's own book, *Poor Charlie's Almanack*, Graham is described as someone who "played a significant role in forming Charlie's investing outlook,"[18] it is not unreasonable to include him in this list, albeit with the qualification above. Regarding the potential objection that this list of direct disciples was "cherry-picked," there were only a handful of investors who worked or studied closely with Graham and then established their own funds. As Buffett clarified in "The Superinvestors of Graham and Doddsville," he did "not select . . . these names from among thousands,"[19] and neither have I. It is also worth noting that there are other successful investors who had direct contact with Graham but whose adherence to his fundamental principles on a consistent basis was/is in doubt. Such investors have been excluded from this survey.

The Buffett Partnership,
the Buffett Limited Partnership,
and Berkshire Hathaway

From 1957 to 1969, both incarnations of the Buffett Partnership, Ltd. (i.e., the partnership itself and its limited partners' entity), Buffett's primary forerunners to the current Berkshire Hathaway holding company, excelled the market by an astounding margin. During that period, while the average annual (compounded) return of the DJIA was 7.4 percent[20] and that of the S&P 500 was 10.22 percent,[21] the average annual return of the Buffett partnership was 29.5 percent[22] and that of his limited partners' entity was 23.8 percent.[23] Buffett assumed control of a Massachusetts company by the name of Berkshire Hathaway, Inc., in 1965. Despite Berkshire's history as a textile company, Buffett had a broader vision for it. In Lowenstein's words, he saw Berkshire as "a corporation whose capital ought to be deployed in the greenest possible pastures."[24] As such, Berkshire began purchasing large stakes in companies across different industries that Buffett deemed to be attractive investment opportunities. By 1970, it had permanently supplanted the Buffett Limited Partnership as Buffett's (and later, Buffett and Munger's) preferred investment vehicle, but there were a few overlapping years while this transition took place during the late 1960s.

A table in Berkshire's 2010 "Chairman's Letter" titled "Berkshire's Corporate Performance vs. the S&P 500"[25] highlights the company's 1965 to 2010 performance relative to that benchmark index. The results, tracking nearly half a century of investment activities, are remarkable in multiple respects. During that period, the average annual return of the S&P 500 was 9.4 percent; Berkshire's was 20.2 percent.[26] While the dramatic difference in performance is obvious, one may arrive at the mistaken conclusion that Buffett, Munger, and company did a little better than twice as well as the market.

However, due to the cumulative power of compounding over a forty-six year period, investors who stayed with Berkshire excelled the market by a much wider margin than that. At the end of 2010,

$2,500 invested in the S&P 500 in 1965 would have appreciated to approximately $156,550. Even adjusting for inflation, that's certainly impressive. However, had that $2,500 been invested in Berkshire instead, it would have appreciated to approximately $1,226,000 during the same time frame,[27] a nearly eightfold improvement over the market! (Forty-three years later, *Forbes*'s headline "How Omaha Beats Wall Street" has proven to be more apt than even that august periodical was likely to have anticipated.) Berkshire's present market capitalization exceeds $180 billion,[28] and the value of its total assets is estimated at over $370 billion.[29]

SEQUOIA FUND: WILLIAM RUANE

In the value-investor community, perhaps the only names held in higher reverence than "Bill Ruane" are those of Graham and Buffett. The Chicago-born Ruane had a brief career as an electrical engineer prior to attending Harvard Business School in the late 1940s. At Harvard, one of his professors encouraged the class to read *Security Analysis*. According to Ruane's obituary in the *Washington Post*, "Although he knew nothing about stocks, he was impressed with the approach by authors Benjamin Graham and David Dodd to financial analysis."[30] A few years later, working on Wall Street, he decided to enroll in Graham's class at Columbia, where, as mentioned earlier, he witnessed the "fireworks" between his new friend Warren and their hero, Ben Graham. Buffett later described Ruane's early development as a superinvestor: "After getting out of Harvard Business School, he [Ruane] went to Wall Street. Then he realized that he needed to get a real business education so he came up to take Ben's course at Columbia."[31]

From 1949 to 1969, Ruane worked at Kidder Peabody (a well-regarded securities firm at the time) before establishing a partnership with Richard Cunniff (Ruane & Cunniff) that, in turn, created the Sequoia Fund. Ruane managed the New York–based fund's investment activities until his death in 2005. Relative to the market, the record of the Sequoia Fund from 1970 to 1984 (when Buffett gave his

"Superinvestors of Graham and Doddsville" address at Columbia) is almost as dazzling as Berkshire's (partly due to the fact that Ruane was savvy enough to invest heavily in Berkshire): Sequoia's compounded average annual return for the period was 17.2 percent versus the S&P 500's 10 percent.[32] The fund's performance since 1984 has remained strong, but, in aggregate, it is somewhat less impressive than its legendary 1970–1984 record.

According to a comparative table published on the Sequoia Fund's website, in its forty-one-year history, the fund has provided its investors with an "average annual total return" of 14.25 percent compared to the S&P 500's 10.32 percent.[33] Considering that, just months prior to his passing in 2005, Bill Ruane described *Security Analysis* as "the greatest book on [investment] research,"[34] there can be little doubt that he was a Graham (and Dodd) devotee throughout his long and illustrious investment career. However, highlighting the seminal contributions of both Graham *and* Buffett to the value-investing framework, Ruane once remarked that "one [Graham] wrote what we call the Bible, and Warren wrote the New Testament."[35] Buffett, Ruane, Cunniff & Goldfarb (Robert Goldfarb became a partner in 1998) is reported to have over $14 billion in assets under management.[36]

TWEEDY, BROWNE PARTNERS:
TOM KNAPP AND ED ANDERSON

Aside from the fact that Tom Knapp had been an employee of Graham-Newman prior to joining this partnership in 1957, the connection between Graham and the entity now known as Tweedy, Browne predates Knapp's involvement by many years. As Jason Zweig wrote in the *Wall Street Journal*, "From the 1930s through the 1950s, Tweedy, Browne—originally Tweedy & Co.—was the favorite brokerage firm of Benjamin Graham, the founding father of value investing."[37] So, by the time Knapp (and, later, Ed Anderson) helped transform the company from a brokerage firm to a value-oriented investment firm, Graham's security-selection methods were hardly foreign to the Tweedy "culture." As published by Tweedy, Browne itself: "The Firm's investment approach derives from the work of the late Benjamin Graham."[38]

In the late 1950s, Tweedy began investing capital pooled by its partners. Then, in 1968, Knapp and Anderson (a Graham devotee who, through Knapp and Buffett, had the opportunity to learn from the "master" in person) helped form an entity through which Tweedy took in, according to the firm's website, "it's first outside money management clients."[39] This is the record that Buffett highlights in his 1984 "Superinvestors" address. The average annual compounded return of Tweedy's limited partnership from 1968 to 1984 was 16 percent, and its overall average annual compounded return (i.e., the combined performance of its limited partnership and its other investment vehicles) was 20 percent.[40] Meanwhile, the S&P 500 offered investors a relatively paltry 7 percent.[41]

Some of Tweedy's more recent results have been less spectacular, although the firm's Value Fund has still managed to outperform the S&P 500 index, albeit by only a slight margin. That fund (established by Tweedy in 1993), has generated an average annual return of 8.04 percent to its investors over its eighteen-year history.[42] Over the same time frame, the S&P 500's average annual return was 7.68 percent.[43] However, the disciples (Knapp and Anderson) are no longer at the helm. As one commentator observed in 2010, "Tweedy, Browne's recent performance isn't as robust as its performance under Tom Knapp and Ed Anderson."[44] As of September 31, 2011, New York–headquartered Tweedy, Browne was reported to manage over $11.5 billion in total assets.[45] Notably, in the original (1980) edition of John Train's classic *The Money Masters*, Train writes that "they [Tweedy, Browne] claim, in fact, to be the only absolutely pure followers of Graham's original doctrine operating on any significant scale."[46] This purity seems to have been compromised somewhat in recent years. In 2009, Robert Wyckoff Jr., one of Tweedy, Browne's current managing directors stated that "our portfolios today are a mix of high-quality, Buffett-type businesses and Ben Graham-type bargains."[47]

WALTER & EDWIN SCHLOSS ASSOCIATES

Most of Graham's "direct disciples" presented here had their first face-to-face encounter with him in the 1950s or 1960s (the 1970s, in the case of Charles Brandes). However, Walter Schloss was among two intellectual heirs whose relationship with Graham commenced in the 1930s. Schloss was working as a "runner" (someone who was responsible for the delivery of stock certificates and other documentation between brokerage firms) on Wall Street at the time when he heard of Graham's evening class at the New York Institute of Finance. Schloss, who never went to college, decided to attend. After taking two courses with Graham, Schloss served in World War II for four years, during which time he maintained a correspondence with his former teacher. When he returned to New York after the war, Schloss worked at Graham-Newman for a number of years before establishing the Walter J. Schloss investment entity in New York toward the end of 1955.

In 1973, his son Edwin came on board and the fund was renamed Walter & Edwin Schloss Associates. The overall record for the fund was outstanding for the period up until 1984, and it continued to be very strong (albeit not quite as extraordinary) afterward. Schloss was actually the first superinvestor highlighted by the Berkshire chairman in his 1984 address, and for good reason. From 1956 to 1984, Schloss Associates generated an average annual compounded return of 21.3 percent, and its limited partnership returned 16.1 percent.[48] As for the market, the S&P 500 returned 8.4 percent.[49] Put another way, $1,000 in the S&P 500 in 1956 would have grown to $8,872 by 1984, while $1,000 entrusted to Schloss would have grown to $231,047! The fund's forty-five-year record (Walter and Edwin closed it in 2001) yielded an average annual compounded return of 15.3 percent, a substantial improvement over the S&P 500's 11.5 percent for the same period.[50] Among the superinvestors, Walter Schloss was among the most faithful to the unalloyed "fifty-cent dollar" Graham approach. As recently as 1998, Walter Schloss identified the source of his highly successful investment philosophy with unambiguous clarity: "Basically we like to buy stocks which we feel are undervalued, and then we have to have the guts to buy more when they go down. And that's really the history of Ben Graham."[51] Walter Schloss passed away on February 19, 2012.

CHARLES MUNGER

A native of Omaha who had established a successful Los Angeles law firm, Munger created his own investment partnership in 1962 and proceeded to run it very successfully prior to his involvement with Berkshire Hathaway. Munger had been close friends with Buffett long before becoming his partner (in fact, it was Buffett who encouraged him to set up an investment partnership of his own in the early 1960s). Through Buffett, aside from being encouraged to read Graham's books, Munger had the opportunity to meet (and, to a limited extent, learn from) Graham on several occasions.

As highlighted above, Munger, a devotee of Phil Fisher, was more of a "focus investor" than a traditional Graham bargain seeker. Nonetheless, Munger acknowledges Graham as a significant influence on his investment approach. Moreover, Buffett cites him as a Graham-and-Doddsville superinvestor because, like the others, Munger focuses on "the difference between the market price of a business and its intrinsic value."[52] From 1962 to 1975, Munger's partnership generated an average annual compounded return of 19.8 percent and its limited partnership yielded 13.7 percent.[53] During that same time, the S&P 500 yielded 6.65 percent.[54]

SUPERINVESTORS 2012

The investing successes of most of Buffett's 1984 superinvestors have been discussed above. Clearly, they all continued to do well (mostly *very* well) after 1984. Two superinvestors who were excluded from the survey above were not really investors per se. Rather, they were investment entities that were managed by Graham devotees: the Washington Post Company Master Trust and the FMC Corporation Pension Fund. Regarding the former, subsequent (i.e., post-1984) results appear not to be available. Regarding the latter, according to the Columbia Business School website, "The pension fund's performance is 6.77% over the last 10 years compared to the S&P 500 . . . down 0.95% over the same period, putting FMC in the top 3% of all funds in the country."[55] Although that is hardly a complete account of FMC's post-1984 performance, it is certainly an encouraging indicator.

There were also two other individual investors, Stan Perlmeter and Rick Guerin, whom Buffett highlighted in his 1984 address. Due to their lack of personal contact with Graham, they were excluded from the above list of Buffett's superinvestors who were/are also direct Graham disciples. Neither Perlmeter nor Guerin have performed very well since.[56] Nonetheless, in 2012, the fact that five of the seven superinvestors continued to excel after 1984 proves that the central argument of Buffett's "Superinvestors of Graham and Doddsville" address remains valid. The address demonstrated that those investors who were steeped in the essentials of Graham's "discount to value" approach (and applied it consistently) outperformed the average market return by a significant margin.

This, in turn, invalidates the arguments of those who promote the efficient market theory (EMT). As Buffett said, "There are no undervalued stocks, these theorists argue, because there are smart security analysts who utilize all available information to ensure unfailingly appropriate prices."[57] Of course, the fact that a particular investment approach would outperform the market by a significant margin certainly calls the universality of EMT into question and strengthens the validity of Graham's core premise that there are superior long-term rewards for identifying and purchasing securities that are underpriced relative to their intrinsic value. As a market commentator wrote in 2010 regarding a more current perspective on "The Superinvestors of Graham and Doddsville," "Overall Warren Buffett beats Eugene

Fama and the Efficient Market Hypothesis crowd by 5–2."[58] Or, in the language of the scientific method, the data is clearly in favor of the "Graham and Dodd" hypothesis (of superior returns through capitalizing upon high price-value discrepancies), not the EMT.

Indeed, the performance of the gold miner equipped with a powerful sensor system is consistently better than the miner who's just taking random stabs in the ground. The "stabber" may get lucky once in a while, but, over the long term, the better-equipped miner will leave that person, quite literally, in the dust. That kind of consistently superior performance is not the product of luck, and neither is the collective performance record of the "Graham and Doddsville" community, whether before or since 1984. After recounting Buffett's legendary purchase of a substantial stake of the then-distressed Washington Post Company (the value of Berkshire's stake in the company peaked at nearly $2 billion in 2004) for only 20 percent of the Post's intrinsic value (i.e., "an 80 percent margin of safety"), noted investment finance professor and author Lawrence Cunningham states that "luck plays a major role in a day trader's portfolio; discipline plays an obvious role in Berkshire's."[59] The discipline that Cunningham is referring to is that of adhering faithfully to Graham's most essential principles, no matter how uncomfortable and unpopular such a contrarian approach may be over the short term.

OTHER DIRECT DISCIPLES

KAHN BROTHERS GROUP, INC.: IRVING AND THOMAS KAHN

Irving Kahn became Graham's full-time teaching assistant in 1931 and remained a close friend for the next forty-five years. At 106 years of age, "the oldest living investment professional,"[60] Irving Kahn continues to be among Graham's greatest champions. Remarkably, Kahn is still active in Kahn Brothers, the firm he established with his sons, Alan and Thomas, in 1978. Presently, Thomas (who also had some direct contact with Graham), his grandson Andrew, and others at the firm practice a value approach that is deeply rooted in Graham's work. I cannot state its aggregate performance relative to the market with certainty, but the New York–headquartered firm has a strong reputation and is reported to manage over $800 million in assets.[61] As Thomas Kahn told me when I interviewed him in September 2011, Kahn Brothers follows a "modified Graham and Dodd approach"[62] that places somewhat more emphasis on a company's management and technological context than Graham did.

Brandes Investment Partners

A native of Pittsburgh, Charles Brandes was working at a San Diego brokerage firm in the early 1970s when a retired Ben Graham came in to purchase some shares. From this chance meeting, an intellectual rapport developed between Graham and his young protégé. Brandes, who did not subscribe to any particular investment philosophy prior to meeting Graham, was treated to several face-to-face value-investing seminars with the master himself and soon became an ardent "believer." Shortly thereafter, Brandes Investment Partners was established. As stated on its website, "Since our inception in 1974, we have applied the value investing approach to security selection pioneered by Benjamin Graham."[63] In the third (2004) edition of his book *Value Investing Today*, Brandes wrote that he is "greatly indebted to Benjamin Graham, my mentor,"[64] and he remains among Graham's most successful pupils. Although I cannot state its aggregate performance relative to the market with certainty, as of September 30, 2011, Brandes Investment Partners managed over $34 billion in assets,[65] making it one of the largest value funds in the world.

OTHER TOP-TIER VALUE INVESTORS

MARIO GABELLI/GAMCO INVESTORS

Mario Gabelli attended Columbia's Graduate School of Business in the mid-1960s, long after Graham's departure for California but early enough to be taught by Roger Murray, a noted value scholar who would later contribute to the fifth (1988) edition of *Security Analysis*. Gabelli established his own fund in 1977 and, as of 2009, Gabelli Asset Management Company (GAMCO) Investors, Gabelli's present investment vehicle, managed $21.4 billion in total assets.[66] In *Value Investing*, Greenwald and his colleagues highlight some of Gabelli's contributions to the field (modifications/updates to some of Graham's original valuation techniques). Nonetheless, Gabelli remains a dedicated Graham devotee and Greenwald and his colleagues describe him as a "value investor . . . schooled in the Benjamin Graham tradition."[67] In fact, Gabelli presents an annual "Graham & Dodd, Murray, Greenwald Award for Distinguished Value Investors."[68]

JOHN BOGLE

The celebrated founder of the Vanguard Group (which manages over $1.7 trillion in assets[69]), John Bogle, now retired, scaled the heights of investment finance for several decades. He is also a proud Graham devotee throughout most of his career. In the acknowledgments to his classic work *Bogle on Mutual Funds: New Perspectives for the Intelligent Investor*, Bogle wrote: "Two centuries ago, it was said that if we stand on the shoulders of giants, we may see further than the giants themselves. The principal giant upon whose shoulders I have stood in writing this book is Benjamin Graham."[70]

JEAN-MARIE EVEILLARD/FIRST EAGLE FUNDS

A native of France who immigrated to the United States in the early 1970s, Jean-Marie Eveillard was once dubbed the "value maestro" by *Fortune* magazine.[71] According to the magazine, during a twenty-six-year period at the helm of a global value fund, Eveillard generated an average annual return of 15.8 percent compared to the S&P 500's 13.7 percent.[72] Eveillard, who quotes Graham in that *Fortune* article and whose investment preferences have been described as "securities whose intrinsic value and long-term potential outweighs market risk,"[73] is clearly a practitioner of Graham-style value investing. At present, Eveillard is the lead investment adviser at First Eagle Funds. First Eagle is reported to manage over $22.7 billion in assets.[74]

HONORABLE MENTIONS

Other notable US-based investors and funds include Longleaf Partners, Charles Royce/Royce Funds, Chris Davis/Davis Funds, Li Lu/Himalaya Capital Partners, Bill Nygren/Oakmark Funds, Glenn Greenberg/Chieftain Capital/Brave Warrior Capital, Howard Marks/Oaktree Capital Management, Seth Klarman/Baupost Group, Michael Price/Franklin Templeton/MFP Investors, Robert Hagstrom/Legg Mason Capital Management, Pat Dorsey/Sanibel Captiva, Monish Pabrai/Pabrai Investment Funds, and Schaffer Cullen Capital Management.

GRAHAM GONE GLOBAL

BUFFETT OF THE NORTH:
PETER CUNDILL/CUNDILL VALUE FUND

Known as the "Canadian Warren Buffett," Peter Cundill was on an airplane in 1973 when he first read about Graham and his methods in *Supermoney*[75] by "Adam Smith" (not the eighteenth-century British economist, of course, but the pseudonym of financial author George Goodman). Apparently, he was so impressed by Graham's concepts that, by the end of that flight, the Vancouver-based accountant knew how he was going to spend the rest of his life. More of a Graham purist than most of the superinvestors, Cundill leveraged his accounting background to seek out "net-net" opportunities. According to financial writer Robert Arffa's *Expert Financial Planning: Investment Strategies from Industry Leaders*, Cundill's focus was on "balance sheet strength and the net-current asset value of a security according to the tenets of Benjamin Graham."[76] Mr. Cundill passed away in January 2011.

VALUE IN "THE LAND OF THE RISING SUN": NOMURA

A value-oriented fund headquartered in Tokyo, Nomura employs over twenty-seven thousand full-time personnel in offices located in thirty-one countries across the world. Its size and global reach is a testament to the international dissemination and practice of Graham's value-investment principles. I had the opportunity to interview two of Nomura's senior asset managers, Mitsunobu Tsuruo and Hideyuki Aoki, at the 2011 Value Investor Conference in Omaha, Nebraska. Mr. Aoki told me of his first exposure to the value school of investing in Japan: "When I was a college student, I read a Japanese translation of John Train's *The Money Masters*, which, of course, highlights Graham quite a bit. That book had a big influence on my career."[77] As of March 2011, Nomura had 24.7 trillion Japanese Yen (approximately $321 billion) under management.[78]

PARISIAN GRAHAM DEVOTEES: AMIRAL GESTION

Among the most notable features of this French group of value-oriented funds is its youth. Established in 2003, Paris-headquartered Amiral Gestion's mission, as stated on its website, is to "realize a solid long term performance by looking for quality companies whose value is clearly undervalued by the markets."[79] I met two analysts from this company, David Poulet and Raphael Moreau, at the 2011 Value Investor Conference in Omaha, Nebraska, and there is no doubt that Amiral's investment philosophy is drawn primarily from the works of Benjamin Graham (and augmented by the investment wisdom of Warren Buffett). As Mr. Moreau told me, "My boss gave me *The Intelligent Investor* when I was an intern. He said read this chapter and this chapter and this chapter and get back to me in two days!"[80] The fact that a French investment entity established in 2003 has anchored itself to Graham speaks to both the timelessness and the universality of his principles.

A WHOLE WORLD OF VALUE:
MARK RUSSO/GARDNER, RUSSO & GARDNER

Portfolio manager Mark Russo of Gardner, Russo & Gardner is a highly successful practitioner of value investing. Although Russo is based in the United States, he specializes in opportunities that capitalize upon the rapid growth of developing economies throughout the world. For example, Russo likes to invest in certain European consumer-products companies with a large presence in rapidly developing regions of sub-Saharan Africa. In this manner, Gardner, Russo & Gardner's investors are able to benefit from this rapid growth through well-established and financially stable European companies. Of course, that is just one of their fascinating applications of Graham's methodologies to an increasingly globalized investment landscape. Through their limited partnership "Semper Vic Partners LP," Gardner, Russo & Gardner have routinely outperformed the market since 1992. Presently, Semper Vic manages over $400 million.[81]

It is important to bear in mind that the profiles above are those of high-profile practitioners of the Graham approach. There are also many thousands of relatively unknown but successful investors (and investment entities) throughout the world owing at least some of their success to these same principles of prudent but opportunistic value investing. After all, aside from being a great investor, Graham also was a prolific author, and, as a lecturer for several decades, he penned dozens of academic papers and articles and gave numerous lectures that were transcribed for posterity. So, unlike many investors who like to "keep their cards close to the chest," Graham was eager to communicate the details of his investment approach.

The ongoing success of value investing lends further credence to Buffett's oft-quoted statement that "if principles can become dated, they are not principles."[82] Considering how well Graham's essential concepts have stood the test of time, they seem to pass Buffett's test. Now that he has several decades of hindsight to review, I asked Buffett what "blind spots" (if any) he now sees in Graham's thinking. His reply was typically illuminating: "I don't really see any blind spots. As I've mentioned in the past, if Graham's three key ideas [looking at stocks as part of a business, "Mr. Market," and the margin of safety] become part of your 'DNA' in investing, you really can't go wrong."[83] Coming from the mouth of the ultimate superinvestor, such words carry a lot of weight. However, even Francis Bacon (who once wrote that "the best proof, by far, is experience"[84]) would have to concede that the impressive record of Graham's disciples and devotees speaks for itself.

Despite attaining considerable wealth through several decades of applying his time-tested ideas, Graham did not "sit still" for long once he moved out to California. In fact, he was soon offering a security-analysis course at UCLA, and he engaged himself in all manner of writing and creative projects (many of which were not even remotely related to investment finance or macroeconomics). More notably, despite a comfortable Beverly Hills home and a seemingly idyllic domestic situation, Graham was about to embark upon the strangest chapter in an already "technicolored" personal life.

CHAPTER 13
STRANGER
THAN FICTION

Notice is hereby given that a special meeting of the stockholders
of Graham-Newman Corporation will be held at the office of the
Corporation, at 122 East 42nd Street, New York, NY, on Monday,
August 20th, 1956 at 10:30 A.M. to take action on a proposition to
liquidate and dissolve the Corporation. ("Notice of Special Meeting
of Stockholders," Graham-Newman Corporation, July 30, 1956)

S o began the end of a legendary investment firm and the storied
investment career of its cofounder and lead analyst, Benjamin
Graham. At the August 1956 meeting, Graham-Newman stockholders elected to commence liquidation, and by September 30, 1957,
the corporation had been dissolved.[1] Regarding investment performance, as highlighted in chapter 9, from 1936 to 1946, Graham-
Newman outperformed the market by over 85 percent.[2] Kahn and
Milne's analysis of performance data gleaned from the corporation's
1945 through 1956 stockholder "letters" (which were actually fairly
detailed annual reports) reveals a strong but not exceptional annual
rate of return of 17.4 percent.[3] This is actually slightly *less* than the
return provided by the S&P 500 during this eleven-year period (18.3
percent[4]). However, before Graham's skills as an investment manager
are called into question, three important provisos are in order.

The first is that, when one fuses the two sets of available performance data (1936–1946 and 1945–1956) and adjusts for the two years of overlap (1945 and 1946), Graham-Newman's average annual performance for the twenty-one year period of 1936–1956 works out to roughly 17.5 percent versus the S&P's 14.3 percent average during that time.[5] Clearly, Graham did, in fact, outperform the market by a significant margin (22.4 percent) for the duration of his active tenure at Graham-Newman.

More important, Graham-Newman shareholders who, after the 1956 dissolution, held on to their proportional allotments of Graham-Newman's large stake in GEICO did extraordinarily well and beat the market by an *enormous* margin. As discussed in chapter 6, Graham was savvy enough to recommend that Graham-Newman purchase 50 percent of GEICO for $736,190.95 in 1948[6]—roughly $7 million in current funds. By August 1995, GEICO had developed into America's sixth largest automobile insurer.[7] Toward the end of that month, Buffett's Berkshire Hathaway, which already owned 51 percent of GEICO, absorbed the entity by purchasing the remaining 49 percent for $2.3 billion[8]—roughly $3.37 billion in current funds! (Of course, the structure of the company had changed since Graham's purchase, so it is not quite an "apples to apples" comparison. However, it does illustrate the exponential appreciation of GEICO's value since 1948.) Moreover, as Janet Lowe wrote in the mid-1990s, "In 1993, Ben's grandson was financing his medical school education by selling some of his grandfather's original GEICO shares."[9]

Secondly, even the record for the period from 1945 to1956 is remarkable in some respects. Its performance exhibited a low 0.39 beta coefficient (i.e., sensitivity to market risks) and an impressive 7.7 alpha coefficient.[10] The latter means that Graham-Newman's results were 7.7 percent better than the statistical norm would have predicted from such a low-risk portfolio. After the terrible sting of his Depression-era losses, the minimization of risk became even more important for Graham. Of course, he also sought to maximize returns, but he would not compromise his low-risk principles to do so. As Janet Lowe observed, "Ben's employees occasionally grumbled that he was overly conservative."[11] So the corporation's returns for the 1945–1956 period may not have been spectacular, but they were attained with admirably low risk and volatility relative to the market. However, as Kahn and Milne write, "It is doubtful, however, that very many of the investors in the Graham-Newman Corporation used this approach to measure the success of their investment. The fabulous success of the GEICO investment far overshadowed everything else."[12] Indeed, Graham's 1945–1956 period may have seemed to err slightly on the side of low risk/low return. However, as the seeds of the 1948 GEICO acquisition bloomed into an enormous bounty in later years, Graham's low-risk decision making ultimately yielded extraordinarily high returns.

GOLDEN YEARS IN THE GOLDEN STATE

In the mid-1950s, Graham made a number of decisions that would shape the remainder of his life. Perhaps most important, after over four decades as a "Wall Street workaholic," he saw that it was time to retire. Having attained the financial security (and, presumably, the acclaim) that he had striven for since his riches-to-rags youth, Graham saw little reason to continue with full-time investment-management activities. However, he would retain some intermittent interest in the market on an intellectual level and would continue lecturing and writing about investment finance during this period. Most significant, he would work on the fourth (1962) edition of *Security Analysis* and the second (1959), third (1965), and fourth (1973) editions of *The Intelligent Investor*, as well as several articles in the *Financial Analysts Journal*, *Barron's*, and other esteemed financial periodicals. A brief biographical overview published in January 1964 (introducing a paper penned by Graham) provides an apt summary of Graham's professional activities during this period:

Benjamin Graham combines extensive business and academic experience. He is presently both professor in residence at the University of California, Los Angeles, and Vice-Chairman of the Government Employees Insurance Group of companies (GEICO) in Washington, DC. He has written extensively on security analysis and on various general economic subjects.[13]

With respect to investing itself, as Charles Brandes told me, "when [Graham] retired, I think that he just moved his money into municipal bonds and he didn't do much investing."[14] As discussed previously, while investing was a genuine interest of Graham's, it was one of many. His son Buz, who recalls the difference between the family's Scarsdale years ("I remember him [Graham] going to the office every day"[15]) and their time in Beverly Hills, confirms Brandes's view:

> I think that my dad sort of had a sense that he wanted enough money to live well but he wasn't interested in accumulating more than that. So, at some point, he got out of the stock market in a personal sense. But I think that what drove him later on was just the intellectual challenge of thinking about the market and communicating those ideas. However, he had many other interests besides the market.[16]

Unshackled from the constraints of full-time office work and the solemn responsibility of managing other people's money, Graham could now explore other interests in his "golden years" to his heart's content. Among other projects, Buz recalls that his father revived an active interest in mathematics through a new invention:

> He spent a lot of time on a slide-rule concept. It was based on similar triangles instead of logarithms. He got people to make prototypes and got it patented and then, finally, when he got it all going and working, the first calculator came out, so he was kind of out of the picture. But he really didn't care so much about that. It was really the intellectual pursuit.[17]

In fact, it seems like all his newly available leisure time made Graham somewhat restless, as his mind seemed to need a stream of new challenges. Buz recalls the interesting ways that his father's natural inventiveness would express itself. Graham's Morse code memorization system is particularly interesting in this regard:

> In Boy Scouts I had to learn Morse code. So my father developed words to remember the Morse code by the syllables. It was quite clever. For my example, *r* is dot dash dot, so he chose the 3 syllable word revolver. Each letter had a particular word with long and short syllables to remember it. He was always doing stuff like that. He had all these projects going, and of course, he read a lot.[18]

With its temperate climate and natural beauty, Southern California seemed like an ideal setting for these pursuits. With his mother gone, two of his three daughters married, and his older two sons no longer alive, the fact that Graham's brothers Leon and Victor (and their respective families) were now in Los Angeles must have been a significant factor in his decision to relocate to the West Coast. There's a touching and revealing passage in Graham's memoirs regarding his brothers. As he tells it, "they had a special fondness for me which was destined to endure sixty years and more."[19] After losing yet another son (however emotionally distant Newton II may have been), it is likely that "reuniting" with his brothers was a source of some much-needed emotional comfort and family support.

The Graham family's move to California was well planned. As mentioned earlier, he, Estey, and Buz all had ample opportunity to sample West Coast living during their extended stay (for half an academic year) in 1955. Presumably, that provisional stay went well and, by its end, all three were comfortable with (and prepared for) a permanent relocation to the Golden State. Restless intellectual that he was, Graham recognized well in advance that he would not be content "smelling the roses" all day and would benefit from some form of academic involvement. As such, as he was parting ways with Columbia University (where he had a remarkable twenty-six-year run), Graham had received enthusiastic assurances from the dean of UCLA's Graduate School of Business Administration that he could continue teaching his renowned security-analysis course at that prestigious institution.

Although he was delighted to have his brothers and their families nearby, it was the family of another relative that would play a much more central role in Graham's family's new life out west. As Dr. Sarnat recounted to me in August 2011,

> When we moved to California we had a modest investment in Graham-Newman (the limited partnership). . . . I depended on our investment to carry us over till I got started out here. Then, to my surprise, I found out that Ben Graham was retiring and moving to California too [*laughs*].[20]

Technically, Dr. Sarnat's wife, Rhoda (Gerard), was Graham's first cousin. However, as a child of Maurice (Gesundheit) Gerard's second marriage, she was closer in age to Graham's older children and had fond memories of spending time with Ben and Hazel and their kids earlier in her life. Although the Sarnats were investors with Graham-Newman, it seems that there was no extensive contact between the Sarnats and the Grahams in the 1950s; the two families' near-simultaneous decisions to move to Los Angeles were made entirely independent of each other. While that is a curious synchronicity in itself, an odd, almost eerie, coincidence would soon follow, as Dr. Sarnat related:

> Then, by strict coincidence, a cousin of mine, totally unrelated to Ben Graham [and who] didn't even know Rhoda particularly well, called me one night and told me that a friend of his, a widow, [was] putting a house up for sale in Beverly Hills. He said, "I think that you ought to look at it before it goes on the market." At that stage, Rhoda had been looking all week long, and she saw three that she liked but I didn't like any of them. Our realtor took me around and then, when I found one that I liked [616 Maple Drive], lo and

behold it was directly across the street from the Grahams [611 Maple Drive].[21]

The Grahams had been living on Maple Drive in Beverly Hills for only a few months before Dr. Sarnat (who had become a noted academic and surgeon by then), Rhoda, and their son, Gerry, moved in across the street. Although there was no ill will between the two men, Graham and Dr. Sarnat didn't quite "hit it off" on the personal level. When I asked Dr. Sarnat what kind of things he would discuss with Ben during the two families' frequent social interactions, he replied, "With Ben? Very little."[22] However, Estey and Rhoda became inseparable friends, as did Buz and Gerry. "Rhoda and Bernie's son is my age," said Buz. "So, we grew up together and we're still very close."[23] It seems that he and Gerry were Boy Scouts under Scoutmaster Glenn Ford! Mr. Ford was among the leading actors of the time (*Torpedo Run*, *Pocketful of Miracles*, and dozens of other successful Hollywood productions).

Indeed, living in one of the country's most upscale neighborhoods in glittery Los Angeles, the Grahams and Sarnats began associating with "the jet set" of the late 1950s and early 1960s. Aside from the dean of the UCLA Graduate School of Business and the president of UCLA itself, other frequent guests at the Grahams' dinner table included famous writers such as Will Durant (*The Story of Civilization*), Irving Stone (*The Agony and the Ecstasy*), and various other notables. As Roger Lowenstein observed, Estey seems to have been more taken by the glamour of West Coast living than her more intellectual husband. "A poor girl from Brooklyn, Estelle was self-educated and enamored of the high life in Los Angeles, where she and Graham shared a box at the Hollywood Bowl and threw lavish parties."[24] Graham himself had little interest in hobnobbing with "the rich and famous" of Los Angeles, but Estey was an eager entertainer.

In retrospect, the most notable of the Grahams' dinner guests was, ironically, not an "Angeleno" at all but a mild-mannered Midwesterner who, outside of Omaha, was hardly known at the time.

As Warren Buffett told me about the Grahams' dinners that he and his wife Susie attended during this period: "I met dozens of friends, including Jack Skirball—of the Skirball Museum; he's become quite famous. And all those people—well, a very significant number of them—became members of my partnership through Ben and Estey. Estey herself was a member of the partnership."[25] In fact, it was during this time that Buffett's relationship with Graham evolved from an amiable academic/professional association to a bona fide friendship. As Buffett recalls:

> We became friends, my wife and I, not only with Ben, but we became friends, very good friends, with his wife, Estey, and when he moved out to California and I moved back to Omaha. My wife and I subsequently went out a great number of times to California to socialize with the Grahams. We would stay at the Beverly Hills Hotel, which was only maybe half a mile or less away from his house. And we would go out there specifically to see them. And then we became not only better friends with them (after I left Graham-Newman) but also with their friends out there. . . . So, the friendship really developed more from our visits to California, which, of course, [were] *after* my employment and after his retirement. I mean he couldn't have been nicer to me when I worked there, but it was not a social sort of affair until after he retired and moved to California.[26]

Graham had indeed retired but, as with many of the opinions he held, his conception of retirement was a departure from the norm. He had little interest in golf, sipping martinis by the pool, or spending hours on end in front of the television screen. Instead, he became involved in many academic and intellectual pursuits. Foremost among these was his fifteen-year post as Regents Professor at UCLA's acclaimed Graduate School of Business. While I was still working on the first draft of the proposal for this book, I was privileged to have a brief phone interview with the late Dr. Fred Weston, the then-ninety-four-year-old UCLA professor emeritus of finance. Dr. Weston was both a colleague and a personal friend of Graham's during this period.

He told me that he was always amazed at the eclecticism of Graham's interests and what seemed to be an insatiable intellectual curiosity. As well, he commented that the span of Graham's multidisciplinary knowledge was awe inspiring.

"He excelled at so many things,"[27] Weston said. Like many of Graham's colleagues, Weston seems to have a deep respect for both the mind and the character of his friend. Weston stated, with equal conviction, that "Graham was one of the brightest people I ever knew" and "I respected him a lot."[28] Perhaps one of the reasons for this respect is the fact that Graham did not accept a single dime for his teaching at UCLA, a highly prestigious university that paid its faculty quite well. After all, he enjoyed teaching and he certainly did not need the money. This was emblematic of his attitude toward money in the later stage of his life. Having moved out to California at age sixty-two, well-cushioned from financial insecurity, he chose projects that appealed to his innate intellectual curiosity, and he progressively withdrew from those that did not. Graham still sat on the board of some companies (GEICO, most notably) and even consulted occasionally, but the vast majority of his time in California (and the post-Graham-Newman period in general) was devoted to nonbusiness pursuits.

As Buz Graham recounted: "When we were living in Beverly Hills, I think he pretty much spent the whole day in his study. We had a study in the back garden and he'd be there most of the time. I just sort of remember him hanging out there during the day."[29] Buz had a particularly revealing and somewhat humorous reflection in this regard. "I'd go in and I'd ask him something and it would take a few seconds while he sort of came from wherever he was to deal with my question. So he was kind of somewhere else, but he was always thinking about something."[30] Henry Ford once wrote that "thinking is the hardest work there is, which is the probable reason why so few engage in it."[31] However, for a perpetual thinker like Graham, Ford's insightful phrase seems to apply inversely—*non*thinking activities were the most tiresome for him.

This dynamic is illustrated best by Dr. Sarnat's recollection of Graham's occasionally eccentric behavior at his wife's lavish dinners:

> He was just a restive person, a strict intellectual. So, when Estey would have a house full of guests, some *high-powered* people, Ben apparently couldn't find much to talk about with them. All of a sudden there would be twelve or fourteen people and Ben just disappeared. Estey would go looking for him, and he would be in his office working on some mathematical puzzle or something abstract.[32]

What I find most interesting about Dr. Sarnat's characterization of Graham as a "strict intellectual" and a borderline recluse is how it contrasts with the warm and sociable Graham recalled by Dr. Robert Hamburger and his wife, Sonia: "We would talk about anything and everything with him."[33] Residents of San Diego and close friends with Irving and Marjorie Janis (Graham's son-in-law and his first daughter), the Hamburgers socialized with Graham extensively when he relocated to that city several years later. The missing link between the "two Grahams" is believed to have been a certain Marie-Louise ("Malou").

A FATEFUL FRIENDSHIP

In his thoughtful introduction to the 1996 publication of Graham's memoirs, Professor Seymour Chatman (professor emeritus, University of California, Berkeley) made the following observation about Graham's post–Wall Street life: "In his later years he increasingly sought for emotional wisdom to match his understanding of the economic and financial ways of the world."[34] In a poetic twist of fate so bizarre that it almost seems like a tale from the Hellenic classics that he so admired, Graham seems to have found this wisdom among the wreckage of one of the worst emotional *tragedies* to befall his family. However, before exploring Graham's relationship with Newton II's former lover, there are a number of important "clues" in the memoirs regarding the less-than-satisfactory elements of his third marriage.

Unlike Graham's multiple criticisms of his first wife and his unambiguous disdain for his second wife, his memoirs are somewhat muted regarding Estey. Yet, when one reads between the lines, an undercurrent of resentment regarding his third wife is unmistakable. When defending his driving record against his critics who were "so near and dear to me by blood or marriage,"[35] he seems to feel most slighted in this regard by her: "And, Estey, you paragon of drivers and my severest critic, was it not you who blithely turned up Park Avenue in the wrong direction?"[36] Although that particular section of Graham's memoirs is written with an air of good humor, the fact that Estey is singled out as the "severest critic" of his driving is significant within the context of other clues he left.

Foremost among these is a passage from the "Self-Portrait" essay that Graham (writing in the past tense and the third person) composed in 1957, one year after moving to California and three years after his first encounter with Malou: "Partly out of real experience, partly perhaps out of imagination, he felt that nearly all women were unreasonable, dominating, unappreciative of his kindness and patience, too insistent on penetrating into the forbidden sanctum of his private self."[37] Graham continues, leaving no doubt as to which women these unflattering adjectives described:

> Only very late in life did B. meet a woman who possessed the qualities of soul and mind, of character and temperament, which he had sought vainly in many others. To her, he felt, he could lower the barriers that had separated him from the rest of humanity. . . . At age sixty and beyond he was to begin his emotional development all over again; he must accept Love not as an experience of life, but as *the* experience of life.[38]

The words "age sixty" make it unambiguously clear that the woman who inspired this emotional renaissance was none other than Malou, whom he first encountered in 1954 (the year he turned sixty). As for

Estey, he had begun dating her in 1940, and he married her in 1944. By all accounts, Estey was less demanding and more attentive than Hazel. However, it seems that, despite her best intentions, there was still something about how Estey related to Graham that made him uneasy and resentful. What's particularly revealing about the passage above is that, as best as can be determined from available information, it was written long before he started spending significant periods of time with Malou. The deep romantic bond between the father and the lover of the troubled Newton II either materialized during Graham's fateful 1954 voyage to France (which, considering that it lasted several weeks, is certainly possible) or took root primarily through written correspondence over the course of those first few years.

AN ENIGMATIC WOMAN

Malou's family name has been reported primarily as Amingues, which is neither French nor Basque. As with many names ending in "es," it is Portuguese. However, she has been described as being Basque (i.e., originating from the Spanish-speaking region of France) and she was fluent in Spanish and French (as well as English). Then again, she and Graham spent considerable periods of time in various Portuguese islands, and it seems that she owned a home in Funchal, Madeira (which probably means that she had some facility with the Portuguese language as well). Of course, even if she had some family connection to Portugal, that would not preclude some partial Basque origins or even disprove others' contention that she was born and raised in the Basque region.

However, Graham's granddaughter Charlotte Reiter supplied me with an interesting piece of information in this regard. Mrs. Reiter has a piece of stationery from 1955 that spells Malou's last name as "Amigues."[39] Apparently, the latter suggests ties to yet another region of the Iberian Peninsula, namely, Catalonia (a region of Spain where both Spanish and the native Catalan are spoken). I find this evidence to be compelling, but it's not sufficient to conclude definitively that her last name was not the oft-reported Amingues. In either case, what is certain is that, ethnically, Malou was not entirely French. Indeed, the color photo of Malou (in her sixties) included herein reveals an olive-skinned woman with distinctly Mediterranean features. France, with its large and comparatively successful economy, has long been home to large numbers of immigrants (or descendants of immigrants) from Spain and Portugal (as well as Italy). So, such Mediterranean surnames are not unusual, even among families that have lived in France for many generations.

It is difficult to place Malou's *origins*, but she was definitely a French citizen. According to the Hamburgers, like many French citizens of her generation, Malou "had great disdain for Americans."[40] Nonetheless, she had attained a high degree of fluency in English, which must have been an important factor in the genesis of her relationship with Newton II. Precisely how she became the lover of this particular American GI is a further enigma. Newton, being roughly twenty years her junior, was probably not far apart in age from her own child (she is reported to have had one son). Such behavior was somewhat unusual in early 1950s provincial France, which was still quite Catholic. However, it is what happened *after* her young lover's suicide that is most peculiar. According to the mores of that time (and, indeed, our own), entering into a romantic relationship with the married father of one's recently departed lover was scandalous. Yet, while Graham had discarded religion and its attendant traditional values entirely (at least as far as romance was concerned), Malou, the Hamburgers informed me, attended Catholic mass intermittently while she was living with Graham in the San Diego area some years later.

Enhancing the mystery of this woman even further, Janet Lowe, writing in 1994, observed: "According to those who knew her, she had been active in the French underground during World War II and had an impressive intellect."[41] Certainly, Malou's involvement in anti-Nazi activities during the war would have elicited Graham's admiration. However, it is the latter point (the "impressive intellect," or what Graham described above as "qualities of mind") that must have been a central element of his powerful attraction to this exotic European woman. For example, both were multilingual, sharing a strong fluency in Spanish, English, and French at the very least. Both Dr. Hamburger and Buz commented on how strong Graham's American accent was in French. "He knew French extremely well, but he had this *terrible* American accent. I mean it was almost a parody of an American trying to speak French," Buz said with a laugh.[42]

As well, it seems that they shared a passion for literature in these various languages. Notably, Graham's final full-length book (excluding new editions of previously published works) was his English translation of a Spanish novel, *La Trega* (i.e., *The Truce*), by Uruguayan author Mario Benedetti, to which Malou's son had introduced him. The novel is about Martin Santome, a middle-aged man who has trouble relating to his own children but then finds salvation through falling in love with a younger woman (this glorious romance being his "truce" with an otherwise antagonistic life) only to see her die an untimely death. For obvious reasons, Graham identified with Benedetti's protagonist to some extent. Graham's translation of *The Truce* was published by Harper & Row in 1969.[43]

Regarding Malou's "qualities of the soul," these are somewhat more difficult to decipher. But her own emotional behavior seems far less than expansive. Buz remembers her as being "a bit stand-offish,"[44] while Sonia Hamburger recalls "a constricted person— Malou was very aloof. It took her such a long time to open up. You couldn't budge her until she was ready."[45] Regarding his wife's relationship with Malou, Dr. Hamburger remarked that "Sonia was one of the few people that Malou became friendly with and opened up to here."[46] However, as the Hamburgers pointed out, the French are not known to open up as readily as many Americans do. So at least part of Malou's apparent "coolness" was probably due to this cultural difference. As well, her apparent reluctance to socialize with a large circle of people might have been off-putting to some, but it probably suited Graham just fine.

However, on the emotional level, Buz's and the Hamburgers' reflections on Malou do not indicate what was special about her. "It was sort of a traditional thing where she was very attentive and took care of him," Buz recalls. "But my mom was kind of that way, too, at least as far as I could tell."[47] Pi Heseltine, Graham's granddaughter (Winnie's daughter), who spent time with her grandfather on several occasions during the final years of his life, has fond memories of Malou: "she was wonderful, and they seemed to have a very endearing relationship."[48] While those who knew her may have had varying opinions regarding Malou personally, there is a clear consensus regarding her positive influence upon Graham's emotional well-being.

The Hamburgers recall that "before Graham met her, he seemed shy and withdrawn. Afterward, it was easier for him to communicate and he was much more relaxed. Malou really helped open him up. Oh my god, the difference was day and night."[49] Oddly, although her own personality did not seem particularly warm (at least to some), she was able to effect a noticeable loosening of Graham's emotional "fortress." Even Buz, who had mixed feelings about the relationship, was impressed by the impact that Malou had on his father. "I was not happy about the break-up [of Graham and Estey] but I was very impressed by how happy he was and how much Malou cared about him and took care of him. So, I was very positive about the whole thing in *that* sense."[50]

THE FALLOUT

Rhoda Sarnat, who had once looked up to Graham as a beloved and admired uncle, had some unflattering words for what she saw as Graham's poor treatment of her dear friend Estey. As Mrs. Sarnat told Buffett biographer Roger Lowenstein in the mid-1990s, "It wasn't all tea and crumpets living with Ben. Just because you're a genius doesn't make you the most caring person in the world."[51] In the early stages of Graham's relationship with Malou, Graham's wife figured that Malou was just another of her husband's "flings" and that the relationship would eventually run its course. She was entirely unprepared for the fact that his relationship with Malou was anything but another "conquest" for her persistently unfaithful husband. On the contrary, the two lovers had forged a deep bond on *all* levels: intellectual and emotional, as well as physical. Indeed, by all accounts, Graham's romance with Malou was the happiest and most successful of all his female relationships.

Rhoda's husband, Dr. Bernie Sarnat, told me how Graham began taking extended trips with Malou in the early 1960s: "They spent time in a couple of the islands off the European coast. He took her to different places and eventually he took her to San Diego."[52] In his memoirs, Graham makes a passing reference to a stay in the Azores (a group of Portuguese islands in the mid-Atlantic), and Buz recalls visiting the couple at Malou's home in Madeira (a Portuguese island off the Moroccan coast). However, Graham still cared for Estelle, although he certainly expressed this in his typically unconventional fashion. He told her that he wanted to spend half the year with her and the other half with Malou. A traditional woman, Estey could never agree to such an arrangement. Instead, deeply embittered by his callous behavior, she demanded a divorce and a large financial settlement. According to Dr. Sarnat, "Estey got one million dollars from Ben around 1965, but she never did get the divorce."[53] Perhaps due in part to the stress of his acrimonious split with Estey, that same year, while skiing with Buz on Mammoth Mountain (in central California), Graham suffered his first heart attack.

Well before 1965, Malou had replaced Estey as the primary companion in Graham's life. After spending some more time in Europe, Graham and Malou would spend part of each year in a condominium Graham purchased in La Jolla, California, and the remainder of the year in France—mostly at a home in Aix-en-Provence that Graham had purchased for Malou. Graham's granddaughter Charlotte Reiter wrote to me that "my father [Irving Janis, Marjorie's husband] took a sabbatical year in La Jolla. I attended La Jolla High for my junior year in 1966/1967. Ben was definitely not living in La Jolla yet."[54] As well, Mrs. Reiter recalls enjoying a European cruise with her grandfather during the summer of 1967. However, in May or June 1968, Buffett, Ruane, Munger, Knapp, and other superinvestors visited Graham in the San Diego area, and Dr. Hamburger recalls a serious medical incident in 1969. So, it seems that Graham must have relocated to La Jolla at some point between the fall of 1967 and the spring of 1968.

From that point on, the couple divided their time between two of the most beautiful places in the world. However, it's notable that neither of their homes was particularly large or opulent. Although they never officially divorced, Graham and Estey lived apart for the last decade of Graham's life. Despite the large financial settlement, Graham's third wife would remain inconsolably heartbroken about her personal loss for the rest of her life. Buz told me that his parents saw very little of each other after the separation and that his mother became somewhat consumed by her bitterness: "I think that was understandable but also very unfortunate, that my mom spent so much time with that."[55] According to Buffett biographer Alice Schroeder, Estey signed all her letters "Mrs. Benjamin Graham"[56] long after her permanent separation (presumably, as a symbolic rejection of her husband's new life with Malou).

Graham did maintain a reasonably close relationship with Buz, but understandably, Graham's sudden departure from Beverly Hills during his son's early adolescence seems to have left a trace of bitterness. Unlike the Sarnats, who expressed their disapproval of Graham's treatment of Estey in no uncertain terms, during my interview with Buz, at his son's home in Berkeley, California, he never expressed any direct condemnation of his father. However, when I asked him about the differences in parenting approaches between his mother and father, the words and tone of his response were revealing: "Of course, my father left sort of midway, so I was really living with my mother when I was in high school. So, it was certainly a closer relationship with my mom in the sense that I spent a lot more time with her growing up."[57]

Buz then proceeded to answer my question about parenting approaches specifically, but considering that I didn't even ask to which parent he felt closest, the preface to his response seemed to be an intentional, albeit subtle, reminder that Graham shirked his duty as a father while his son was still growing up. However, in Graham's partial defense, it is likely that he lived half of the year in La Jolla (only a two-hour drive from Beverly Hills) to help maintain his relationship with his son. Indeed, Buz remembers visiting him there frequently as well as spending a fair amount of time with him in Europe. After completing high school, Buz became very active in the civil-rights movement. In fact, during the pivotal 1964–1965 period, he travelled to Mississippi, where he was thrown in jail three times. Andrew Goodman, the activist son of Robert Goodman, whom Graham knew and liked a great deal, had recently disappeared in that state (he would later be found dead) just prior to Buz's arrival, so it was a harrowing time for all concerned. Graham certainly shared his son's views on racial equality, but understandably, he was alarmed by the dangers involved in such activism at that time. Fortunately, Buz made it back home safely and Benjamin Graham Jr., MD, eventually established a bilingual medical clinic in the rural region of Mendocino, California.

It is telling that even Irving Kahn, one of Graham's most vocal champions and the man who told me that Graham is still "greatly underappreciated,"[58] recognized Graham's marital shortcomings. He wrote in 1977, in an essay titled "Some Reflections on Ben Graham's Personality," that "while Ben was a devoted father, he was really more married to his business and cultural interests than the normal husband."[59] Indeed, despite the tragedy of Newton II's death, Graham's behavior as a parent seems reasonably conscientious and well-meaning overall. However, it is difficult to defend his behavior as a husband, particularly in his third marriage. Aside from his involvement with Malou, he was routinely chasing women throughout his time with Estey. Professor Chatman pointed out correctly that there didn't seem to be "much point in defending someone born in 1894 against charges of sexism."[60] Nonetheless, considering that Estey, unlike Hazel, was thoroughly devoted and faithful, it is difficult to rationalize his behavior.

Graham's failings in one particular area of an otherwise honorable personal life are all the more startling in light of his exemplary, almost saintly, track record in ethical matters where money was concerned. The next chapter will highlight this critical aspect of Graham's legacy.

CHAPTER 14

THE ETHICS OF MONEY

W hile Graham's romantic life was unusually adventurous (particularly for the era in which he lived), his professional life was unusually virtuous: he was highly active on Wall Street for forty-two years. Unlike some other notables in the financial-services industry, he retired with an unblemished record of personal integrity and honesty in a field that is known for neither. However, what's especially admirable about Graham's professional scruples is that they were governed not by optics (i.e., how others viewed his actions) but by true *ethics*—a set of moral principles. The question of the universality or objectivity of morality is a complex one, which, of course, is well beyond the scope of this book. However, perhaps the best and most universally accepted definition of ethics is that which is found, in various forms and wordings, across multiple cultures/ traditions throughout the world. In Western civilization, it is best known as the "Golden Rule" or, as the German enlightenment philosopher Immanuel Kant recast it, the categorical imperative: "Act only according to that maxim whereby you can at the same time will that it should become a universal law."[1]

For example, an investment firm decides to engage in some practice that, while legal, is clearly injurious to its clientele. Obviously, the managers of such a firm would not choose to have their *personal* funds handled in such a manner. However, if their stewardship of their clients' money became "universal law," they would be compelled to "drink from the same bottle that they put on the tray," so to speak. So their conduct, while legal, is nonetheless a violation of the categorical imperative mentioned above. After all, these managers would not want the practice to become a generally implemented one that would impact their own personal savings. Graham, on the other hand, saw his clients not only as his customers but also as people whose resources it was his solemn duty to protect. Considering the fact that he contemplated committing suicide the first time that he lost significant sums of money for a client (Professor Tassin in 1917) due to an external and entirely unintended misfortune (which, of course, was not due to any ethical lapse), it is difficult to imagine Graham being able to live with himself after intentionally "fleecing" his clientele in *any* manner, regardless of how legal or "common" it may have been.

So, judging from both his behavior and his writings (and speeches) on these matters, Graham's career as an investment manager adhered to the categorical imperative with a steadfastness and consistency that, particularly in the financial-services industry, was exceptional. With respect to matters not only of money, but of employee promotions, student grades, and various other aspects of his professional and academic life, this ethical principle governed his every word and deed. As Irving Kahn wrote in a 1977 essay titled "Some Reflections on Ben Graham's Personality," his recently departed friend, employer, and mentor possessed "a very fair mind, entirely objective, in distinguishing between what was fair rather than what was self-serving."[2] (Of course, behaving according to fairness, in an objective sense, as opposed to "what was self-serving," is the essence of the categorical imperative.)

This unfailing sense of fairness and objectivity is well illustrated in Graham's frank disclosure of his financial misdeeds, what he describes in his memoirs as "my peculations"[3] (*peculation* being roughly synonymous with *embezzlement*). As he wrote, these are "incidents which are somewhat painful to my pride to recall."[4] However, what follows is hardly the series of "bombshell confessions" typical of some posthumously published white-collar memoirs of his own time or our own. Rather, a remorseful Graham proceeds, in chronological order, to present the three most heinous financial crimes of his life. He recalls how, as a "very little boy,"[5] he wanted more candy than his "mademoiselle" (this was prior to his father's death, when the Grossbaum family still enjoyed such luxuries) would allow. "Every now and then I would filch a penny from Mother's purse and exchange it for candy in a slot machine."[6] However, after accidentally "filching" a $5 gold piece (which he soon returned discreetly to her purse) instead of a penny, Graham recalls that he was "so shaken by the thought that I had stolen $5 instead of a penny that I never filched again."[7]

Then, jumping ahead a decade or so to the summer of 1910, when Graham worked as a vaudeville theater usher, his memoirs tell of his acceptance of "a few small bribes to give people better seats than they were entitled to."[8] Perhaps worse (as it was a form of outright theft from the theater), Graham recounts what was probably the only time when he applied his natural inventiveness to nefarious ends: "I also discovered a way to make ten tickets admit eleven people, and during some weeks of financial stringency I used this device to misappropriate a few dollars. I felt so uncomfortable about it, however, that I quickly stopped the practice."[9] Last, Graham addresses the one incident that actually took place while he was neither a candy-starved toddler nor a briefly wayward adolescent. In his words, it was "the only action in my business career proper about which I have serious ethical regrets."[10]

It seems that Graham-Newman had an investment in a company that had sold land to a state government that needed the land for some new roads. As part owners of the company, the partners of Graham-Newman were, in Graham's words, "entitled to fair compensation for it" (the land sale).[11] However, the state that purchased the land was "run by a party machine"[12] and, with a nod and a wink, they told Graham and Jerry Newman that "in order to get results both quick and satisfactory"[13] for the transaction at hand, Graham-Newman would be well-advised to "hire the 'right' firm of lawyers at a substantial fee."[14] The partners acquiesced, and one of the entirely legal transactions that followed (at least with respect to Graham-Newman's actions, the state government's activities are another matter entirely) became, in all likelihood, the sole ethical lapse of Graham's long and varied Wall Street career:

> Acting like most business firms in such circumstances, we followed this [the state's] practical advice. My partner, who was a member of the bar, later received part of the fee as a "forwarder." Since we had a general agreement for dividing earnings, he offered me half his share. I should not have accepted that money, but I did—and I have regretted it ever since.[15]

Certainly, all three *were* incidents of unethical behavior (to varying degrees). From a legal perspective, the first incident might be classified as theft (although, considering that Graham was barely out of his infancy at the time, it's of little consequence anyway), the second, particularly pocketing money that was rightfully the theater's, certainly *was* a kind of petty theft (*very* petty, of course, but theft nonetheless), and the third, while unseemly, was well within the bounds of the law. Graham recognized that, overall, his "reputation for scrupulous honesty"[16] was "fairly earned."[17] Nonetheless, the heartfelt remorse that his few misdeeds seemed to have caused reveals much about the makeup of Graham's singular character, which seemed to be the inverse of an unrepentant criminal. Despite being such a noncriminal that he adhered to a more stringent set of professional ethics than those prescribed by the law itself, Graham seems to have been far more repentant than many wrongdoers!

Not only was his own conduct strictly above reproach, but, unlike many in the industry, Graham also had an uncanny knack for discerning the character of others with remarkable accuracy and foresight. As such, at least in the professional realm, *almost* all of Graham's associations were with similarly high-minded people (though his memoirs make reference to an early employee who had been caught misappropriating the company's money, and there are also some vague insinuations about possible misdeeds committed by at least one other unnamed professional associate). When Jerry Newman resigned from the GEICO board in 1971 (six years after Graham's resignation), the GEICO chairman sought Graham's opinion regarding having Warren Buffett take Newman's place on the board. What he wrote to Chairman David Kreeger reveals much about the importance Graham placed on ethical behavior (as well as competence): "I am 100% for that idea. I have known Buffett intimately for many years, and I must say I have never met anyone else with his combination of high character and brilliant business qualities."[18]

It is notable that Graham's laudatory letter cites his friend's "high character" *prior* to his "brilliant business qualities" despite the fact that, in the same letter, he states that Buffett's "record as an investment fund manager is probably unequalled."[19] Obviously, Graham held Buffett's investment prowess in the highest regard, but he seemed to have respected the latter's uncommon integrity even more. Graham understood that investment managers, entrusted with the solemn responsibility of protecting others' savings, must be judged as much on character as on competence. In his memoirs he declares his contempt for "those who abuse positions of trust and honor. For example, in my eyes, Jimmy Walker's behavior as mayor of New York City [1925 to 1932] was disgraceful. His enormous popularity after his downfall, and his virtual canonization after death, make me despair of my fellow man."[20] For Graham, investment managers who abused *their* "positions of trust" were merely lesser-known "Jimmy Walkers."

Regarding his choice of partner for his own investment-management firm, it is instructive that Graham chose to partner with a lawyer (Jerry Newman) during most of his time on Wall Street and for all the time during which he was the steward of substantial sums of money. Graham knew that he could rely upon himself to handle all financial matters *ethically*. However, having a Columbia Law School graduate and member of the New York bar as an equal partner was helpful in ensuring that Graham-Newman's activities would be handled *legally* (as well as ethically). As Graham was savvy enough to recognize, there is a positive but imperfect correlation between generally accepted norms of ethical behavior and the letter of the law. As highlighted in previous chapters, not only was Graham-Newman highly respected as a responsible Wall Street firm, but it treated its clients with a level of integrity and transparency that was exceptional.

It was Graham who was responsible for directing the more sensitive aspects of Graham-Newman's operations (investment allocations, dividend payments to stockholders, and the like) and his conscientiousness and transparency were legendary. Certainly, the firm's exemplary record of ethical behavior is reflective, to a great extent, of Graham's own conduct. Indeed, if his few and generally meager "skeletons" of lifetime financial misconduct were the norm in Wall Street's "closets," several thousand securities regulators and attorneys would hardly be necessary. That is why Graham was so troubled by the egregious lapses in financial ethics that he witnessed—within both the investment industry itself and the many "issuing companies" of all industries that acted contrary to their shareholders' interests. Moreover, as discussed in the following section, he took it upon himself to help protect not only Graham-Newman's investors, but the wider investing public as well.

INVESTOR ADVOCATE

"Corporation treasurers sleep soundly while stockholders walk the floor."[21] So wrote a thirty-eight-year-old Benjamin Graham in the first installment of a three-part series that his esteemed publisher described as follows: "*Forbes* takes pleasure in offering this expose of injustice and maladjustment in the stock and corporation world, presented in a fearless, frank, and interesting series."[22] As a successful and prudent investor who was able to write in a manner easily understood by the lay investor, Graham saw it as his duty to help educate the public on the myriad risks of investing. Aside from providing a framework for low-risk yet reliably profitable investing, he was also an impassioned advocate of fair treatment for investors. Fair-minded person that he was, it is likely that, no matter what field Graham would have worked in, he would have done what he could to highlight any inequitable treatment his penetrating intellect uncovered. As it happened, Graham worked on Wall Street, where the interests of the most vulnerable party (shareholders) were undermined with alarming frequency.

Among other outrages, Graham's 1932 series in *Forbes* drew attention to the fact that the stock prices of many US companies were selling for substantially less than "their pro rata of cash in the company's treasury"[23] (that is, the proportional ownerships of a company's total cash represented by a single share/stock proportional ownership). However, shareholders, seemingly oblivious to this important fact, were effectively allowing each of these companies to "give its present cash away."[24] An exasperated Graham wondered why shareholders failed to see themselves as partial owners of these businesses, which now had shareholders' capital "tied up unproductively in excessive cash balances while [shareholders] themselves are in dire need of funds."[25] Graham made a strong case for his contention that, if investors were to insist on being treated as "proprietors" (which, of course, is precisely what they are), "we would not have before us the insane spectacle of treasuries bloated with cash and their proprietors in a wild scramble to give away their interest (i.e., their shares) on any terms they can get."[26] In other words, owners of a business bursting with cash would generally prefer to have some of that cash distributed to them. So, the managers of some shareholder-controlled companies who were not distributing that cash were not acting in the best interests of their employers—the shareholders.

Judging from one of his contributions to the *Magazine of Wall Street*, fair treatment for shareholders was a matter of some concern for Graham as early as January 1925: "A good many reasons are advanced by companies for their failures to publish statements as frequently as promised."[27] Indeed, management malfeasance, in its various forms, was a central theme of most of Graham's writings on investment finance. He possessed a healthy dose of skepticism, which, aside from his extraordinary intelligence, may have been his greatest advantage amid the smoke and mirrors of Wall Street. He had a remarkable ability to strip away all artifice and reveal the true intention behind seemingly benign, even benevolent, maneuvers undertaken by management. As stated in *Security Analysis*, "Modern financing methods are not far different from a magician's bag of tricks; they can be executed in full view of the public without it being very much the wiser."[28] Graham considered the use of option warrants to be among the most egregious of these tricks. Option warrants are financial instruments that, when exercised, grant their owners (typically members of "the organizing interest,"[29] that is, the company's management) a certain share of future profits at the expense of earnings that would otherwise be due to the company's shareholders. As he (and Dodd) wrote:

> The option warrant is a fundamentally dangerous and objectionable device because it effects an indirect and usually unrecognized dilution of common-stock values. . . . The public's failure to comprehend that all the value of option warrants is derived at the expense of the common stock has led to a practice which would be ridiculous if it were not so mischievous. . . . A properly managed business sells additional stock only when new capital is needed. [30]

For example, in its analysis of a utility company by the name of First American and Foreign Power Company, *Security Analysis* provides one of the most vivid illustrations of just how outrageous and dangerously misleading the use of such option warrants (and Wall Street arithmetic, in general) can be: "By the insane magic of Wall Street, earnings of $6,500,000 were transmuted into a market value of $320,000,000 for the common shares and $1,240,000,000 for the [option] warrants, a staggering total of $1,560,000,000."[31] These numbers are especially staggering considering that they are quoted from the original (1934) edition of *Security Analysis*. Clearly, Wall Street promoters were working their magic on "Mr. Market" and the company's stock price had risen well beyond a level justified by its earnings.

However, the implications of option warrants that were by then collectively inflated to almost quadruple that of the common stock (which, of course, was also highly inflated) were not lost on Graham. Indeed, he noticed that Wall Street's "insane magic" was hardly random. In fact, it had a peculiar tendency to serve the interests of a company's management at the expense of its shareholders. So such maneuvers were not necessarily "insane" from the perspective of management, but, as Graham recognized, they were certainly gross violations of fiduciary responsibility toward management's employers (the shareholders).

Similarly, with regard to the position of preferred stockholders (i.e., shareholders who, with respect to frequency and size of dividends and their ownership claim on a company's assets and earnings, are supposed to enjoy preferential treatment relative to common shareholders), Graham and Dodd clarified that management's typical treatment of these investors was, in fact, somewhat less than "preferential":

> It is considered an approved financial policy to sacrifice the preferred stockholder's present income to what he is told is his future welfare; in other words, to retain cash available for dividends in the treasury to meet future emergencies or even for future expansion. . . . It is a point worth noting that in all cases where the dividend could be continued, but instead is withheld "for the sake of the stockholders' future advantage," the quoted price suffers a severe decline, indicating that the investment market does not agree with the directors as to what is really in the best interests of the preferred stockholders.[32]

In other words, despite the fact that, as preferred shareholders, such owners have a reasonable expectation of receiving regular dividends, management often disregards its fiduciary duty to even its most "elite" shareholders.

Of course, both the conflict of interest inherent in management's governance of shareholder-owned entities and the use of questionable accounting methods remain vexing problems to this day. Two years prior to his passing in 2006, noted economist John Kenneth Galbraith's second-to-last full-length book was published. In *The Economics of Innocent Fraud*, Galbraith explains how many US companies, ostensibly operated for the benefit of their shareholders, are, in practice, run *by* management *for* management. The eminent economist and public-policy figure discusses the unhealthy "passage of power"[33] (or, *further* power) from shareholders to management.

While Galbraith was working on that book, America was beset by some of the most outrageous corporate accounting scandals in its history. As Galbraith writes, "There are few times when an author can have such affirmation of what he or she has written."[34] Indeed, from 2001 to 2004, Enron (massive hidden losses[35]), WorldCom ("personal loans"[36] to the CEO), Tyco (enormous theft by the CEO and CFO[37]), and Health South (wildly inflated earnings[38]) dominated the headlines. Since 2004, the scandals have continued unabated, with such headline-grabbers as AIG ($1.7 billion in loans were recorded as "revenue"[39]), Bernard Madoff (massive Ponzi scheme[40]), and Lehman Brothers (hidden losses prior to the firm's bankruptcy[41]). Of course, these are the most egregious, even sensational, examples. Nonetheless, Graham would have been disappointed regarding the persistence of what Lawrence Cunningham describes as the "small population of true owner-orientated U.S. managers"[42] and the various forms of shareholder abuse that result from this systemic weakness.

As evidenced by Graham's writings, as well as instances of shareholder activism in his own career (e.g., Graham's dogged pursuit of a fair deal for shareholders in the Northern Pipeline affair cited in chapter 7), he had very little patience for management chicanery. Graham had even less tolerance for the deceptive practices of Wall Street itself. For example, the following passage from *Security Analysis* is an apt reflection of Graham's cynical attitude toward unscrupulous underwriters (i.e., those who administer the "flotation" or issuance of new securities): "Gross overvaluations can be made plausible enough to sell. In the liquor flotations of 1933 the degree of overvaluation depended entirely upon the conscience of the sponsors."[43] Writing in the early 1970s, almost forty years later, Graham was dismayed (but hardly surprised) that Wall Street's unprincipled pursuit of short-term gain at investors' long-term expense (as the market eventually corrects its initial mistake and the stock price sinks down to a level that is more commensurate with the true value of the company) continued unabated. As he wrote in the 1973 edition of *The Intelligent Investor* regarding those that issue and promote securities of high price and low quality:

> The years 1960–1961 and, again, 1968–1969 were marked by an unprecedented outpouring of issues of lowest quality, sold to the public at absurdly high offering prices and in many cases pushed much higher by heedless speculation and some semi-manipulation. A number of the more important Wall Street houses have participated to some degree in these less than creditable activities, which demonstrates that the familiar combination of greed, folly, and irresponsibility has not been exorcized from the financial scene.[44]

That is why, as Irving Kahn told me, one of Graham's most important contributions to investment finance was "the promotion of certain elemental standards of safety for securities."[45] Graham accomplished this through his writings, his lectures, and his indispensable role in the establishment of an accreditation system (presently known as the Chartered Financial Analyst [CFA] accreditation) for the profession. Graham was decidedly unimpressed with the generally low level of competence and integrity exhibited by many Wall Street professionals of his era. Indeed, regarding the advice doled out by brokerage houses to their clients, Graham observes in *The Intelligent Investor* that the typical Wall Street firm devotes most of its efforts to "help its customers make money in a field (day-to-day trading) where they are condemned almost by mathematical law to lose in the end."[46] Of course, such "day-to-day trading" was the antithesis of Graham's more methodical system, revolving around a long-term investment approach and the "margin of *safety*."

A 1973 exchange between Graham and representatives of a

younger generation of money managers is telling in this regard. As John Quirt recalls in an article published in *Institutional Investor*,

> Graham asked one of the money managers if he were convinced that the market was due to drop severely, what effect would it have on his operations? "None," came the reply. "Relative performance is all that matters to me. If the market collapses and my funds collapse less, that's okay with me. I've done my job." "That concerns me," Graham admonished him. "Doesn't it concern you?" . . . On another occasion a participant pleaded that he really couldn't distinguish between an investor and a speculator. Graham responded, almost inaudibly, "That's the sickness of the time."[47]

CITIZEN GRAHAM

Remarkably, Graham not only concerned himself with the safety of the investing public, but, as reflected in his work on the commodity reserve currency plan (see chapter 10), he was also mindful of the overall economic welfare of society as a whole, particularly its more vulnerable segments. Graham's economic philosophy was just about equidistant from Karl Marx on one end and Ayn Rand on the other. While he certainly did not concur with the former's assertion that the quest for profit was inherently unjust and exploitive, he similarly rejected the latter's notion that the capitalist bore no responsibility for anyone's welfare but his or her own. In fact, Graham viewed the cataclysm of 1929 as a consequence of decades of unrestrained laissez-faire capitalism. Of course, as demonstrated by the entrepreneurialism of his own career and his drive for, in his words, "large earnings and large spending"[48] (at least in his younger years), Graham was certainly an eager capitalist himself, and he believed in the overall merits of the American "free enterprise" system.

However, he was skeptical of those with a quasi-religious faith in the unmitigated societal benefits of unrestrained capitalism. Regarding Adam Smith's oft-quoted principle of the "invisible hand" (in which participants in a capitalist economy make decisions that, though motivated by personal profit, ultimately benefit society at large), Graham made the following observation at an address he delivered just months after retiring from Graham-Newman:

> This point of view [Smith's "invisible hand"] still has validity, but not in the unqualified over-enthusiastic way in which the proponents of *laissez-faire* presented it. It is now being offset by a complementary point of view, expressed by Peter F. Drucker . . . : "No policy is likely to benefit the business itself unless it benefits society."[49]

Indeed, in matters of socioeconomic policy, Graham was an ardent believer in enlightened self-interest. As an avid reader of history (particularly European history), Graham may have been wary of what could transpire when the condition of the "masses" deteriorates beyond a certain point. More practically, he was of the opinion that unemployed, underemployed, or otherwise impoverished consumers were hardly a boon to business. As he stated in the same speech, "I think we have found that the basic welfare activities of government—those centering in various forms of social security, including unemployment insurance—are worth to business more than their cost in high taxes."[50] Unlike many of his contemporaries in the American business community, Graham was actually heartened by the more muscular government regulation and intervention initiated by Franklin Delano Roosevelt and maintained/expanded upon by subsequent administrations.

As stated in the 1962 edition of *Security Analysis* (cowritten with both David Dodd and Sidney Cottle), Graham was pleased that, in the "post-World War II world,"[51] the US government has "assumed large responsibilities in preventing or remedying mass unemployment. This Federal involvement is a new factor, and we consider it important in its potential effect on the business cycle and on stock values."[52] When it came to ensuring certain basic levels of social well-being (particularly employment), Graham was certainly a firm believer in government activism. Friedrich Hayek may have been a greater admirer of

Graham's currency proposals than John Maynard Keynes, but there is little doubt that Graham's general perspective on macroeconomics was in far greater accord with that of Keynes. As Graham declared in 1956, "Nothing is more beneficial for business as a whole than the improvement in the living standards and the purchasing power of our poorer people."[53]

An almost-forgotten 1964 piece (that can be perused only at the New York Public Library's main reading room) is most enlightening with respect to Graham's thinking on such issues. Titled "Benjamin Graham on the Flexible Work-Year: An Answer to Unemployment"[54] and published by a US think tank (now no longer active) that referred to itself as the Center for the Study of Democratic Institutions, the piece posits that significant progress could be made in reducing unemployment through a moderate reduction of the number of hours in the work year. After laying out a fairly convincing case for this hypothesis in his typically methodical and detailed manner ("a cut of fifty hours in the work-year—equivalent to one hour a week—could have reduced the unemployment of 1962 by about one-half"[55]), Graham concludes that "if it is formulated with imagination and practicality, and if it is applied with skill, the flexible work-year should give us the power to control the unemployment rate instead of being controlled by it."[56] In other words, by reducing the number of paid hours, employers would be better able to retain a greater number of workers, thereby minimizing unemployment. It is a testament to the sincerity of Graham's concern for his fellow citizens that, long after retiring from business himself, and with only a small proportion of his money still invested in other businesses, Graham took the (unpaid) time to grapple with such issues as unemployment and their impact upon society's most economically disadvantaged members. On this matter, another passage from his work on the flexible work year offers a revealing glimpse into his acute social conscience (a trait that has also defined the life and work of his son "Buz" and, of course, his protégé Warren Buffett):

The relative percentages [of unemployment] have not changed much over the fifteen-year period from 1947 to 1962. The deplorable exception is the Negro, whose unemployment rate rose from 5.2 per cent to 11 per cent while that of Whites was advancing only from 3.2 per cent to 4.9 per cent.[57]

A CHARITABLE MAN

In 1844, Charles Dickens wrote that "charity begins at home and justice begins next door."[58] In other words, the same people who call out for a more benevolent and just society should serve this worthy cause by practicing those values themselves. Obviously, the great novelist was irked by the hypocrisy of those who professed their "social conscience" with much fanfare while, on the personal level, their conduct expressed little of the charity and kindness of which they spoke. Graham had his flaws, but hypocrisy of any sort (even in romantic matters—according to Buffett, Graham had offered Estey the opportunity to pursue extramarital relationships of her own[59]) was just not part of his makeup. As such, Graham's impassioned words regarding social issues were reflective not only of his personal integrity in financial matters but of an uncommon generosity as well.

Charlotte Reiter wrote to me about her grandfather's generosity: "Ben gave my parents a three- to six-thousand-dollar tax-free gift per year [a significant sum back then]. They used the money to travel every summer, during my father's months off from Yale—enough to last 10 weeks!"[60] She added that "it is my understanding that Ben was honorable and fair, and he gave the same gift to his other adult children."[61] Of course, he was also generous with his grandchildren, and not only in the material sense. Pi Heseltine (whose mother named her after the mathematical constant), recalls her maternal grandfather as "gentle and warm,"[62] and she remembers spending many hours playing fun mathematical games with him. However, Pi, born in 1964, knew Graham only during the last phase of his life. Charlotte, the daughter of Graham's first daughter (born some sixteen years prior to Pi's mother, Winnie), stated that, although "grandpa Ben" was consistently *kind* to her, his personal warmth evolved over time: "When I was older, he was very welcoming and generous to me."[63]

The same generosity applied to his friends as well. Dr. Hamburger, whom I interviewed (along with his wife Sonia) at their charming La Jolla home, told me how Graham helped them purchase that home in the spring of 1961:

> I had a mortgage loan, a secondary loan, and a $5,000 loan for the pool. Ben Graham lived in Beverly Hills at the time, but he came down to visit quite a bit even back then, and he bailed me out of a really bad situation. I mean I was really in trouble and he loaned me a *significant* amount of money. I got the house finished, refinanced everything, and then paid him back. But at the time, it didn't look like he'd ever get it back, but he wasn't worried. He was very generous but not the least bit cavalier—he was a very serious businessman and he thought that I was just ludicrous in my financial behavior![64]

I asked Irving Kahn about this charitable aspect of Graham's personality. Recounting Graham's various charitable activities (financing the African American church in Connecticut, his work as president of the Jewish Guild for the Blind, and so forth), Kahn remarked that "he did a lot of charity and he gave to people of all races."[65] Perhaps because he had experienced the pain of poverty firsthand, for Graham, beyond providing a certain level of financial comfort for himself and his family, money was not a prestige item. Rather, it provided an opportunity to help others. As Buffett biographer Lowenstein wrote, "[Graham] gave much of his money to charity and offered that anyone who died with more than $1 million to his name was a fool."[66] It is notable that Buffett, who has resolved to give away almost all of his wealth to charity prior to his passing,[67] subscribes to a similar view.

Buffett held Graham's intellect in the highest regard, but, as revealed in a tribute he penned for the *Financial Analysts Journal* in 1977, Buffett was even more impressed by Graham's generosity:

> I knew Ben as my teacher, my employer, and my friend. In each relationship—just as with all his students, employees and friends—there was an absolutely open ended, no-scores-kept generosity of ideas, time, and spirit. If clarity of thinking was required, there was no better place to go. And if encouragement or counsel was needed, Ben was there.[68]

To this day, Warren Buffett remains astonished at just how generous and selfless his former teacher, employer, and friend was. Aside from Graham's personal generosity (e.g., the expensive gifts he gave when the Buffetts had their first child), Buffett marveled at Graham's eagerness to share the "treasures" of his mind:

> You can argue that—well, in fact, it's absolutely true—Ben was creating his competitors by the day. When he taught a course down at the New York Institute of Finance, which he did regularly, Wall Streeters used to take his course just to pick up ideas from the current examples he was using. Of course, this would negatively impact his own income, but he didn't care. . . . He never conveyed any impression that I owed him anything, and, of course, I owed him an *enormous* amount. It's interesting that way. He was a teacher at heart. He was a fabulous human being, really one of a kind.[69]

Indeed, Graham's generosity was not limited to money. He felt a natural empathy toward those who were encountering difficulties, and sometimes it was his time and counsel, rather than his money, that were needed most. For example, German World War II refugees in New York City found an unusually helpful, empathetic, *and* financially generous friend in Benjamin Graham. Similarly, Kahn recalls that "a needy colleague would always be helped—and always anonymously."[70] This last observation is particularly revealing, as it demonstrates that, for Graham, helping others was an end in itself, not a means to the adulation of his peers. At a family event for his eightieth birthday, Graham delivered a brief but memorable address. The transcript of this speech includes a revealing nod to his hero Benjamin Franklin: "[Franklin] had all the characteristics to which I aspire—high intelligence, application, inventiveness, humor, kindness, and tolerance of others' faults. Perhaps too—without trying—I shared some of his weaknesses, especially for the fair sex."[71]

A SAINT WHO SINNED

Graham's weakness for "the fair sex" is just as undeniably evident as his angelic behavior in other aspects of his life. However, I believe that the fair-minded person who examines *all* the evidence would be hard-pressed to conclude that Graham was a "bad" person. Even Rhoda Sarnat, the same relative who has declared her disdain for Graham's behavior toward Estey, attests to the indisputable fact that her late cousin's professional ethics were beyond reproach. She once remarked that when it came to all matters related to money (or any other aspect of his business affairs), "he had integrity that wouldn't quit."[72] There is a passage in Benjamin Franklin's autobiography (among Graham's favorite books) regarding integrity that could apply equally well to most aspects of Graham's life: "I grew convinc'd that *Truth, Sincerity, & Integrity* in Dealings between Man & Man, were of the utmost importance to the Felicity of Life."[73] Aside from the relatively confrontational Northern Pipeline episode, one wonders if Graham ever exchanged so much as a cross word with another *man* (women, particularly wives, being another matter entirely).

In his 1976 tribute to Graham in the *Financial Analysts Journal*, Buffett highlighted a revealing phrase uttered by Graham not long before his death: "Several years ago Ben Graham, then almost eighty, expressed to a friend the thought that he hoped every day to do 'something foolish, something creative and something generous.'"[74] In November 1987, *Fortune* magazine published an article, titled "The

Father of Value Investing," about how fashionable Graham's ideas had become. Regarding Graham's above quote about being foolish, creative, and generous, and making light of Graham's reputation as a ladies' man, the *Fortune* writer quipped that "inventing security analysis and value investing is evidence enough of Graham's creativity and generosity. And the foolish? Graham usually took care of that before getting out of bed."[75] Humorous as it is, the two-dimensional caricature implied by that wisecrack is not quite accurate.

In fact, it would be deeply unfair to Graham to see him as a kind of "Jekyll and Hyde" character whose goodness vanished when he exited the office (or the classroom) and stepped outside (at which point he would revert to his wicked and sinful ways). I saw Graham in a similar light when I commenced work on this book. However, I've since learned that the truth is far more nuanced than such a hero/villain dichotomy might suggest. He could be (or at least *seem* to be) somewhat aloof, even insensitive, in some of his personal relationships (such as may have been the case with Newton II). Moreover, at least in the case of Estey, he proved to be deeply inconsiderate of his wife's feelings and her more conventional understanding of marriage. (The marriage to Hazel, in which she might have been the first to "stray," was, from an ethical perspective, far more complex.) Nonetheless, as far as I know, he never verbally or physically abused any of his children or spouses (vocal arguments with Hazel notwithstanding). Moreover, although he was not the most emotionally expressive individual, Graham made sincere attempts to maintain strong relationships with all of his surviving children.

So, even as a family man, an area of comparative failure for Graham, he was hardly a villain. In my estimation, the most unambiguously immoral incident of Graham's life that we know of was his attempt to seduce Edythe Saffron, who, as Graham knew, was married at the time. Especially if that incident was indicative of a wider pattern of seducing married women, such behavior is impossible to defend and must be recognized as a deeply unfortunate moral "blind spot" in Graham's makeup. Of course, as a married man, Graham's seduction of unmarried women was inherently inappropriate as well. However, particularly during his first marriage (in which neither Graham nor his spouse were faithful), one may at least understand, if not necessarily empathize with, such behavior. As discussed previously, his extramarital activities during his third marriage were less defensible, and they certainly demonstrated a capacity for insensitive behavior.

Overall, Graham was neither "angel" nor "devil." Yet, on balance, his behavior (on both the professional *and* personal levels) was commendable far more often than it was deplorable. As the late Marjorie Graham Janis told me, regarding both of her parents (Graham and Hazel):

> I feel more positive than I used to about them, at the time. I was upset that they weren't getting along, but, looking back, they were both, I think, remarkable people. Each functioned in the world in a way to take part and try to help make the world better—not only for them personally but for people around them and the people that they worked with and helped.[76]

Of course, the ongoing "dividends" of Graham's professional legacy, manifesting in multiple fields and applications, are further proof that he did "help make the world better." These will be explored further in the following chapter.

CHAPTER 15
OF *PERPETUAL* VALUE

During his final years, Graham was beset (although generally not incapacitated) by multiple health problems. Charles
Brandes, who met him during this time, recalls that he suffered from
gout. Dr. Robert Hamburger, Graham's friend (through a longstanding friendship with Graham's son-in-law and daughter, Irving
and Marjorie Janis) and fellow La Jolla resident, explained to me
that "the gout caused Graham's kidney problem. Graham had kidney
disease, BPH (Benign Prostate Hyperplastia), and hypertension/heart
disease."[1] Dr. Hamburger recalls how he became Graham's unofficial
physician during these years:

> I was Ben's secret weapon. I'm a pediatrician, so I didn't take per-
> sonal responsibility for him, but we were so close with the Janises
> and then with him that he was family. And, as a family member, he,
> no matter what, would never call his doctor, but he would call me,
> and I would get in touch with an internist here in town, a very good
> friend of mine, who managed him.[2]

These multiple conditions required a sophisticated treatment
program involving a delicate balance of various drugs. As
Dr. Hamburger recalls, many of Graham's problems, at least during
the years in which Graham and Malou split their time between La

Jolla and Aix-en-Provence, were due to the seeming inability of the physicians who cared for him in Provence to manage that balance properly:

> He would go to France in perfect health and come back completely out of control. He was digitalized, and digitalis requires very fine adjustments. Digitoxin is a drug for the heart. The French doctors would never make the darn adjustments, so he'd come home undigitalized in heart failure. They wouldn't bother to regulate him. When he would go to France, Malou would bring in her favorite doctors. What was good about them was that they would come to the house, but American doctors would no longer come to the house. However, the American doctors were superb, but the French doctors were providing terrible care. I would never say that out loud if it wasn't true. At least for Graham, the care was atrocious in France. So, he'd come back ill. Every six months, he'd return here ill. My internist and I would spend three to six weeks getting him back in shape.[3]

"MAYBE IT'S TIME TO TURN ME TO THE WALL"

Considering that most of Graham's health crises occurred either in France or shortly after his return from there, it does seem that the elderly retiree was not being cared for properly when he was abroad. Indeed, as others have noted, Dr. Hamburger almost certainly saved Graham's life on multiple occasions. One instance occurred in 1970. At the time, the La Jolla pediatrician was the dean of the University of California, San Diego (UCSD), medical school, which was significant, considering that UCSD was (and is) an institution with multiple hospitals throughout San Diego County.

> That time, in 1970, he was so bad when he came back from France that his internist immediately hospitalized him at my hospital. So Ben was in the hospital on the eleventh floor, the only private floor.

All the other floors were public. It's the UCSD hospital in Hillcrest [a neighborhood in central San Diego]. I go in and I say, "Ben, it's Bob." He was full of fluid, he was short of breath, he was panting for his life, and he was sure that he was dying. So he says, "Maybe it's time to turn me to the wall." I told him, "I don't know anything about money but you sure don't know anything about medicine. All you need is a few days of meds here and you'll be walking around as good as new." As I promised, within three days, he was up and running and back in La Jolla.[4]

Graham was a lifelong admirer of the great stoic philosophers of antiquity (particularly Marcus Aurelius) and, in his 1957 "Self-Portrait," he wrote that, since his youth, he had embraced stoicism as a "gospel sent . . . from heaven."[5] At its core, the message of stoicism is to accept one's fate without complaint. For example, if one goes out for a walk on a sunny day and it starts to rain, one might get upset and think "that's not *fair*, just as I was going to enjoy the day . . ." In contrast, a stoic response would be simply to accept the circumstances as they are and adapt the best way possible. In the health crisis described above, Graham's willingness to accept what he believed to be his imminent death, without any evident anguish or complaint, is a revealing illustration of Graham's commitment to his beliefs.

Indeed, despite his many health problems, Graham still managed to enjoy his final years, perhaps more than any other period of his life. His daughter Marjorie has been quoted as observing that her father's "last years were his happiest. He became warmer. . . . The family really did gather around him . . . but not just as a duty. We looked forward to it."[6] Graham's granddaughter (Marjorie's daughter) Charlotte has an amusing anecdote from this period regarding her grandfather's burgeoning gregariousness, which she shared with me:

Patrick (later my first husband), myself, and our friend Jacques Schlumberger drove to La Jolla on our way to Mexico in 1970 or 1971. Grandpa took the three of us out to lunch at Anthony's Fish

Grotto, a nice seafood restaurant in downtown La Jolla. He made a witty remark about our friend's name, and, of course, Grandpa covered the check with his usual good grace.[7]

MR. MARKET BECKONS

Graham's hospitalization in 1970 is noteworthy because it prompted a bedside visit from Warren Buffett. That same year, Buffett agreed to help Graham prepare the fourth edition of *The Intelligent Investor*, which was published in 1973. Since his work on the fourth edition of *Security Analysis* (published in 1962), Graham had written very little about the market, preferring to apply his prodigious intellect and writing skill to such matters as "The Flexible Work-Year," English translations of *La Trega* and various Hellenic classics (e.g., works by the Roman poet Ovid), and sundry other projects, including sizable portions of his memoirs. It seems that, during this eight-year period, Graham derived his greatest intellectual and artistic satisfaction from projects that seemed to be as far removed from the stock market as possible.

It's not entirely clear what renewed Graham's interest in the market. When I asked Buz about this period, he said, "I didn't have the sense that he was trying to promote himself much or that he was enhancing his legacy or that kind of thing." On the contrary, instead of promoting his ideas to others, it seems that others were coming to him for advice. As Buz described: "Many people were approaching him about various ideas and funds during those years. For my dad, I think that he just saw the stock market as one of the intellectual challenges that he enjoyed."[8] Despite his health complications, Graham's final spurt of intellectual activity regarding investment finance proved to be among his most prolific. Completing work on the fourth edition of *The Intelligent Investor* was his most significant achievement during this time.

However, Graham also devoted considerable time in the early and middle 1970s to a fifth edition of *Security Analysis*, which, unfortunately, was not completed prior to his death (and would not be published until 1988). Graham also found the time to formulate and test some new investment techniques. Most notably, just months prior to his passing, he cofounded a new fund with James Rea, a California-based fund manager with whom Graham had taught several investment-finance classes at UCLA. However, the Rea-Graham fund, as it was named, proved to be an unfortunate misnomer, since Graham passed away soon after its establishment, and its subsequent performance was poor.

A 1999 *Forbes* piece evaluated "Rea-Graham" (which has since been renamed and sold off) and concluded that "the fund is a clunker. . . . [It] eked out a 7% average annual return. . . . The fund's assets peaked in the late 1980s at $50 million."[9] Moreover, assessing one of the recent transactions of its then manager (a relative of Rea's), *Forbes* asks (rhetorically), "Would a value investor buy a stock like this one? . . . How does that mixed metaphor go? Something like: If Graham were alive today, he'd be spinning in his grave."[10] Fortunately, Graham's association with another West Coast investor proved to be more faithful to his investment philosophy and hence more reflective of his legacy.

WHEN THE STUDENT IS READY . . .

A native of Pittsburgh, Charles Brandes moved out to the West Coast in the mid-1960s to pursue graduate studies at San Diego State University. In 1971, he was working as a stockbroker at Roberts, Scott & Co. Inc., a member firm of the New York Stock Exchange, located on Prospect Street in the heart of downtown La Jolla. This locale happened to be just a few blocks from Graham and Malou's La Jolla condo. Graham, prompted by the research that he was conducting that year for the fourth edition of *The Intelligent Investor*, decided to make one of his rare post-1956 stock purchases. He took a quick stroll to the firm's office, where a young man took his order for the common stock of National Presto Industries (a company highlighted as an example of an attractive current "net-net" opportunity in the fourth edition of *The Intelligent Investor*). As Brandes, now a San Diego billionaire, described it to me, this seemingly inconsequential encounter with an elderly Graham led to a tutelage that, in retrospect, was a landmark moment in his career:

> We began talking when he purchased National Presto. He had an office in a small apartment in La Jolla on Eads Avenue, and I proceeded to meet with him several times over there. We met in his study (it always had a lot of books and papers all around). Anyway, he definitely enjoyed sharing his knowledge with me. At the time when I was going over there to learn, I wasn't thinking "wow, this is a life-changing event," but, of course, it ended up being that. His principles are still *very* applicable to today in many ways.[11]

Just as Graham refused to accept a penny of compensation for his teaching work at UCLA, the informal value-investing seminar that he conducted for Brandes was motivated strictly by the joy that Graham took in sharing his knowledge with others. Brandes was so impressed by his elderly teacher's principles that he proceeded to read and reread *Security Analysis* and *The Intelligent Investor* to solidify his understanding of Graham's methodologies and how they apply in various investment scenarios. Within a few years of the chance encounter with the father of value investing, Brandes established Brandes Investment Partners. Since 1974, the firm has since climbed to the top echelon of global value-oriented investment entities, with over $34 billion under management.[12] Brandes attributes much of this enormous growth directly to Graham. In his 2004 book titled *Value Investing Today*, Brandes writes, "I am greatly indebted to Benjamin Graham, my mentor. His basic principles formed the solid foundations for my worldwide investment success."[13] Brandes remains Graham's preeminent West Coast disciple and *champion*. At his firm's San Diego headquarters, Brandes named the main conference room "The Benjamin Graham Room."

A GRANDFATHERLY RENAISSANCE MAN

May 9, 1974, marked Benjamin Graham's eightieth birthday. The occasion was celebrated a few weeks earlier (on April 11) at an event organized by his daughter Marjorie. Attendees included his children, grandchildren (who numbered in the double digits by then), Malou, his brother Victor, and, in Graham's words, "the other dear ones who are here with me."[14] According to Charlotte Reiter, who was in attendance, the occasion was held at an ornate private room in a downtown La Jolla hotel. Along with the many heartfelt speeches by family members and friends, Graham delivered a wonderfully inspiring address that, fortunately, has been transcribed for posterity.

In characteristic Graham fashion, even his relatively brief eightieth-birthday address made reference to such assorted literary and historical notables as Alexander the Great, Virgil, Homer, Cicero, Julius Caesar, Napoleon, Alfred Lord Tennyson, Benjamin Franklin, and Mark Twain. Renaissance man par excellence, Graham took the opportunity to exhort his audience, particularly the large gathering of grandchildren, to enjoy "the life of culture"[15]—that is, literature, philosophy, and the arts. Then he proceeded to quote Cicero, the great Roman orator and philosopher: "These studies nourish our youth and comfort our age."[16] What's most notable about this speech is its frank self-reflection. Despite suffering his share of setbacks and tragedies, he expresses the thought that, contrary to the rather dim view he held of his own future as a child, his life had turned out to be "unusually successful, even happy."[17] Considering that Graham's life was marked by both tremendous professional success (on multiple levels) *and* calamitous personal tragedy, it is notable that, toward its end, he chose to reflect upon it with contentment rather than the self-deprecating regret that permeated much of his 1957 "Self-Portrait."

Interestingly, the speech also betrays a measure of the doomsday pessimism of the cold war era. "The world seems to me to be going to Hell in a hansom [as in 'hansom cab']," Graham laments.[18] He goes on to express his grave concern for his grandchildren's future.

This seems to have been one of Graham's less prescient moments (although he certainly would not have minded to be proven wrong in this instance). After all, relative to his own era of global bloodbaths (i.e., World Wars I and II) and unprecedented economic calamity (i.e., the Great Depression), his grandchildren have lived (and are living) through a time of relative peace and prosperity. Nonetheless, to Graham's credit, he was conscientious enough (especially considering the audience he was addressing) to end his address on an uplifting note by quoting a passage from Alfred Lord Tennyson's 1833 poem *Ulysses*, which begins, "Come, my friends, 'tis not too late to seek a newer world."[19]

BOTTOM OF THE NINTH HOME RUN

Graham delivered another extraordinary speech, this one in a professional context, later that same year. As the keynote speaker for a seminar held by the Institute of Chartered Financial Analysts on September 23, 1974, Graham gave a rousing and, as one would expect, well-researched lecture on the "Renaissance of Value," which was later printed in the *Financial Analysts Journal*. The market was experiencing one of its most prolonged downturns during 1973 and 1974, and Graham took the opportunity to illustrate just how much value was being ignored in the prices of some stocks during that particular bear market. He stated that the historically low prices provided an ideal opportunity to purchase "shares at less than their working-capital value,"[20] citing the fact that "100 such issues"[21] were listed in the August 1974 edition of the well-known investment periodical *Value Line*. However, Graham, ever leery of excessive debt and its impact upon the safety of securities, had cautionary words regarding some bonds: "We now have a situation in which all bonds sell at high yields, but many companies have an overextended debt position."[22]

Much of the lecture was quoted in *Barron's* magazine and then reprinted throughout the financial press of the day. It seems that Graham's call for the investment community to buy up strong stocks in a depressed market had more impact than even he could have imagined. According to Janet Lowe, the market proceeded to pick up on the increased investor activity urged by the "Dean of Wall Street" himself: "Ben inspired a disheartened investment community to go on a buying campaign that led to a revival of the stock market."[23] Although Graham was advocating the purchase of underpriced securities specifically (and not the market indices per se), it is worth noting that the Dow Jones Industrial Average climbed almost 40 percent over the next five years, and over 100 percent over the next ten years.[24]

AN EYE ON ETERNITY

Graham had suffered another acute health crisis earlier in 1974, again during that portion of the year when he and Malou lived in France. As with his 1970 hospitalization, Graham was convinced that his latest complications would be fatal. Although he managed to survive yet again, both the reflective theme of his eightieth-birthday address and the title of Graham's last contribution to the *Financial Analysts Journal*—"The Future of Common Stocks" (September 1974)— are telling. Contemplative by nature ("he lived inside his mind,"[25] as Dr. Hamburger told me), an elderly and frail Graham seems to have been very conscious of his mortality at this time. "The Future of Common Stocks" conveys the impression that its writer did not expect to be opining about the market for very many years to come:

> It should be obvious from my overall approach to the future of equities that I do not consider such much-publicized problems as the energy crisis, environmental pressures, foreign exchange instability, etc. as central determinations of financial policy. . . . Their weight for the future may be assessed by economists and security analysts, presumably with the same accuracy, or lack of it, as has characterized such predictive work in the past. . . . Experience suggests therefore that the various [recent] threats to equities . . . are

not very different from other obstacles that common stocks have faced and surmounted in the past.[26]

Some eighteen months later, on March 6, 1976, this tone of weathered resignation was more evident than ever. In an interview with Hartman L. Butler Jr., CFA, of the *Financial Analysts Journal*, he declared that "Wall Street hasn't changed at all. The present optimism is going to be overdone, and the next pessimism will be overdone, and you are back on the Ferris Wheel."[27] He also delivered one of his most stinging criticisms of Wall Street (as highlighted in the previous chapter, his voluminous writings on investment finance are bursting with them): "I have no confidence whatever in the future behavior of the Wall Street people. I think this business of greed—the excessive hopes and fears and so on—will be with us as long as there will be people."[28] Not surprisingly, it seems that Graham's "perspective of eternity" (along with his deep skepticism regarding Wall Street) only grew more prominent toward the end of his life.

A TRUE INTELLECTUAL

In the latter part of Albert Einstein's career, the eccentric physicist was willing to abandon and even discredit his own theories when they no longer made sense to him. For example, in 1926, Einstein complained to a friend about a certain "new fashion"[29] in physics. His friend pointed out that what Einstein was complaining about was actually "invented by you in 1905!"[30] to which Einstein retorted, "a good joke should not be repeated too often."[31] Apparently, by 1926, Einstein considered his special theory of relativity to be "a good joke." His thinking on a number of matters had changed so dramatically that he came to question, even belittle, his previous conclusions (a process Einstein would undergo more than once during his rich intellectual life). As biographer Walter Isaacson clarifies in *Einstein: His Life and Universe*, the Nobel Prize winner's "about face" on these matters has yet to be proven correct. Nonetheless, this willingness to dissociate oneself from previously embraced ideas (especially one's own) in the pursuit of a greater truth is the mark of a true intellectual (i.e., one for whom greater understanding, not personal gain or fame, is the primary end of intellectual pursuits).

Graham, whom Irving Kahn described as possessing a mind that was "entirely objective,"[32] exemplified such intellectual purity. Toward the end of his life, he embarked upon a significant intellectual "about face" of his own. By the mid-1970s, Graham no longer believed that the thorough security-selection methodologies presented in *Security Analysis* or *The Intelligent Investor* were the best ones for the great majority of investors. Less than seven months prior to his death, Graham made this admission to Butler: "I have lost most of the interest I had in the details of security analysis which I devoted myself to so strenuously over many years. I feel that they are relatively unimportant, which, in a sense, has put me opposed to developments in the whole [financial analysis] profession."[33] Instead, the man who popularized individual security selection for the masses now favored what he described as an "apparently too-simple investment program."[34]

This program involved evaluating groups of securities according to "some simple criterion"[35] for being underpriced (e.g., those selling for 67 percent or less of their book value) "regardless of the industry and with very little attention to the individual company."[36] As he revealed in a 1976 interview with *Medical Economics*:

> For the past few years I've been testing the results of selecting undervalued stocks according to a few simple criteria. My research shows that a portfolio put together using such an approach would have gained twice as much as the Dow Jones Industrial Average over the long run.[37]

However, just as Einstein's latter-day views never got the same traction as his earlier breakthroughs, among both professional and novice investors, Graham's legacy is similarly defined by his earlier approach to (individual) security analysis and selection. The most renowned of his followers, Warren Buffett (who, as a student of Graham's life and work, is well aware of these more simplified methods), certainly prefers his mentor's earlier and more detailed approach. At the 2007 Berkshire Hathaway annual meeting, Buffett told his fellow Berkshire shareholders that "at age 19, I read a book [*The Intelligent Investor* by Benjamin Graham], and what I'm doing today, at age 76, is running things through the same thought process I learned from the book I read at 19."[38] Nevertheless, whether or not Graham's latter-day conclusions were correct, his willingness to challenge his own intellectual legacy is admirable.

CONTRARIAN TO THE END

Aside from his skepticism of Wall Street in general, Graham had little enthusiasm for the efficient market theory (EMT) that had become gospel among many academics and investors. As he told Mr. Butler:

> They [EMT proponents] would claim that if they are correct in their basic contentions about the efficient market, the thing for people to do is to try to study the behavior of stock prices and try to profit from these interpretations. To me, that is not a very encouraging conclusion because if I have noticed anything over these 60 years on Wall Street, it is that people do not succeed in forecasting what's going to happen to the stock market.[39]

Graham's contrariness was still very much intact during that interview, as was his ready wit: "It is surprising how many of the large companies have managed to turn in losses of $50 million or $100 million in one year, in these last few years. . . . You have to be a genius to lose that much money."[40] Graham's towering stature in his field is amply reflected in the reverent tone of Mr. Butler's questions ("When did you decide to write your classic text, *Security Analysis*?"[41]) and the fact that in the previous year (1975), the Financial Analysts Federation had awarded Graham its most prestigious honor, the Molodovsky Award, at its annual conference. According to the CFA Institute (the current incarnation of the federation), the award is presented to "those individuals who have made outstanding contributions of such significance as to change the direction of the [financial-analyst] profession and to raise it to higher standards of accomplishment."[42]

A QUIET EXIT

Almost two years to the day after his acclaimed "Renaissance of Value" address, Graham died peacefully in his sleep on September 21, 1976, at Malou's home in Aix-en-Provence. According to the Hamburgers, a death mask was made of Graham's face (presumably kept by Malou) before he was cremated. Graham's remains were sent back to America, where they were buried beside his "sweetest, bravest, most beloved" Isaac Newton Graham (or Newton I) in a Jewish cemetery north of New York City. (Newton II is interred in the Graham family plot in the same cemetery, as are Graham's brothers, mother, and various other relatives.)

On October 10 of that year, Irving Kahn organized a memorial service for Graham at Columbia University, a place of immense significance in Graham's life. The Ivy League institution was both his alma mater and his forum for communicating (and refining) his methods throughout most of his career. Kahn and Milne, writing just a few months later, described the event as follows:

> A hundred old and close friends of Ben attended—his partner Jerome Newman, Columbia's President, William McGill, David Dodd, Professor James Bonbright, Ben's colleagues for half a century, and many from the investment and academic communities. Friends from other areas of his life also attended. A group of ten from the Mt. Zion Baptist Church of Bridgeport, Connecticut, gave homage to the stranger who made it possible for them to worship in their own church.[43]

"COMPOUND INTEREST":
AN EVER-EXPANDING LEGACY

The value of Graham's estate has been estimated at approximately $3 million (as mentioned in the previous chapter, according to Roger Lowenstein, Graham gave much of his wealth away prior to his death). According to Janet Lowe, the bulk of the money was bequeathed to his second wife Estelle.[44] However, Dr. Sarnat stated that Graham had paid out a $1 million settlement to Estey long before his death. In any case, it seems probable that Malou received some portion of the money, along with the condominium in La Jolla (and the home in Aix-en-Provence that Graham had purchased for her some years earlier). Graham's daughters Marjorie, Elaine, and Winnie probably received some portion of the inheritance as well. (By then, Winnie had been diagnosed with cancer; tragically, she would succumb to the disease less than three years after her father's passing.) Buz was awarded Graham's book royalties, which, as he told me, have paid exceptionally well over the years, a success that he credits primarily to Buffett's relentless promotion of *The Intelligent Investor*.

While Graham's loved ones may have been enriched by his wealth, millions of others have been enriched by his intellectual legacy. Graham's impact as a seminal thinker in a vital field of endeavor (investment finance) cannot be understated. The most obvious illustrations of this impact are the Buffett phenomenon, the growth of the CFA (Chartered Financial Analyst) profession (which Graham played a primary role in establishing), and the millions of investors who have benefited from his sage insights in *Security Analysis*, *The Intelligent Investor*, and numerous other publications.

Moreover, in the expanding realm of academic finance, Graham's stature has never been more prominent. For example, Richard W. Roll, a professor of applied finance at UCLA (and the most recent recipient of the *Financial Analysts Journal*'s Graham and Dodd Best Perspectives Award) wrote to me that Graham remains a "pioneer in finance" and that the "Graham/Dodd approach is now found in modern asset pricing [academic] literature."[45] Meanwhile, Graham's views on other related issues, most notably macroeconomics, still reverberate decades later in the highest echelons of academia and public policy. However, in the rampant speculation and fraud that mar today's investment world, Graham's sterling professional reputation for honesty and personal integrity is also a crucial facet of his legacy. As someone who was both scrupulously honest and extraordinarily successful, he serves as the ideal role model for young investment professionals and business persons in general.

In 1997, Warren Buffett made the following observation regarding the long-term soundness of Graham's principles:

> We will continue to ignore political and economic forecasts, which are an expensive distraction for many investors and businessmen. Thirty years ago, no one could have foreseen the huge expansion of the Vietnam War, wage and price controls, two oil shocks, etc. . . . But, surprise—none of these blockbuster events made the slightest dent in Ben Graham's investment principles. . . . Fear is the foe of the faddist but the friend of the fundamentalist [i.e., one who adheres to Graham's fundamental principles]. A different set of major shocks is sure to occur in the next thirty years. We will neither try to predict these nor to profit from them.[46]

As Buffett and many other successful value investors are happy to report, Graham's principles endure, even through the momentous political, military, and economic "shocks" of the early twenty-first century. In fact, not only have they endured, but their application continues to expand, not only numerically and geographically, but *intellectually* as well (e.g., Joseph Calandro's 2009 book *Applied Value Investing*,[47] which applies Graham's principles to mergers and acquisitions, alternative investments, and other phenomena to which they have generally not been applied before).

In 2005, Warren Buffett responded to the question, "Is there a Ben Graham today?" with "You don't need another Ben Graham. You don't need another Moses. There were only Ten Commandments; we're still waiting for the eleventh. His investing philosophy is still alive and well."[48] The inscription on Graham's headstone, like the concluding passage of his eightieth-birthday address, draws from Tennyson's *Ulysses*: The words *And Not To Yield* are carved into the granite (just below the dates of his birth and death). Clearly, Graham's intellectual legacy is not likely to *ever* yield. As with all pioneering intellects who set forth their ideas in writing, the brilliance of Benjamin Graham will illuminate in perpetuity.

APPENDIX

Merck & Company, Inc., Common Stock (MRK)

(in millions)

	Historical Data	Forecast Data											Terminal (Perpetual) Value	
	Y2010	Y2011	Y2012	Y2013	Y2014	Y2015	Y2016	Y2017	Y2018	Y2019	Y2020			
Net Income[1]	982	6,465	7,755	9,303	11,159	13,385	16,055	19,258	23,101	27,710	33,238	34,235	20%
Depreciation[2]	2,638	2,901	3,191	3,510	3,860	4,246	4,670	5,136	5,649	6,213	6,833	7,038	10%
Amortization[3]	4,743	4,600	4,500	4,500	4,300	3,700	3,300	2,900	2,500	2,100	1,700	-	0%
Change in Working Capital[4]	(632)	(771)	(941)	(1,149)	(1,402)	(1,710)	(2,087)	(2,547)	(3,108)	(3,793)	(4,629)	(4,768)	22%
Capital Expenditures[5]	(1,678)	(1,925)	(2,209)	(2,535)	(2,908)	(3,337)	(3,829)	(4,393)	(5,041)	(5,784)	(6,637)	(6,836)	15%
Free Cash Flow		11,270	12,296	13,629	15,009	16,283	18,109	20,354	23,100	26,445	30,506	29,670	
Period[6]		1.0	2.0	3.0	4.0	5.0	6.0	7.0	8.0	9.0	10.0		
Discount Rate[7]		0.91	0.83	0.75	0.68	0.62	0.56	0.51	0.47	0.42	0.39		
PV		10,246	10,162	10,240	10,251	10,110	10,222	10,445	10,776	11,215	11,761	423,857	

Discount Rate	10%	
Growth Rate	3%	
Operating Value (PV)	105,429	
Terminal Value (PV)	163,415	
Total	**268,844**	
Debt[8]	17,882	2010 Annual Report
Equity Value (PV)	**250,962**	
Shares Outstanding[9]	3,576,948,356	2010 Annual Report
Value per Share	**70.16**	

NOTES

1. 2011 estimated net income is annualized from the 2011 Third Quarter Report.

September 2011 (9 months)	(12 months)
4,849	6,465

Net income from 2012 to 2020 is forecasted by employing the average growth rate of the past five years (2010~2006) of net annual income figures.

Net income for terminal value assumes a rate of 3 percent (average US GDP rate).

2. The 2010 real (i.e., historical) depreciation figure is from Merck's 2010 Annual Report.

Estimated depreciation is forecasted by employing the average growth rate of the past five years (2010~2006) of annual depreciation figures.

Depreciation for terminal value (perpetuity) is calculated using a rate of 3 percent.

3. The 2010 real amortization figure is from Merck's 2010 Annual Report.

Estimated depreciation from 2011 to 2015 is from the 2010 Annual Report.

Estimated depreciation from 2016 to 2020 deducted $400 million every year.

Amortization for terminal value is calculated using a rate of 3 percent.

4. The 2010 real working capital figure is from Merck's 2010 Annual Report.

Working capital from 2012 to 2020 is forecasted by employing the average growth rate of the past five years (2010~2006) of annual revenue figures.

Working capital for terminal value is calculated using a rate of 3 percent.

5. The 2010 real capital expenditure figure is from Merck's 2010 Annual Report.

Estimated capital expenditures are forecasted by employing the average growth rate of the past five years (2010~2006) of capital expenditure figures.

Capital expenditures for terminal value are calculated using a rate of 3 percent.

6. Assume that free cash flow occurs at the end of the year.

7. Apply 10 percent discount rate (since Merck is a large-cap company).

8. Apply interest-bearing debt figure from the 2010 Annual Report

Loan Payable and current portion of long-term debt   2,400

Long-term debt (notes)   15,482

                                                           17,882

9. The figure for the number of shares outstanding is from the 2010 Annual Report.

GLOSSARY

alpha (in an investment context): A measure of a security's (or a fund's) risk-adjusted performance. High alpha indicates that the security has exceeded its expected performance as suggested by its volatility (i.e., its *beta*).

book value per share (BVPS): A per-share measure of a company's equity, BVPS (also known as "net asset value") is calculated by dividing the value of total common equity (i.e., total assets – [total liabilities + preferred stock + intangible assets]) by the number of common shares outstanding.

charge-off: A one-time unusual expense (e.g., writing off a debt owed to the company by another party that is now believed to be uncollectible) that reduces earnings for the period in question.

current assets: A balance-sheet figure representing all assets that are likely to be converted into cash within one year. Examples include marketable securities, inventory, and cash itself.

current liabilities: A balance-sheet figure representing all liabilities that must be paid within one year. Examples include short-term debt and accounts payable.

diluted earnings: A stringent earnings metric, diluted earnings is calculated by dividing total earnings by a fully diluted base. This includes common stock, preferred stock, and unexercised convertible securities (unexercised stock options, warrants, and some forms of convertible bonds).

discount cash flow method: A valuation method that discounts all future per-share earnings projections to their present value, the discount cash flow (DCF) method is widely used among value investors. The aggregate result is considered to be the intrinsic (present) value of the stock, which can then be compared with the current stock price to weigh its attractiveness as an investment.

dividend yield: The dividend yield is calculated by dividing per-share dividends by the stock's current market price.

earned surplus: More commonly known today as "retained earnings" or "accumulated earnings," earned surplus consists of the earnings that are left over after dividends have been paid out.

earnings yield: The inverse of the Price to Earnings (P/E) ratio, the earnings yield is calculated by dividing per-share earnings (of the most recent twelve-month period) by the stock's current market price.

fixed charges: Expenses that recur consistently as part of the regular course of business (e.g., insurance payments, loan payments, etc.).

goodwill: Unlike such tangible assets such as cash or inventory, goodwill is a balance-sheet item that represents intangible assets such as brand-name recognition, strength of client (or supplier) relationships, and the like.

intangible assets: Nonphysical resources such as goodwill, intellectual property, and so forth.

liquidity: The extent to which an asset can be converted, both quickly and wholly (i.e., without a price discount), to its cash equivalent.

long-term debt: Loans and financial obligations due in over one year.

margin trading: The practice of purchasing stock with borrowed funds.

market correction: A short-term decline of 10 percent or less in overall stock-market prices (a decline of over 10 percent is classified as a *crash*); often linked to negative economic, political, or geopolitical news.

mean reversion (or "reversion to the mean"): The theory that the value of a particular entity (such as that of a security) will, over time, return to its *mean* (i.e., its average).

net present value: This metric reveals the difference between the present value of all future cash inflows and cash outflows.

short-term debt: Loans and financial obligations due within one year.

working capital: This critical metric of financial health is calculated by subtracting a company's current liabilities from its current assets.

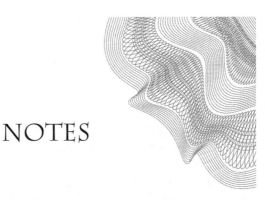

NOTES

INTRODUCTION

1. Lewis Braham, "True Believers in Value Investing," *Bloomberg Businessweek*, March 24, 2003.

2. Rich Karlgaard, "Microsoft's IQ Dividend," *Wall Street Journal*, July 28, 2004.

3. David Luhnow and Russell Adams, "Corporate News: Slim Brings Eye for Value to New York Times Co.," *Wall Street Journal*, September 12, 2008.

4. James K. Glassman, "As a Shareholder, Think of Yourself as an Owner or a Partner in a Business," *Kiplinger's Personal Finance Magazine*, February 2005.

5. Chris Farrell, "Equities: Dead, or Just Resting?" *Bloomberg Businessweek*, March 10, 2009.

6. Jonathan Burton, "Funds That Emulate Buffett," *Wall Street Journal*, March 25, 2006.

7. Jeff Sommer, "Market Predictions, with Many Grains of Salt," *New York Times*, January 9, 2011.

8. James K. Glassman, "Talk about a Smart Investment," *Kiplinger's Personal Finance Magazine*, April 2008.

9. Steve Johnson, "Jim Cullen: Value Investing Delivers Superior Returns," *Financial Times*, October 24, 2010.

10. Benjamin Graham, *The Memoirs of the Dean of Wall Street* (New York: McGraw-Hill, 1996), p. 293.

CHAPTER 1. LOSING IT ALL

1. Benjamin Graham, *The Memoirs of the Dean of Wall Street* (New York: McGraw-Hill, 1996), p. 20.

2. Ibid., p. 2.

3. Ibid, p. 9.

4. Ibid.

5. Ibid.

6. Rebecca Weiner, "The Virtual Jewish History Tour: Warsaw," Jewish Virtual Library, http://www.jewishvirtuallibrary.org/jsource/vjw/Warsaw.html (accessed April 6, 2012).

7. Isidore Singer and Cyrus Adler, eds., *The Jewish Encyclopedia* (New York: McGraw-Hill, 1912), 12:472.

8. Ibid.

9. Pete E. Lestrel, *Bernard G. Sarnat: 20th Century Plastic Surgeon and Biological Scientist* (Hackensack, NJ: World Scientific Publishing, 2008), p. 238.

10. Graham, *Memoirs of the Dean of Wall Street*, p. 26.

11. R. W. Gerard, Clyde Kluckhohn, and Anatol Rapoport, "Biological and Cultural Evolution: Some Analogies and Explorations," *Behavioral Science* 1, no. 1 (1956): 6–34.

12. R. W. Gerard, Archibal Hill, and Y. Zotterman, "The Effect of Frequency of Simulations on the Heat Production of the Nerve," *Journal of Physiology* 63 (1927): 130–43.

13. Graham, *Memoirs of the Dean of Wall Street*, p. 12.

14. Jacob Riis, *How the Other Half Lives: Studies among the Tenements of New York* (1890; repr., New York: Penguin, 1997).

15. Graham, *Memoirs of the Dean of Wall Street*, p. 6.

16. Ibid., pp. 19–20.

17. Ibid., p. 6.

18. Ibid., p. 19.

19. Ibid., p. 26.

20. Ibid., pp. 26–27.

21. Ibid., p. 27.

22. Ibid., p. 37.

23. Ibid., p. 39.

24. Ibid.

25. Ibid.

26. Ibid.

27. Ibid., p. 31.

28. Ibid.

29. Ibid., p. 30.

30. Ibid., p. 65.

31. Ibid., p. 27.

32. Ibid., pp. 27–28.

33. Ibid., p. 33.

34. Live interview with Dr. Bernard Sarnat and Rhoda Gerard Sarnat, July 18, 2011, Los Angeles, CA.

35. John Train, *The Money Masters* (New York: Harper & Row, 1980), p. 83.

36. Graham, *Memoirs of the Dean of Wall Street*, p. 71.

37. Ibid., p. 26.

38. Ibid., p. 77.

CHAPTER 2. THE MARGIN OF SAFETY

1. Benjamin Graham, *The Intelligent Investor*, 4th ed. (New York: Harper & Row, 1973), p. 277.

2. Ibid.

3. Berkshire Hathaway, Inc., 1990 Annual Report, p. 17.

4. Telephone interview with Warren Buffett, June 25, 2011.

5. Benjamin Graham, "Current Problems in Security Analysis: Excerpts from Lectures, 1946–1947, New York Institute of Finance," in *The Rediscovered Benjamin Graham*, edited by Janet Lowe (New York: John Wiley & Sons, 1999), p. 226.

6. Benjamin Graham and David Dodd, *Security Analysis*, 1st ed. (New York: McGraw-Hill, 1934), p. 54.

7. Telephone interview with Warren Buffett, June 25, 2011.

8. Graham, *Intelligent Investor*, pp. 204–205.

9. Ibid., p. 287.

10. Ibid., p. 95.

11. Ibid.

12. Ibid., p. 281.

13. Lawrence C. Strauss, "Trucking down the Long Value Highway," *Barron's*, May 14, 2011.

14. Graham and Dodd, *Security Analysis*, p. 610.

15. Ibid., p. 17.

16. Ibid.

17. Graham, *Intelligent Investor*, p. 85.

18. Ibid., p. 103.

19. Ibid., p. 161.

20. Pat Dorsey, *The Five Rules for Successful Stock Investing* (Hoboken, NJ: John Wiley & Sons, 2004), p. 144.

21. Robert Hagstrom, *The Essential Buffett* (Hoboken, NJ: John Wiley & Sons, 2002), p. 58.

22. Telephone interview with Pat Dorsey, May 5, 2011.

23. Graham, *Intelligent Investor*, p. 95.

24. Lawrence Cunningham, *How to Think Like Benjamin Graham and Invest Like Warren Buffett* (New York: McGraw-Hill, 2001), p. 143.

25. Charles H. Brandes, *Value Investing Today* (New York: McGraw-Hill, 2003), p. 5.

26. Graham and Dodd, *Security Analysis*, p. 613.

27. Robert Hagstrom, *The Warren Buffett Way*, 2nd ed. (Hoboken, NJ: John Wiley & Sons, 2005), p. 14.

28. Greg Sandoval, "Furniture.com a Case Study in E-tail Problems," *CNET News*, July 31, 2000, http://news.cnet.com/2009-1017-243395.html (accessed April 6, 2012).

29. Graham, "Current Problems in Security Analysis," p. 174.

30. Cunningham, *How to Think Like Benjamin Graham and Invest Like Warren Buffett*, p. 143.

31. Warren Buffett, "The Superinvestors of Graham and Doddsville" (speech to Columbia Business School, May 17, 1984), *Hermes* (Columbia Business School Magazine), May 17, 1984.

32. Howard Marks, *The Most Important Thing* (New York: Columbia University Press, 2011), p. 47.

33. Irving Kahn and Robert Milne, *Benjamin Graham: The Father of Financial Analysis* (Charlottesville, VA: Financial Analysts Research Foundation, 1977).

34. Alfred Dupont Chandler and Stephen Salsbury, *Pierre S. Du Pont and the Making of the Modern Corporation* (Washington, DC: Beard Books, 2000), p. 433.

35. Kahn and Milne, *Benjamin Graham*, p. 11.

36. Marks, *Most Important Thing*, p. 47.

37. L. J. Davis, "Buffett Takes Stock," *New York Times*, April 1, 1990.

38. Phillip A. Fisher, *Common Stocks and Uncommon Profits* (New York: Harper & Brothers, 1958).

39. Janet Lowe, *Damn Right! Behind the Scenes with Berkshire Hathaway Billionaire Charlie Munger* (New York: John Wiley & Sons, 2000), p. 78.

40. Telephone interview with Warren Buffett, June 25, 2011.

41. Telephone interview with Thomas Russo, May 17, 2011.

42. Jonathan Burton, "WSJ: A Monthly Analysis—Stress-Test Your Portfolio: How to Prepare for Risks Known and Unknown," *Wall Street Journal*, May 2, 2011.

43. Ibid.

CHAPTER 3. TOP OF THE CLASS

1. Benjamin Graham, *The Memoirs of the Dean of Wall Street* (New York: McGraw-Hill, 1996), p. 14.

2. Ibid.

3. Ibid., p. 23.

4. Ibid., p. 46.

5. Seymour Chatman, "Introduction," in Graham, *Memoirs of the Dean of Wall Street*, p. xiii.

6. Graham, *Memoirs of the Dean of Wall Street*, p. 15.

7. Ibid.

8. Ibid.

9. Ibid., p. 46.

10. W. S. Clinton, "Dr. Maxwell's Examinations," *New York Times*, July 18, 1905.

11. Live interview with Benjamin Graham Jr., June 20, 2011, Berkeley, CA.

12. Graham, *Memoirs of the Dean of Wall Street*, p. 47.

13. Ibid., pp. 48–49.

14. Ibid., p. 49.

15. Ibid., p. 53.

16. Ibid.

17. "The Top Ten," *New York Post*, September 1, 2010.

18. Graham, *Memoirs of the Dean of Wall Street*, p. 56.

19. Ibid., p. 68.

20. Jason Zweig, "Benjamin Graham," Columbia University, http://c250 .columbia.edu/c250_celebrates/your_columbians/benjamin_graham.html (accessed April 6, 2012).

21. Benjamin Graham, *The Intelligent Investor*, 4th ed. (New York: Harper & Row, 1973), inset page.

22. Benjamin Graham and David Dodd, *Security Analysis*, 1st ed. (New York: McGraw-Hill, 1934), inset page.

23. Graham, *Memoirs of the Dean of Wall Street*, pp. 58–59.

24. Ibid., p. 59.

25. Ibid.

26. Live interview with Dr. Robert Hamburger and Sonia Hamburger, July 21, 2011, La Jolla, CA.

27. John Train, *The Money Masters* (New York: Harper & Row, 1980), p. 83.

28. Graham, *Memoirs of the Dean of Wall Street*, p. 60.

29. Ibid., p. 68.

30. Ibid.

31. Ibid., p. 70.

32. Ibid.

33. Ibid.

34. Ibid., p. 74.

35. Ibid., p. 78.

36. Ibid., p. 81.

37. Ibid., p. 79.

38. Ibid., p. 86.

39. Ibid.

40. Ibid., p. 87.

41. Ibid.

42. Ibid.

43. Janet Lowe, *Benjamin Graham on Value Investing* (Chicago: Dearborn Financial Publishing, 1994), p. 17.

44. Graham, *Memoirs of the Dean of Wall Street*, p. 88.

45. Robert A. McCaughey, appendix, "Columbia and the 'Jewish Problem,'" in *Stand, Columbia* (New York: Columbia University Press, 2003).

46. As some indication of how Jews were viewed during Graham's years at Columbia (1911–1914), in 1911, the school's president and trustees voted against allowing use of the school chapel by "non-Christian" student organizations (ibid.). Then, in 1913, the trustees and president voted against "electing a Jew to the Board" (not a particular Jewish person who was running at the time but any Jew) (ibid.).

47. Graham, *Memoirs of the Dean of Wall Street*, p. 88.

48. Ibid.

49. Ibid., p. 90.

50. Ibid.

51. Ibid., p. 57.

52. Ibid., p. 91.

53. Ibid., p. 92.

54. Ibid.

55. Ibid., p. 93.

56. Telephone interview with Warren Buffett, June 25, 2011.

57. Graham, *Memoirs of the Dean of Wall Street*, p. 100.

58. Ibid.

59. Ibid., pp. 96–97.

60. Ibid., p. 97.

61. Ibid.

62. Ibid.

63. Ibid., p. 101.

64. Ibid., p. 113.

65. Live interview with Dr. Bernard Sarnat and Rhoda Gerard Sarnat, July 18, 2011, Los Angeles, CA.

66. Graham, *Memoirs of the Dean of Wall Street*, p. 114.

67. Ibid., p. 115.

68. Ibid.

69. Ibid., p. 116.

70. Ibid.

71. Ibid., p. 117.

72. Ibid.

73. Irving Kahn and Robert Milne, *Benjamin Graham: The Father of Financial Analysis* (Charlottesville, VA: Financial Analysts Research Foundation, 1977), p. 2.

CHAPTER 4. NUMBERS DON'T (USUALLY) LIE

1. John Train, *The Money Masters* (New York: Harper & Row, 1980), p. 106.

2. Benjamin Graham and David Dodd, *Security Analysis*, 1st ed. (New York: McGraw-Hill, 1934), p. 37.

3. Telephone interview with Irving Kahn, September 13, 2011.

4. Lawrence Cunningham, *How to Think Like Benjamin Graham and Invest Like Warren Buffett* (New York: McGraw-Hill, 2001), p. 137.

5. Ibid.

6. Ibid.

7. Benjamin Graham and Spencer B. Meredith, *The Interpretation of Financial Statements* (New York: HarperBusiness, 1937), p. 76.

8. Graham and Dodd, *Security Analysis*, 1st ed., p. 37.

9. Ibid., p. 40.

10. Ibid., p. 11.

11. Ibid.

12. Ibid., p. 474.

13. Charles H. Brandes, *Value Investing Today* (New York: McGraw-Hill, 2003), p. 22.

14. Ibid.

15. Harrison Hong and Jeffrey D. Kubik, "Analyzing the Analysts: Career Concerns and Biased Earnings Forecasts," *Journal of Finance* 58, no. 1 (February 2003): 315.

16. Harrison Hong, Jeffrey D. Kubik, and Amit Solomon, "Security Analysts' Career Concerns and Herding of Earnings Forecasts," *RAND Journal of Economics* 31, no. 1 (Spring 2000): 122.

17. Graham and Dodd, *Security Analysis*, 1st ed., p. 48.

18. Benjamin Graham, *The Intelligent Investor*, 4th ed. (New York: Harper & Row, 1973), p. xiii.

19. Ibid., pp. xiii, 184–85.

20. Ibid., p. 209.

21. Benjamin Graham, *The Intelligent Investor*, rev. ed., updated with new commentary by Jason Zweig (New York: Harper, 2003), p. 369.

22. Ibid.

23. YCharts (NYSE:MAT), December 20, 2011.

24. Ibid.

25. Ibid.

26. Ibid.

27. Ibid.

28. Ibid.

29. Ibid.

30. Ibid.

31. Ibid.

32. Ibid.

33. Graham and Zweig, *Intelligent Investor*, rev. ed., p. 369.

34. YCharts (NYSE:ITT), December 21, 2011.

35. Ibid.

36. Ibid.

37. Ibid.

38. Ibid.

39. Benjamin Graham, "Current Problems in Security Analysis: Excerpts from Lectures, 1946–1947, New York Institute of Finance," in *The Rediscovered Benjamin Graham*, edited by Janet Lowe (New York: John Wiley & Sons, 1999).

40. Graham and Dodd, *Security Analysis*, 1st ed., p. 58.

41. Graham, *Intelligent Investor*, 4th ed.p. 104.

42. Ibid.

43. Graham and Dodd, *Security Analysis*, 1st ed., p. 85.

44. Graham, *Intelligent Investor*, 4th ed., p. 149.

45. Graham and Dodd, *Security Analysis*, 1st ed., p. 85.

46. Ibid., p. 126.

47. "Form 10-K for Fiscal Year Ending June 30, 2011," Archer-Daniels-Midland Company, November 2011.

48. Graham and Zweig, *Intelligent Investor*, rev. ed., p. 283.

49. Graham, *Intelligent Investor*, 4th ed., p. 158.

50. Ibid., p. 200.

51. Graham and Dodd, *Security Analysis*, 1st ed., p. 20.

52. Graham and Meredith, *Interpretation of Financial Statements*, p. vii.

53. Ibid., p. viii.

54. Ibid., p. 23.

55. Ibid., p. 48.

56. Ibid., p. 165.

57. Graham and Dodd, *Security Analysis*, 1st ed., pp. 418–19.

58. Graham, *Intelligent Investor*, 4th ed., p. 167.

59. Graham and Dodd, *Security Analysis*, 1st ed., p. 648.

60. Graham, *Intelligent Investor*, 4th ed., p. 167.

61. Ibid.

62. Ibid.

63. Ibid.

64. Benjamin Graham, David Dodd, and Sidney Cottle, *Security Analysis*, rev. 4th ed. (New York: McGraw-Hill, 1962), p. 222.

65. Ibid.

66. Graham and Meredith, *Interpretation of Financial Statements*, pp. 50–51.

CHAPTER 5. THE ORIGINAL SECURITY ANALYST

1. Saul Friedlander, *Nazi Germany and the Jews*, vol. 1, *The Years of Persecution 1933–1939* (New York: HarperCollins, 1997), p. 109.

2. Benjamin Graham, *The Memoirs of the Dean of Wall Street* (New York: McGraw-Hill, 1996), p. 63.

3. Ibid.

4. Elsdon Coles Smith, *American Surnames* (Baltimore, MD: Genealogical Publishing, 1986), p. 30.

5. Graham, *Memoirs of the Dean of Wall Street*, p. 127.

6. Ibid., p. 54.

7. Telephone interview with Warren Buffett, June 25, 2011.

8. Live interview with Charles H. Brandes, May 19, 2011, San Diego, CA.

9. Live interview with Dr. Bernard Sarnat and Rhoda Gerard Sarnat, July 18, 2011, Los Angeles, CA.

10. William L. Silber, "What Happened to Liquidity When World War I Shut the

NYSE?" *Journal of Financial Economics* (2001), Asset Management Research Group: NYU Stern School of Business, March 2007, http://people.stern.nyu.edu/wsilber/Article%20What%20Happened%20When%20%20JFE%205%2020%2005%20FINAL%20PAPER.pdf.

11. Graham, *Memoirs of the Dean of Wall Street*, p. 136.

12. Simon Doolittle, "A Lifetime of Perspective on Wall Street's Hard Times," *New York Times*, April 4, 2009.

13. Ibid.

14. Graham, *Memoirs of the Dean of Wall Street*, p. 127.

15. Ibid., p. 139.

16. Ibid., p. 138.

17. Lawrence Chamberlain, *The Principles of Bond Investment* (New York: Henry Holt, 1911), p. 120.

18. Graham, *Memoirs of the Dean of Wall Street*, p. 139.

19. Ibid.

20. Irving Kahn and Robert Milne, *Benjamin Graham: The Father of Financial Analysis* (Charlottesville, VA: Financial Analysts Research Foundation, 1977), p. 4.

21. Ibid.

22. Ibid.

23. Ibid., p. 5.

24. Seymour Chatman, "Introduction," in Graham, *Memoirs of the Dean of Wall Street*, p. xii.

25. "The Father of Value Investing," *Fortune*, November 2, 1987.

26. Graham, *Memoirs of the Dean of Wall Street*, p. 142.

27. Ibid.

28. Benjamin Graham, "The New Speculation in Common Stocks: Address to the Financial Analysts Society Stock Market Luncheon [June 1958]," in *The Rediscovered Benjamin Graham*, edited by Janet Lowe (New York: John Wiley & Sons, 1999), p. 38.

29. Graham, *Memoirs of the Dean of Wall Street*, p. 146.

30. Ibid., p. 147.

31. Ibid.

32. Ibid., p. 146.

33. Ibid., p. 147.

34. Kahn and Milne, *Benjamin Graham*, p. 5.

35. Graham, *Memoirs of the Dean of Wall Street*, p. 149.

36. Ibid.

37. Live interview with Marjorie Graham Janis, June 28, 2011, Palo Alto, CA.

38. Ibid.

39. Ibid.

40. Benjamin Graham, "Some Calculus Suggestions by a Student," *American Mathematical Monthly* 24, no. 6 (June1917): 265–71.

41. Kahn and Milne, *Benjamin Graham*, p. 6.

42. Benjamin Graham, "Current Problems in Security Analysis: Excerpts from Lectures, 1946–1947, New York Institute of Finance," in *The Rediscovered Benjamin Graham*, edited by Janet Lowe (New York: John Wiley & Sons, 1999).

43. Kahn and Milne, *Benjamin Graham*, p. 7.

44. Ibid., p. 6.

45. Graham, *Memoirs of the Dean of Wall Street*, p. 174.

46. Ibid., p. 167.

47. Ibid.

48. Ibid., p. 153.

49. Ibid.

50. Ibid., pp. 153–54.

51. Ibid., p. 154.

52. Friedrich Nietzsche, *Twilight of the Idols* (1888; repr., New York: Penguin Classics, 1990), p. 33.

53. Kahn and Milne, *Benjamin Graham*, p. 8.

54. Ibid., p. 9.

55. Graham, *Memoirs of the Dean of Wall Street*, p. 182.

56. Ibid., p. 180.

57. Live interview with Dr. Bernard Sarnat and Rhoda Gerard Sarnat, July 18, 2011, Los Angeles, CA.

58. Graham, *Memoirs of the Dean of Wall Street*, p. 177.

59. Ibid.

60. Ibid., p. 174.

61. Kahn and Milne, *Benjamin Graham*, p. 19.

CHAPTER 6. ALL OR NOTHING

1. Benjamin Graham, *The Intelligent Investor*, 4th ed. (New York: Harper & Row, 1973), p. 286.

2. Robert Hagstrom, *The Essential Buffett* (Hoboken, NJ: John Wiley & Sons, 2001), p. 121.

3. Lawrence Cunningham, *How to Think Like Benjamin Graham and Invest Like Warren Buffett* (New York: McGraw-Hill, 2001), p. 244.

4. Hagstrom, *Essential Buffett*, p. 212.

5. Telephone interview with Pat Dorsey, May 5, 2011.

6. Benjamin Graham, *The Intelligent Investor*, rev. ed., updated with new commentary by Jason Zweig (New York: Harper, 2003), p. 546.

7. Ibid.

8. Benjamin Graham and David Dodd, *Security Analysis*, 1st ed. (New York: McGraw-Hill, 1934), pp. 305–306.

9. Benjamin Graham, "Curiosities of the Bond List," in *Benjamin Graham on Investing: Enduring Lessons from the Father of Value Investing*, edited by Rodney G. Klein, with updates and commentary by David M. Darst (New York: McGraw-Hill, 2009), p. 10.

10. Graham and Dodd, *Security Analysis*, p. 432.

11. Benjamin Graham, "Hidden Assets of Consolidated Gas," in *Benjamin Graham on Investing: Enduring Lessons from the Father of Value Investing*, edited by Rodney G. Klein, with updates and commentary by David M. Darst (New York: McGraw-Hill, 2009), p. 83.

12. Benjamin Graham, "Is American Business Worth More Dead Than Alive?" in *The Rediscovered Benjamin Graham*, edited by Janet Lowe (New York: John Wiley & Sons, 1999), p. 13.

13. Graham and Dodd, *Security Analysis*, p. 432.

14. Ibid.

15. T. H. Chu, C. C. Lin, and L. J. Prather, "An Extension of Security Price Reactions around Product Recall Announcements," *Quarterly Journal of Business & Economics* 44, no. 3–4 (2005): 33–47.

16. Charles H. Brandes, *Value Investing Today* (New York: McGraw-Hill, 2003), p. 13.

17. Hagstrom, *Essential Buffett*, p. 124.

18. Gregory J. Millman, *The Day Traders* (New York: Times Books, 1999), pp. 126–27.

19. Cunningham, *How to Think Like Benjamin Graham and Invest Like Warren Buffett*, p. 63.

20. Michael Mackenzie, "High-Frequency Trading under Scrutiny," *Financial Times*, July 28, 2009.

21. Charles Duhigg, "Stock Traders Find Speed Pays, in Milliseconds," *New York Times*, July 23, 2009.

22. Millman, *Day Traders*, p. 186.

23. Matt Krantz, "Rolling the Dice: Day Trading Is Gambling," *USA Today*, January 31, 2006.

24. Graham and Dodd, *Security Analysis*, p. 492.

25. Graham, *Intelligent Investor*, 4th ed., pp. 517–18.

26. Telephone interview with Pat Dorsey, May 5, 2011.

27. Hagstrom, *Essential Buffett*, p. 185.

28. Graham, *Intelligent Investor*, 4th ed., p. 102.

29. Frederic P. Miller, Agnes F. Vandome, and John McBrewster, *Barbara Marx* (Saarbrucken, Germany: VDM Publishing House, 2010).

30. Graham and Dodd, *Security Analysis*, p. 48.

31. Benjamin Graham, "Inflated Treasuries and Deflated Stocks: Are Corporations Milking Their Owners?" in *The Rediscovered Benjamin Graham*, edited by Janet Lowe (New York: John Wiley & Sons, 1999), p. 7.

32. Ibid., p. 14.

33. Telephone interview with Warren Buffett, June 25, 2011.

34. Ibid.

35. Ibid.

36. Warren Buffett, "Chairman's Letter," Berkshire Hathaway, Inc., 2010 Annual Report, February 26, 2011, p. 8.

37. Warren Buffett, "The Superinvestors of Graham and Doddsville" (speech to Columbia Business School, May 17, 1984), *Hermes* (Columbia Business School Magazine), May 17, 1984.

38. Walter Schloss, "Sixteen Golden Rules for Investing (1994)," Guru Focus, October 25, 2009, http://www.gurufocus.com/news/72536/walter-schloss-16-golden -rules-for-investing (accessed April 13, 2012).

39. Graham and Zweig, *Intelligent Investor*, rev. ed., p. 217.

40. Graham, *Intelligent Investor*, 4th ed., p. 106.

41. Graham and Dodd, *Security Analysis*, p. 48.

42. Irving Kahn and Robert Milne, *Benjamin Graham: The Father of Financial Analysis* (Charlottesville, VA: Financial Analysts Research Foundation, 1977), p. 27.

43. Graham, *Intelligent Investor*, 4th ed., p. 288.

44. Ibid.

45. "Stockholder's Letter," Graham-Newman Corporation, February 25, 1949, p. 6.

46. Graham, *Intelligent Investor*, 4th ed., p. 289.

47. "GEICO History: An American Success Story," GEICO, http://www.geico .com/about/corporate/history/ (accessed October 25, 2011).

48. Buffett, "Chairman's Letter."

49. Graham, *Intelligent Investor*, 4th ed., p. 289.

50. Nikki Ross, *Lessons from the Legends of Wall Street* (Chicago: Dearborn Financial Publishing, 2000), p. 36.

51. Charlie Munger and Peter D. Kaufman, *Poor Charlie's Almanack: The Wit and Wisdom of Charles T. Munger*, 3rd ed. (Virginia Beach, VA: Donning Company Publishers, 2008), p. 67.

52. Warren Buffett, "Chairman's Letter," Berkshire Hathaway, Inc., 1993 Annual Report, March 1, 1994.

53. Graham, *Intelligent Investor*, 4th ed., p. 106.

54. Graham and Dodd, *Security Analysis*, p. 17.

CHAPTER 7. DIZZYING HEIGHTS AND SHUDDERING DEPTHS

1. Allen Weinstein and David Rubel, *The Story of America* (New York: Agincourt Press, 2002), p. 488.

2. Benjamin Graham, *The Memoirs of the Dean of Wall Street* (New York: McGraw-Hill, 1996), p. 189

3. Ibid., p. 188.

4. Ibid., p. 190.

5. Ibid., p. 173.

6. Ibid., p. 192.

7. Irving Kahn and Robert Milne, *Benjamin Graham: The Father of Financial Analysis* (Charlottesville, VA: Financial Analysts Research Foundation, 1977), p. 12.

8. Graham, *Memoirs of the Dean of Wall Street*, p. 193.

9. Ibid., p. 190.

10. Ron Chernow, *Titan: The Life of John D. Rockefeller Sr.* (New York: Random House, 1998), p. xx.

11. Kahn and Milne, *Benjamin Graham*, pp. 12–13.

12. Graham, *Memoirs of the Dean of Wall Street*, pp. 200–201.

13. Ibid., p. 201.

14. Ibid.

15. Kahn and Milne, *Benjamin Graham*, p. 13.

16. Graham, *Memoirs of the Dean of Wall Street*, p. 203.

17. Ibid., p. 211.

18. Ibid.

19. "The Wealthiest Americans Ever," *New York Times*, July 15, 2007.

20. Graham, *Memoirs of the Dean of Wall Street*, p. 214.

21. Ibid., p. 215.

22. Ibid.

23. Ibid.

24. Ibid., p. 251.

25. Ibid.

26. Ibid., p. 252.

27. Ibid., p. 253.

28. Live interview with Marjorie Graham Janis, June 28, 2011, Palo Alto, CA.

29. Graham, *Memoirs of the Dean of Wall Street*, p. 230.

30. Morton N. Swartz, "Bacterial Meningitis—A View of the Past 90 Years," *New England Journal of Medicine* 351, no. 18 (2004): 1826–28.

31. Graham, *Memoirs of the Dean of Wall Street*, p. 231.

32. Ibid.

33. Ibid.

34. Live interview with Marjorie Graham Janis, June 28, 2011, Palo Alto, CA.

35. Graham, *Memoirs of the Dean of Wall Street*, pp. 231–32.

36. Ibid., p. 232.

37. Ibid.

38. Ibid.

39. Live interview with Benjamin Graham Jr., June 20, 2011, Berkeley, CA.

40. Telephone interview with Irving Kahn, September 13, 2011.

41. Kahn and Milne, *Benjamin Graham*, p. 19.

42. Telephone interview with Irving Kahn, September 13, 2011.

43. Ibid.

44. Telephone interview with Warren Buffett, June 25, 2011.

45. Kahn and Milne, *Benjamin Graham*, p. 18.

46. Graham, *Memoirs of the Dean of Wall Street*, p. 232.

47. Weinstein and Rubel, *Story of America*, p. 488.

48. Ibid., p. 490.

49. John Train, *The Money Masters* (New York: Harper & Row, 1980), p. 86.

50. Benjamin Graham and David Dodd, *Security Analysis*, 1st ed. (New York: McGraw-Hill, 1934), pp. 8–9.

51. Ibid., p. 9.

52. Roger Lowenstein, *Buffett: The Making of an American Capitalist* (New York: Random House, 1995), p. 38.

53. Graham, *Memoirs of the Dean of Wall Street*, p. 264.

54. Telephone interview with Irving Kahn, September 13, 2011.

55. Graham and Dodd, *Security Analysis*, 1st ed., p. 195.

56. Ibid., p. 124.

57. See the cover description for Benjamin Graham and David Dodd, *Security Analysis: The Classic 1951 Edition* (New York: McGraw-Hill, 2004).

58. Graham, *Memoirs of the Dean of Wall Street*, p. 239.

59. Benjamin Graham, "Inflated Treasuries and Deflated Stocks: Are Corporations Milking Their Owners?" in *The Rediscovered Benjamin Graham*, edited by Janet Lowe (New York: John Wiley & Sons, 1999), p. 9.

CHAPTER 8. THE FOLLY OF "MR. MARKET"

1. Benjamin Graham, *The Intelligent Investor*, 4th ed. (New York: Harper & Row, 1973), p. 108.

2. Ibid.

3. Kelly Evans, "Ahead of the Tape," *Wall Street Journal*, April 2, 2010.

4. Graham, *Intelligent Investor*, 4th ed., p. 108.

5. John C. Bogle, *Common Sense on Mutual Funds* (Hoboken, NJ: John Wiley & Sons, 2009), p. 28.

6. Pat Dorsey, *The Five Rules for Successful Stock Investing* (Hoboken, NJ: John Wiley & Sons, 2004), p. xvii.

7. Gary P. Brinson, Randolph L. Hood, and Gilbert P. Beebower, "Determinants of Portfolio Performance," *Financial Analysts Journal* (July/August 1986).

8. Dorsey, *Five Rules for Successful Stock Investing*, p. xvii.

9. Benjamin Graham, *The Intelligent Investor*, rev. ed., updated with new commentary by Jason Zweig (New York: Harper, 2003), p. 217.

10. Steven L. Jones and Jeffery M. Netter, "Efficient Capital Markets," *The Concise Encyclopedia of Economics* (Indianapolis, IN: Liberty Fund, 2008).

11. Lawrence Cunningham, *How to Think Like Benjamin Graham and Invest Like Warren Buffett* (New York: McGraw-Hill, 2001), p. 51.

12. Howard Marks, *The Most Important Thing* (New York: Columbia University Press, 2011), p. 8.

13. Cunningham, *How to Think Like Benjamin Graham and Invest Like Warren Buffett*, p. 51.

14. Ibid.

15. Live interview with Charles H. Brandes, May 19, 2011, San Diego, CA.

16. Telephone interview with Warren Buffett, June 25, 2011.

17. Benjamin Graham and David Dodd, *Security Analysis*, 1st ed. (New York: McGraw-Hill, 1934), pp. 321–22.

18. Marks, *Most Important Thing*, pp. 174–75.

19. Graham and Zweig, *Intelligent Investor*, rev. ed., p. 215.

20. Steven M. Sears, "A Trade to Play the Market's Swings," *Barron's*, June 2, 2011.

21. Telephone interview with Warren Buffett, June 25, 2011.

22. Graham, *Intelligent Investor*, 4th ed., p. 109.

23. Steve Forbes and Rob Arnott, "Steve Forbes Interview: Fundamental Index Pioneer Rob Arnott," *Forbes*, August 8, 2011.

24. Marks, *Most Important Thing*, p. 75.

25. Nikhil Hutheesing, "The Graham & Dodders," *Forbes*, February 23, 2009.

26. Ibid.

27. Graham and Dodd, *Security Analysis*, p. 322.

28. Parag Parikh, *Value Investing and Behavioral Finance* (New Delhi, India: Tata McGraw-Hill, 2009), p. 61.

29. Steven Sears, "A Hearty Options Play on Medtronic," *Barron's*, August 30, 2010.

30. James Montier, *Value Investing: Tools and Techniques for Intelligent Investment* (West Sussex, United Kingdom: John Wiley & Sons, 2009), p. 136.

31. Marks, *Most Important Thing*, p. 27.

32. Nikki Ross, *Lessons from the Legends of Wall Street* (Chicago: Dearborn Financial Publishing, 2000), p. 54.

33. Graham, *The Intelligent Investor*, 4th ed., p. 106.

34. Benjamin Gallander, *The Contrarian Investor's Thirteen* (Toronto, Canada: Insomniac Press, 2003), p. 8.

35. Charles H. Brandes, *Value Investing Today* (New York: McGraw-Hill, 2003), p. 187.

36. Graham, *Intelligent Investor*, 4th ed., p. 110.

37. Telephone interview with Pat Dorsey, May 5, 2011.

38. Harley-Davidson, Inc., "Harley-Davidson Reports 2008 Third Quarter Results," October 16, 2008.

39. See Graham, *Intelligent Investor*, 4th ed., p. 106.

CHAPTER 9. NEW BEGINNINGS

1. Benjamin Graham, "Is American Business Worth More Dead Than Alive?" in *The Rediscovered Benjamin Graham*, edited by Janet Lowe (New York: John Wiley & Sons, 1999), p. 9.

2. Irving Kahn and Robert Milne, *Benjamin Graham: The Father of Financial Analysis* (Charlottesville, VA: Financial Analysts Research Foundation, 1977), p. 13.

3. Live interview with Marjorie Graham Janis, June 28, 2011, Palo Alto, CA.

4. Benjamin Graham and David Dodd, *Security Analysis*, 1st ed. (New York: McGraw-Hill, 1934), p. 6.

5. Live interview with Dr. Bernard Sarnat and Rhoda Gerard Sarnat, July 18, 2011, Los Angeles, CA.

6. Benjamin Graham, *The Memoirs of the Dean of Wall Street* (New York: McGraw-Hill, 1996), p. 268.

7. Graham-Newman Corporation Letter, 1946.

8. Kahn and Milne, *Benjamin Graham*, p. 21.

9. Benjamin Graham, "Stabilized Reflation," *Economic Forum* (Spring 1933): 186–93.

10. Benjamin Graham, "Summarization of the Multiple Commodity Reserve Plan," in *The Rediscovered Benjamin Graham*, edited by Janet Lowe (New York: John Wiley & Sons, 1999).

11. Graham, *Memoirs of the Dean of Wall Street*, p. 279.

12. Ibid.

13. Ibid., p. 281.

14. Ibid., p. 282.

15. Ibid.

16. Ibid.

17. "Buerger's Disease," Mayo Clinic, http://www.mayoclinic.com/health/buergers-disease/DS00807 (accessed December 9, 2011).

18. Graham, *Memoirs of the Dean of Wall Street*, p. 282.

19. Ibid., p. 283.

20. Ibid.

21. Ibid., p. 284.

22. Benjamin Graham and David Dodd, *Security Analysis*, 6th ed. (New York: McGraw-Hill, 2008).

23. Graham, *Memoirs of the Dean of Wall Street*, p. 284.

24. Ibid., p. 235.

25. Ibid., p. 236.

26. Ibid., p. 235.

27. Ibid., p. 288.

28. "Baby Talk," *New York Times*, December 28, 1934.

29. Graham, *Memoirs of the Dean of Wall Street*, p. 290.

30. See the preface in Benjamin Graham and Spencer B. Meredith, *The Interpretation of Financial Statements* (New York: HarperBusiness, 1937).

31. Ibid., p. 23.

32. Ibid., p. 56.

33. Live interview with Marjorie Graham Janis, June 28, 2011, Palo Alto, CA.

34. Live interview with Dr. Bernard Sarnat and Rhoda Gerard Sarnat, July 18, 2011, Los Angeles, CA.

35. Ibid.

36. Graham, *Memoirs of the Dean of Wall Street*, p. 180.

37. Ibid., p. 279.

38. Susan B. Carter, Scott Sigmund Gartner, Michael R. Haines, Alan L. Olmstead, Richard Sutch, and Gavin Wright, *Historical Statistics of the United States:*

Marriage and Divorce Rates, 1920–1995 (Cambridge, United Kingdom: Cambridge University Press, 2006).

39. Live interview with Marjorie Graham Janis, June 28, 2011, Palo Alto, CA.

40. Graham, *Memoirs of the Dean of Wall Street*, p. 230.

41. Ibid., p. 273.

42. Ibid., p. 275.

43. Ibid., p. 276.

44. Ibid., p. 277.

45. Ibid.

46. Ibid., p. 274.

47. Kahn and Milne, *Benjamin Graham*, p. 26.

48. CFA Institute, https://www.cfainstitute.org/pages/index.aspx (accessed January 10, 2012).

49. Live interview with Dr. Bernard Sarnat and Rhoda Gerard Sarnat, July 18, 2011, Los Angeles, CA.

50. "Irving Janis Dies at 72; Coined 'Group Think,'" *New York Times*, November 18, 1990.

51. Daniel Bell, *The End of Ideology: On the Exhaustion of Political Ideas in the Fifties* (Cambridge, MA: Harvard University Press, 1962).

52. Daniel Bell, *The Coming of Post-Industrial Society: A Venture in Social Forecasting* (New York: Basic Books, 1973).

53. Roberto Foa and Thomas Meaney, "The Last Word," *Utopian*, February 10, 2011 (interview with Daniel Bell conducted on September 21, 2010).

54. Cyril Sofer, *Men in Mid-Career: A Study of British Managers and Technical Specialists* (Cambridge, United Kingdom: Cambridge University Press, 1970).

55. Cyril Sofer, *Organizations in Theory and Practice* (Portsmouth, NH: Heinemann Educational Publishers, 1973).

56. Elaine Graham Sofer, *The Psychological Impact of School Experience* (New York: Basic Books, 1969).

57. Elaine Graham Sofer, "Inner-Direction, Other-Direction, and Autonomy: A Study of College Students," in *Culture and Social Character*, edited by Seymour Martin Lipset and Leo Lowenthal (New York: Free Press, 1961), pp. 316–48.

58. Marjorie Graham Janis, *A Two-Year-Old Goes to Nursery School: A Case Study of Separation Reactions* (New York: National Association for the Education of Young Children, 1966).

59. Live interview with Marjorie Graham Janis, June 28, 2011, Palo Alto, CA.

60. Janet Lowe, ed., *The Rediscovered Benjamin Graham* (New York: John Wiley & Sons, 1999).

61. Live interview with Benjamin Graham Jr., June 20, 2011, Berkeley, CA.

CHAPTER 10. KEYNES, HAYEK, AND GRAHAM?

1. Benjamin Graham, *The Memoirs of the Dean of Wall Street* (New York: McGraw-Hill, 1996), p. 293.

2. Telephone interview with Irving Kahn, September 13, 2011.

3. "Diagnosing Depression: What Is the Difference between a Recession and a Depression?" *Economist*, December 30, 2008.

4. Andrew Atkeson and Patrick J. Kehoe, "Deflation and Depression: Is There an Empirical Link?" Federal Reserve Bank of Minneapolis, Research Department Staff Report 331, January 2004, http://minneapolisfed.org/research/sr/sr331.pdf.

5. Graham, *Memoirs of the Dean of Wall Street*, p. 294.

6. Ibid.

7. Ibid.

8. Ibid.

9. Lyman Judson Gage, "The Gold Standard Act (1900)," in *American History Told by Contemporaries: Welding of the Nation, 1845–1900,* edited by Albert Bushnell Hart (London, United Kingdom: MacMillan, 1910), p. 539.

10. Graham, *Memoirs of the Dean of Wall Street*, p. 294.

11. Irving Fisher, *The Money Illusion* (New York: Adelphi, 1928), p. 169.

12. Graham, *Memoirs of the Dean of Wall Street*, p. 295.

13. Kenneth Roose, "The Recession of 1937–38," *Journal of Political Economy* 56, no. 3 (June 1948): 239–48.

14. Benjamin Graham, *Storage and Stability* (New York: McGraw-Hill, 1937), pp. 53–54.

15. Ibid., p. 51.

16. Graham, *Memoirs of the Dean of Wall Street*, p. 297.

17. John Maynard Keynes, *General Theory of Employment, Interest, and Money* (London, United Kingdom: MacMillan, 1936).

18. John A. Hobson, *The Economics of Unemployment* (London, United Kingdom: Allen Publishing, 1922).

19. Graham, *Memoirs of the Dean of Wall Street*, p. 289.

20. Graham, *Storage and Stability*, p. 40.

21. Graham, *Memoirs of the Dean of Wall Street*, p. 298.

22. Milton Friedman and Anna Jacobson Schwartz, *A Monetary History of the United States, 1867–1960* (Princeton, NJ: Princeton University Press, 1963), p. 299.

23. Ibid.

24. Allen Weinstein and David Rubel, *The Story of America* (New York: Agincourt Press, 2002), p. 490.

25. Graham, *Memoirs of the Dean of Wall Street*, p. 298.

26. Jan Goudriaan, *How to Stop Deflation* (N.p.: University of Rotterdam/ Search Publishing, 1922).

27. Irving Kahn and Robert Milne, *Benjamin Graham: The Father of Financial Analysis* (Charlottesville, VA: Financial Analysts Research Foundation, 1977), p. 24.

28. William Stanley Jevons, *Money and the Mechanisms of Exchange* (New York: D. Appleton, 1877), p. 328.

29. Graham, *Memoirs of the Dean of Wall Street*, p. 298.

30. Benjamin Graham, "Stabilized Reflation," *Economic Forum* (Spring 1933): 186–93.

31. Graham, *Memoirs of the Dean of Wall Street*, p. 300.

32. Graham, *Storage and Stability*, p. 3.

33. Ibid., p. 9.

34. Live interview with Charles H. Brandes, May 19, 2011, San Diego, CA.

35. Graham, *Storage and Stability*, p. 11.

36. Ibid., p. 13.

37. Ibid., p. 14.

38. "Roosevelt, Franklin D.," Encyclopedia Britannica Profiles the American Presidency, http://www.britannica.com/presidents/article-23944 (accessed May 3, 2012).

39. *United States v. Butler*, Oyez, http://www.oyez.org/cases/1901-1939/1935/ 1935_401 (accessed December 22, 2011).

40. Dwight Macdonald, *Henry Wallace: The Man and the Myth* (New York: Vanguard Press, 1948), p. 59.

41. Graham, *Storage and Stability*, p. 26.

42. Ibid., p. 20.

43. Ibid., p. 25.

44. Ibid., p. 37.

45. Ibid., p. 148.

46. Franklin D. Roosevelt, "White House Statement on Proclamation 2072," January 31, 1934.

47. Graham, *Storage and Stability*, p. 59.

48. Ibid., p. 58.

49. Ibid., pp. 60–61.

50. Ibid., p. 61.

51. Ibid., p. 147.

52. Ibid., p. 89.

53. Ibid., p. 88.

54. Ibid.

55. Ibid., p. 89.

56. Ibid.

57. Benjamin Graham, *World Commodities and World Currencies* (New York: McGraw-Hill, 1944), p. 1.

58. Ibid., pp. 42–43.

59. Ibid., p. 44.

60. Ibid.

61. Ibid., pp. 44–46.

62. Todd G. Buchholz, *From Here to Economy* (New York: Penguin, 1996), p. 183.

63. Graham, *World Commodities and World Currencies*, p. 101.

64. Ibid.

65. Peter Klein, "Biography of F. A. Hayek (1899–1992)," Ludwig Von Mises Institute, 1998, http://mises.org/page/1454/Biography-of-F-A-Hayek-18991992 (accesssed April 9, 2012).

66. Ibid.

67. John Hicks, "The Hayek Story," in *Critical Essays in Monetary Theory* (Oxford, United Kingdom: Oxford University Press, 1967), p. 203.

68. Hyman P. Minsky, *John Maynard Keynes: Hyman P. Minsky's Influential Re-interpretation of the Keynesian Revolution* (New York: McGraw-Hill, 2008), p. 1.

69. Ibid.

70. Graham, *World Commodities and World Currencies*, p. 110.

71. F. A. Hayek, "A Commodity Reserve Currency," *Economic Journal* 53, no. 210/211 (June–September 1943): 176–84.

72. Janet Lowe, ed., *The Rediscovered Benjamin Graham* (New York: John Wiley & Sons, 1999), p. 232.

73. Kahn and Milne, *Benjamin Graham*, p. 25.

74. Lowe, *Rediscovered Benjamin Graham*, p. 233.

75. "Bretton Woods Conference Collection," IMF Online Archives, http://www.imf.org/external/np/arc/eng/fa/bwc/overview.htm (accessed December 22, 2011).

76. Graham, *Memoirs of the Dean of Wall Street*, p. 307.

77. David Ranson, "The Volatile Dollar: The Floating Dollar Needs an Anchor," *New York Times*, November 19, 1989.

78. Ibid.

79. Ibid.

80. Robert Heilbrunn, "Fixing the Dollar," *New York Times*, December 24, 1989.

81. David Boyle, *The Money Changers: Currency Reform from Aristotle to E-Cash* (London, United Kingdom: Earthscan Publications, 2002), p. 196.

82. John W. Allen, "China's Role in Creating a New Reserve Currency" (lecture, London School of Economics, January 22, 2011).
83. Ibid.
84. Ibid.
85. Ibid.

CHAPTER 11. AN EAGER YOUNG STUDENT FROM OMAHA

1. Benjamin Graham, *The Memoirs of the Dean of Wall Street* (New York: McGraw-Hill, 1996), p. 157.
2. Telephone interview with Irving Kahn, September 13, 2011.
3. Irving Kahn and Robert Milne, *Benjamin Graham: The Father of Financial Analysis* (Charlottesville, VA: Financial Analysts Research Foundation, 1977), p. 27.
4. Telephone interview with Warren Buffett, June 25, 2011.
5. "The Intelligent Investor, Rev. Ed.," Amazon.com, http://www.amazon.com/The-Intelligent-Investor-Definitive-Investing/dp/0060555661 (accessed December 27, 2011).
6. Benjamin Graham, *The Intelligent Investor*, 1st ed. (New York: Harper, 1950), p. 5.
7. Ibid., p. 8.
8. Ibid., p. 21.
9. Warren Buffett, "Preface," in Benjamin Graham, *The Intelligent Investor*, 4th ed. (New York: Harper & Row, 1973).
10. Telephone interview with Warren Buffett, June 25, 2011.
11. Roger Lowenstein, *Buffett: The Making of an American Capitalist* (New York: Random House, 1995), p. 6.
12. John Train, *The Money Masters* (New York: Harper & Row, 1980), p. 4.
13. Lowenstein, *Buffett*, p. 10.
14. Live interview with Scott Widman, Omaha, NE, April 2011.
15. Lowenstein, *Buffett*, p. 23.
16. Ibid., p. 20.
17. Ibid., p. 16.
18. Live interview with Benjamin Graham Jr., June 20, 2011, Berkeley, CA.
19. Andrew Kilpatrick, *Of Permanent Value: The Story of Warren Buffett* (Birmingham, AL: AKPE, 1994), p. 32.
20. Alice Schroeder, *The Snowball: Warren Buffett and the Business of Life* (New York: Bantam, 2008), p. 144.

21. Ibid., p. 127.

22. Kilpatrick, *Of Permanent Value*, p. 58.

23. Berkshire Hathaway, Inc., 1995 Annual Report, p. 17.

24. Telephone interview with Warren Buffett, June 25, 2011.

25. Bill Ruane, quoted in Andrew Kilpatrick, *Of Permanent Value: The Story of Warren Buffett*, 2006 Literary Edition (Birmingham, AL: AKPE, 2005), p. 81.

26. Janet Lowe, *Benjamin Graham on Value Investing* (Chicago: Dearborn Financial Publishing, 1994), p. 158.

27. Live interview with Dr. Bernard Sarnat and Rhoda Gerard Sarnat, July 18, 2011, Los Angeles, CA.

28. Lowenstein, *Buffett*, p. 43.

29. Ibid., p. 45.

30. Train, *Money Masters*, p. 6.

31. Telephone interview with Irving Kahn, September 13, 2011.

32. Amey Stone and Mike Brewster, *King of Capital: Sandy Weill and the Making of Citigroup* (New York: John Wiley & Sons, 2002), p. 43.

33. Schroeder, *Snowball*, p. 150.

34. Ibid.

35. Ibid., p. 197.

36. Telephone interview with Warren Buffett, June 25, 2011.

37. Ibid.

38. Live interview with Dr. Bernard Sarnat and Rhoda Gerard Sarnat, July 18, 2011, Los Angeles, CA.

39. Ibid.

40. Telephone interview with Warren Buffett, June 25, 2011.

41. Graham-Newman Corporation Letter, 1946.

42. Graham-Newman Corporation Letter, 1954.

43. Benjamin Graham, "Toward a Science of Security Analysis," in *The Rediscovered Benjamin Graham*, edited by Janet Lowe (New York: John Wiley & Sons, 1999), p. 118.

44. Graham-Newman Corporation Letter, 1954.

45. Graham, "Toward a Science of Security Analysis," p. 98.

46. Ibid.

47. Ibid., p. 90.

48. Ibid., p. 98.

49. "Jewish Drive Total Rises to $5,332,040," *New York Times*, May 16, 1926.

50. Graham, *Memoirs of the Dean of Wall Street*, description of photo no. 16.

51. Telephone interview with Irving Kahn, September 13, 2011.

52. Lowe, *Benjamin Graham on Value Investing*, p. 125.

53. Ibid., p. 188.

54. Graham, *Memoirs of the Dean of Wall Street*, p. 237.

55. Lowe, *Benjamin Graham on Value Investing*, p. 125.

56. E-mail interview with Charlotte Reiter, January 28, 2012.

57. Graham, *Memoirs of the Dean of Wall Street*, p. 323.

58. Lowe, *Benjamin Graham on Value Investing*, pp. 187–88.

59. Graham, *Memoirs of the Dean of Wall Street*, p. 309.

60. Ibid., p. 237.

61. Ibid., p. 238.

62. Ibid., p. 64.

63. Ibid., p. 311.

64. Ibid.

65. Live interview with Benjamin Graham Jr., June 20, 2011, Berkeley, CA.

66. Robert W. Coren, Mary Rephlo, David Kepley, and Charles South, "Records of the Committee on Banking and Currency, 1913–1968," Guide to the Records of the US Senate at the National Archives, National Archives and Records Administration, Washington, DC, 1989, http://www.archives.gov/legislative/guide/senate/chapter-05.html.

67. Ibid.

CHAPTER 12. DISCIPLES OF VALUE

1. Perez Zagorin, *Francis Bacon* (Princeton, NJ: Princeton University Press, 1998), p. 126.

2. Ibid., cover inset, quoted from Bacon's *The New Organon*.

3. Ibid., p. 127.

4. Ibid., cover inset, quoted from Bacon's *The New Organon*.

5. Benjamin Graham, "Toward a Science of Security Analysis," in *The Rediscovered Benjamin Graham*, edited by Janet Lowe (New York: John Wiley & Sons, 1999), p. 98.

6. Bruce Greenwald, Judd Kahn, Paul Sonkin, and Michael Van Biema, *Value Investing: From Graham to Buffett and Beyond* (New York: John Wiley & Sons, 2001), p. 9.

7. Gabriel Wisdom, *Wisdom on Value Investing* (Hoboken, NJ: John Wiley & Sons, 2009), p. 71.

8. Adair Turner et al., *The Future of Finance: The LSE Report* (London, United Kingdom: London School of Economics and Political Science, 2010), p. 133.

9. "How Omaha Beats Wall Street," *Forbes*, November 1, 1969.

10. Ibid.

11. Robert G. Hagstrom, *The Warren Buffett Portfolio* (New York: John Wiley & Sons, 1999), p. 2.

12. Telephone interview with Warren Buffett, June 25, 2011.

13. Greenwald et al., *Value Investing*, p. 266.

14. Warren Buffett, "The Superinvestors of Graham and Doddsville" (speech to Columbia Business School, May 17, 1984), *Hermes* (Columbia Business School Magazine), May 17, 1984.

15. Ibid.

16. "Great Investors: Philip Fisher—Fisher's Investment Philosophy," Morningstar.com, http://news.morningstar.com/classroom2/course.asp?docId=145 662&page=2&CN=com (accessed April 9, 2012).

17. Buffett, "Superinvestors of Graham and Doddsville."

18. Charles T. Munger, *Poor Charlie's Almanack: The Wit and Wisdom of Charles T. Munger*, expanded 3rd ed., ed. Peter D. Kaufman (Florence, KY: Wadsworth, 2005), p. 63.

19. Buffett, "Superinvestors of Graham and Doddsville."

20. Ibid.

21. Robert Shiller (Yale University Economics Department) and Yahoo! Finance, "CAGR of the Stock Market (Annualized Returns)," MoneyChimp, http://www.moneychimp.com/features/market_cagr.htm (accessed November 14, 2011).

22. Buffett, "Superinvestors of Graham and Doddsville."

23. Ibid.

24. Roger Lowenstein, *Buffett: The Making of an American Capitalist* (New York: Random House, 1995), p. 135.

25. Warren Buffett, "Chairman's Letter," Berkshire Hathaway, Inc., 2010 Annual Report, February 26, 2011, p. 2.

26. Ibid.

27. Ibid.

28. "Berkshire Hathaway, Inc (BRK-A)," Yahoo! Finance, http://finance.yahoo .com/q?s=BRK-A (accessed November 28, 2011).

29. "World's 20 Most Valuable Companies," *Rediff Business*, July 25, 2011.

30. Joe Holley, "Sequoia Fund Manager, Philanthropist William J. Ruane," *Washington Post*, October 6, 2005.

31. Buffett, "Superinvestors of Graham and Doddsville."

32. Ibid.

33. "Comparison of the Investment Return of the Sequoia Fund (from Inception) vs. the Standard & Poor's 500," Sequoia Fund, Inc., http://www.sequoiafund .com/fp-investment-return-table.htm (accessed January 5, 2012).

34. Doctor Zen, "William J. Ruane—The Making of a Superinvestor," Guru Focus, May 19, 2011, http://www.gurufocus.com/news/133912/william-j-ruane-the-making-of-a-superinvestor (accessed April 13, 2012).

35. Janet Lowe, *Benjamin Graham on Value Investing* (Chicago: Dearborn Financial Publishing, 1994), p. 172.

36. Deeshesh Chheda, "Acacia Partners Buys Stake in Net4 India," *DealCurry*, February 3, 2011.

37. Jason Zweig, "Christopher H. Browne: 1946–2009—A Career Spent Finding Value," *Wall Street Journal*, December 16, 2009.

38. "About Tweedy, Browne," Tweedy, Browne Company, LLC, http://www.tweedy.com/about/ (accessed December 10, 2011).

39. Ibid.

40. Buffett, "Superinvestors of Graham and Doddsville."

41. Ibid.

42. "Value Fund: Investment Performance and Expense Ratio," Tweedy, Browne Company, LLC, http://www.tweedy.com/funds/vf/performance.php (accessed January 6, 2012).

43. Ibid.

44. Meena Krishnamsetty, "Warren Buffett Knew These 9 Fund Managers Would Outperform the Market," Insider Monkey, December 1, 2010, http://www.insidermonkey.com/blog/2010/12/01/warren-buffett-knew-these-9-fund-managers-would-outperform-the-market/ (accessed April 9, 2012).

45. "About Tweedy, Browne."

46. John Train, *The Money Masters* (New York: Harper & Row, 1980), p. 109.

47. Nikhil Hutheesing, "The Graham & Dodders," *Forbes*, February 23, 2009.

48. Buffett, "Superinvestors of Graham and Doddsville."

49. Ibid.

50. Greenwald et al., *Value Investing*, p. 273.

51. "Fall Investment Conference," *Grant's Interest Rate Observer*, Fall 1998.

52. Buffett, "Superinvestors of Graham and Doddsville."

53. Ibid.

54. Shiller and Yahoo! Finance, "CAGR of the Stock Market (Annualized Returns)."

55. "CIMA Guest Speaker: Randall Woods Director, Pension Investment, FMC Corporation," Columbia University, http://www4.gsb.columbia.edu/events/view/725225/CIMA+Guest+Speaker:+Randall+Woods+-+Director,+Pension+Investments,+FMC+Corporation (accessed April 9, 2012).

56. Krishramsetty, "Warren Buffett Knew These 9 Fund Managers Would Outperform the Market."

57. Buffett, "Superinvestors of Graham and Doddsville."

58. Krishnamsetty, "Warren Buffett Knew These 9 Fund Managers Would Outperform the Market."

59. Lawrence Cunningham, *How to Think Like Benjamin Graham and Invest Like Warren Buffett* (New York: McGraw-Hill, 2001), p. 13.

60. "Irving Kahn Adds New York Times, Sallie Mae, and Citigroup," Guru Focus, August 10, 2011, http://www.gurufocus.com/news/141914/irving-kahn-adds-new-york-times-sallie-mae-and-citigroup (accessed April 13, 2012).

61. "Low P/E Stocks from Irving Kahn: SLM, C, BP, CVX, KEY," Guru Focus, January 5, 2012, http://www.gurufocus.com/news/157458/low-pe-stocks-from-irving-kahn-slm-c-bp-cvx-key (accessed April 13, 2012).

62. Telephone interview with Thomas Kahn, September 13, 2011.

63. "About Us," Brandes Investment Partners, http://www.brandes.com/Pages/AboutUs.aspx (accessed December 12, 2011).

64. Charles H. Brandes, *Value Investing Today* (New York: McGraw-Hill, 2003), p. ix.

65. "About Us," Brandes Investment Partners (total asset figures are stated as of September 30, 2011).

66. Daniel Tovrov, "Gabelli Taps an Assistant for a $2 Billion Fund," Mutual FundWire.com, September 8, 2009, http://www.mutualfundwire.com/article.asp?storyID=22536&template=article&bhcp=1 (accessed April 9, 2012).

67. Greenwald et al., *Value Investing*, p. 197.

68. GAMCO Investors, Inc., 2005 Annual Report.

69. "Who We Are," Vanguard, https://personal.vanguard.com/us/content/Home/WhyVanguard/AboutVanguardWhoWeAreContent.jsp (accessed April 25, 2012).

70. John C. Bogle, *Bogle on Mutual Funds: New Perspectives for the Intelligent Investor* (New York: Dell, 1994), p. v.

71. John Birger, "Eveillard: A Value Maestro's Encore," *Fortune*, June 19, 2007.

72. Ibid.

73. "Jean-Marie Eveillard: Profile/Performance," Guru Focus, February 11, 2012, http://www.gurufocus.com/StockBuy.php?GuruName=Jean-Marie+Eveillard (accessed April 13, 2012).

74. Ibid.

75. Adam Smith, *Supermoney* (New York: Random House, 1972).

76. Robert C. Arffa, *Expert Financial Planning: Investment Strategies from Industry Leaders* (New York: John Wiley & Sons, 2001), p. 96.

77. Live interview with Mitsunobu Tsuruo and Hideyuki Aoki of Nomura Asset Management, Omaha, NE, April 29, 2011.

78. Nomura Reports for Quarter and Full Year Financial Results, March 31, 2011.

79. "Welcome to Amiral Gestion," Amiral Gestion, http://www.amiralgestion.fr/ENG/index.php (accessed December 21, 2011).

80. Live interview with David Poulet and Raphael Moreau of Amiral Gestion, Omaha, NE, April 28, 2011.

81. "Performance Review: December 31, 1992, to December 31, 2010," Semper Vic Partners LP, March 2011.

82. Warren Buffett and Janet Lowe, *Warren Buffett Speaks: Wit and Wisdom from the World's Greatest Investor* (Hoboken, NJ: John Wiley & Sons, 2007), p. 117.

83. Telephone interview with Warren Buffett, June 25, 2011.

84. Zagorin, *Francis Bacon*, p. 127.

CHAPTER 13. STRANGER THAN FICTION

1. "Notes to Financial Statements: Note A—Liquidation-Dissolution-Liquidating Distributions," Graham-Newman Corporation, January 31, 1958.

2. Letter, Graham-Newman Corporation, 1946.

3. Irving Kahn and Robert Milne, *Benjamin Graham: The Father of Financial Analysis* (Charlottesville, VA: Financial Analysts Research Foundation, 1977).

4. Robert Shiller (Yale University Economics Department) and Yahoo! Finance, "CAGR of the Stock Market (Annualized Returns)," MoneyChimp, http://www.moneychimp.com/features/market_cagr.htm (accessed November 14, 2011).

5. Ibid.

6. "Stockholder's Letter," Graham-Newman Corporation, February 25, 1949, p. 6.

7. Michael Quint, "Buffett Moves to Acquire All of GEICO," *New York Times*, August 26, 1995.

8. Ibid.

9. Janet Lowe, *Benjamin Graham on Value Investing* (Chicago: Dearborn Financial Publishing, 1994), p. 156.

10. Kahn and Milne, *Benjamin Graham*, p. 44.

11. Lowe, *Benjamin Graham on Value Investing*, p. 165.

12. Kahn and Milne, *Benjamin Graham*, p. 45.

13. Benjamin Graham, "Benjamin Graham on the Flexible Work-Year: An Answer to Unemployment," *Center for the Study of Democratic Institutions*, January 1964, p. 1.

14. Live interview with Charles H. Brandes, May 19, 2011, San Diego, CA.

15. Live interview with Benjamin Graham Jr., June 20, 2011, Berkeley, CA.

16. Ibid.

17. Ibid.

18. Ibid.

19. Benjamin Graham, *The Memoirs of the Dean of Wall Street* (New York: McGraw-Hill, 1996), p. 38.

20. Live interview with Dr. Bernard Sarnat and Rhoda Gerard Sarnat, July 18, 2011, Los Angeles, CA.

21. Ibid.

22. Ibid.

23. Live interview with Benjamin Graham Jr., June 20, 2011, Berkeley, CA.

24. Roger Lowenstein, *Buffett: The Making of an American Capitalist* (New York: Random House, 1995), p. 68.

25. Telephone interview with Warren Buffett, June 25, 2011.

26. Ibid.

27. Telephone interview with Fred Weston, March 2009.

28. Ibid.

29. Live interview with Benjamin Graham Jr., June 20, 2011, Berkeley, CA.

30. Ibid.

31. Henry Ford and Ray Leone Faurote, *My Philosophy of Industry* (Detroit: Forum Publishing, 1928), p. 25.

32. Live interview with Dr. Bernard Sarnat and Rhoda Gerard Sarnat, July 18, 2011, Los Angeles, CA.

33. Live interview with Dr. Robert Hamburger and Sonia Hamburger, July 21, 2011, La Jolla, CA.

34. Seymour Chatman, "Introduction," in Graham, *Memoirs of the Dean of Wall Street*, p. xxxii.

35. Graham, *Memoirs of the Dean of Wall Street*, p. 160.

36. Ibid., p. 161.

37. Ibid., p. 310.

38. Ibid., pp. 310–11.

39. E-mail interview with Charlotte Reiter, January 28, 2012.

40. Live interview with Dr. Robert Hamburger and Sonia Hamburger, July 21, 2011, La Jolla, CA.

41. Lowe, *Benjamin Graham on Value Investing*, p. 208.

42. Live interview with Benjamin Graham Jr., June 20, 2011, Berkeley, CA.

43. Mario Benedetti, *The Truce*, trans. Benjamin Graham (New York: Harper & Row, 1969), cover page.

44. Live interview with Benjamin Graham Jr., June 20, 2011, Berkeley, CA.

45. Live interview with Dr. Robert Hamburger and Sonia Hamburger, July 21, 2011, La Jolla, CA.

46. Ibid.

47. Live interview with Benjamin Graham Jr., June 20, 2011, Berkeley, CA.

48. Telephone interview with Pi Heseltine, July 20, 2011.

49. Live interview with Dr. Robert Hamburger and Sonia Hamburger, July 21, 2011, La Jolla, CA.

50. Live interview with Benjamin Graham Jr., June 20, 2011, Berkeley, CA.

51. Lowenstein, *Buffett*, p. 68.

52. Live interview with Dr. Bernard Sarnat and Rhoda Gerard Sarnat, July 18, 2011, Los Angeles, CA.

53. Ibid.

54. E-mail interview with Charlotte Reiter, January 28, 2012.

55. Live interview with Benjamin Graham Jr., June 20, 2011, Berkeley, CA.

56. Alice Schroeder, *The Snowball: Warren Buffett and the Business of Life* (New York: Bantam, 2008), p. 892.

57. Live interview with Benjamin Graham Jr., June 20, 2011, Berkeley, CA.

58. Telephone interview with Irving Kahn, September 13, 2011.

59. Irving Kahn, "Some Reflections on Ben Graham's Personality," in *Benjamin Graham: The Father of Financial Analysis*, by Irving Kahn and Robert D. Milne (Charlottesville, VA: Financial Analysts Research Foundation, 1977), p. 31.

60. Chatman, "Introduction," p. xxv.

CHAPTER 14. THE ETHICS OF MONEY

1. Howard Caygill, *A Kant Dictionary* (Malden, MA: Blackwell Publishing, 1995), p. 100.

2. Irving Kahn, "Some Reflections on Ben Graham's Personality," in *Benjamin Graham: The Father of Financial Analysis*, by Irving Kahn and Robert D. Milne (Charlottesville, VA: Financial Analysts Research Foundation, 1977), p. 40.

3. Benjamin Graham, *The Memoirs of the Dean of Wall Street* (New York: McGraw-Hill, 1996), p. 102.

4. Ibid., p. 101.

5. Ibid.

6. Ibid.

7. Ibid., p. 102.

8. Ibid.

9. Ibid.

10. Ibid.

11. Ibid.

12. Ibid.

13. Ibid.

14. Ibid.

15. Ibid.

16. Ibid., p. 101.

17. Ibid.

18. Benjamin Graham, quoted in Janet Lowe, *Benjamin Graham on Value Investing* (Chicago: Dearborn Financial Publishing, 1994), p. 152.

19. Ibid.

20. Graham, *Memoirs of the Dean of Wall Street*, p. 103.

21. Benjamin Graham, "Selling America for 50 Cents on the Dollar," in *The Rediscovered Benjamin Graham*, edited by Janet Lowe (New York: John Wiley & Sons, 1999), p. 8.

22. Ibid., p. 7.

23. Ibid., p. 8.

24. Ibid., p. 13.

25. Ibid., p. 14.

26. Ibid.

27. Benjamin Graham, "Is United Drug Cheap at 53?" in *Benjamin Graham on Investing: Enduring Lessons from the Father of Value Investing*, edited by Rodney G. Klein, with updates and commentary by David M. Darst (New York: McGraw-Hill, 2009), p. 191.

28. Benjamin Graham and David Dodd, *Security Analysis*, 1st ed. (New York: McGraw-Hill, 1934), p. 558.

29. Ibid., p. 554.

30. Ibid., p. 552.

31. Ibid., p. 569.

32. Ibid., p. 561.

33. John Kenneth Galbraith, *The Economics of Innocent Fraud* (New York: Houghton Mifflin, 2004), p. x.

34. Ibid.

35. "Three Biggest Accounting Scandals in Corporate History," Hakeshet Business Centre, November 8, 2011, http://www.hakeshet.org/financian-tips/3-biggest-accounting-scandals-in-corporate-history-486.html (accessed April 10, 2012).

36. Ibid.

37. "10 Major Accounting Scandals," Bizcovering, January 12, 2009, http://bizcovering.com/history/10-major-accounting-scandals/ (accessed April 10, 2012).

38. Ibid.

39. Ibid.

40. "A Timeline of the Madoff Fraud," *New York Times*, June 29, 2009.

41. Shahien Nasiripour, "Lehman Bankruptcy Report: Top Officials Manipulated Balance Sheets, JPMorgan and Citi Contributed to Collapse," *Huffington Post*, May 5, 2010, http://www.huffingtonpost.com/2010/03/11/lehman-bankruptcy-report_n_495668.html (accessed April 10, 2012).

42. Lawrence Cunningham, *How to Think Like Benjamin Graham and Invest Like Warren Buffett* (New York: McGraw-Hill, 2001), p. 181.

43. Graham and Dodd, *Security Analysis*, 1st ed., p. 561.

44. Benjamin Graham, *The Intelligent Investor*, 4th ed. (New York: Harper & Row, 1973), pp. 141–42.

45. Telephone interview with Irving Kahn, September 13, 2011.

46. Graham, *Intelligent Investor*, 4th ed., p. 136.

47. John Quirt, "Benjamin Graham: The Grandfather of Investment Value Is Still Concerned," in *The Rediscovered Benjamin Graham*, edited by Janet Lowe (New York: John Wiley & Sons, 1999), p. 252.

48. Graham, *Memoirs of the Dean of Wall Street*, p. 54.

49. Benjamin Graham, "The Ethics of American Capitalism," in *The Rediscovered Benjamin Graham*, edited by Janet Lowe (New York: John Wiley & Sons, 1999), p. 32.

50. Ibid.

51. Benjamin Graham, David Dodd, and Sidney Cottle, *Security Analysis*, rev. 4th ed. (New York: McGraw-Hill, 1962), p. vii.

52. Ibid.

53. Graham, "Ethics of American Capitalism," p. 32.

54. Benjamin Graham, "Benjamin Graham on the Flexible Work-Year: An Answer to Unemployment," *Center for the Study of Democratic Institutions*, January 1964.

55. Ibid., p. 4.

56. Ibid.

57. Ibid., p. 9.

58. Charles Dickens, *The Life and Adventures of Martin Chuzzlewit* (London: Chapman and Hall, 1844), p. 335.

59. Andrew Kilpatrick, *Of Permanent Value: The Story of Warren Buffett* (Birmingham, AL: AKPE, 1994), p. 67.

60. E-mail interview with Charlotte Reiter, January 28, 2012.

61. Ibid.

62. Telephone interview with Pi Heseltine, July 20, 2011.

63. E-mail interview with Charlotte Reiter, January 28, 2012.

64. Live interview with Dr. Robert Hamburger and Sonia Hamburger, July 21, 2011, La Jolla, CA.

65. Telephone interview with Irving Kahn, September 13, 2011.

66. Roger Lowenstein, *Buffett: The Making of an American Capitalist* (New York: Random House, 1995), p. 58.

67. Warren Buffett, "My Philanthropic Pledge," *Fortune*, June 16, 2010.

68. Warren Buffett, "Benjamin Graham (1894–1976)," *Financial Analysts Journal* 32, no. 6 (November/December 1976): 19.

69. Telephone interview with Warren Buffett, June 25, 2011.

70. Kahn, "Some Reflections on Ben Graham's Personality," p. 31.

71. Benjamin Graham, "Benjamin Graham's Eightieth Birthday Speech—April 11, 1974," in *The Memoirs of the Dean of Wall Street* (New York: McGraw-Hill, 1996), p. 313.

72. Rhoda Sarnat, quoted in Janet Lowe, ed., *The Rediscovered Benjamin Graham* (New York: Wiley & Sons, 1999), p. 5.

73. Benjamin Franklin, *Autobiography of Benjamin Franklin*, edited by Louis Mazur (Boston: Bedford/St. Martin's Press, 2003), p. 74.

74. Buffett, "Benjamin Graham (1894–1976)."

75. "The Father of Value Investing," *Fortune*, November 2, 1987.

76. Live interview with Marjorie Graham Janis, June 28, 2011, Palo Alto, CA.

CHAPTER 15. OF *PERPETUAL* VALUE

1. Live interview with Dr. Robert Hamburger and Sonia Hamburger, July 21, 2011, La Jolla, CA.

2. Ibid.

3. Ibid.

4. Ibid.

5. Benjamin Graham, "Benjamin Graham's Self-Portrait at Sixty-Three," in *The Memoirs of the Dean of Wall Street* (New York: McGraw-Hill, 1996), p. 309.

6. Janet Lowe, *Benjamin Graham on Value Investing* (Chicago: Dearborn Financial Publishing, 1994), p. 222.

7. E-mail interview with Charlotte Reiter, January 28, 2012.

8. Live interview with Benjamin Graham Jr., June 20, 2011, Berkeley, CA.

9. Thomas Easton, "Graham.RIP," *Forbes*, March 8, 1999.

10. Ibid.

11. Live interview with Charles H. Brandes, May 19, 2011, San Diego, CA.

12. "About Us," Brandes Investment Partners (total asset figures are stated as of September 30, 2011), http://www.brandes.com/Pages/AboutUs.aspx (accessed December 12, 2011).

13. Charles H. Brandes, *Value Investing Today* (New York: McGraw-Hill, 2003), p. ix.

14. Benjamin Graham, "Benjamin Graham's Eightieth Birthday Speech—April 11, 1974," in *The Memoirs of the Dean of Wall Street* (New York: McGraw-Hill, 1996), p. 312.

15. Ibid., p. 314.

16. Ibid.

17. Ibid.

18. Ibid.

19. Ibid., p. 315.

20. Benjamin Graham, *Renaissance of Value: The Proceedings of a Seminar on the Economy, Interest Rates, Portfolio Management, and Bonds vs. Common Stocks, September 18, 1974* (Charlottesville, VA: Financial Analysts Research Foundation, 1974).

21. Ibid.

22. Ibid.

23. Janet Lowe, *Benjamin Graham on Value Investing* (Chicago: Dearborn Financial Publishing, 1994), pp. 213–14.

24. "Dow Jones Industrial Average (1900—Present Monthly)," Stockcharts .com, http://stockcharts.com/freecharts/historical/djia1900.html (accessed April 9, 2012).

25. Live interview with Dr. Robert Hamburger and Sonia Hamburger, July 21, 2011, La Jolla, CA.

26. Benjamin Graham, "The Future of Common Stocks," *Financial Analysts Journal* 30, no. 5 (September/October 1974).

27. Hartman Butler, "An Hour with Mr. Graham," *Financial Analysis Journal* (March 6, 1976).

28. Ibid.

29. Walter Isaacson, *Einstein: His Life and Universe* (New York: Simon & Schuster, 2007), p. 332.

30. Ibid.

31. Ibid.

32. Irving Kahn, "Some Reflections on Ben Graham's Personality," in *Benjamin Graham: The Father of Financial Analysis*, by Irving Kahn and Robert D. Milne (Charlottesville, VA: Financial Analysts Research Foundation, 1977), p. 32.

33. Butler, "Hour with Mr. Graham," p. 36.

34. Graham, "Future of Common Stocks."

35. Butler, "Hour with Mr. Graham," p. 36.

36. Ibid.

37. Benjamin Graham, quoted in "The Simplest Way to Select Bargain Stocks," by Bart Sheridan and Laton McCartney, in *The Rediscovered Benjamin Graham*, edited by Janet Lowe (New York: John Wiley & Sons, 1999), pp. 259–60.

38. Warren Buffet, quoted in Whitney Tilson, "Investment Advice from Buffett & Munger," *Value Investor Insight*, June 7, 2007.

39. Butler, "Hour with Mr. Graham," p. 39.

40. Ibid., p. 33.

41. Ibid., p. 35.

42. "Nicholas Molodovsky Award: Daniel Kahneman," CFA Institute, May 17, 2010, http://www.cfainstitute.org/about/press/release/Pages/05172010_30073 .aspx (accessed April 10, 2012).

43. Irving Kahn and Robert D. Milne, *Benjamin Graham: The Father of Financial Analysis* (Charlottesville, VA: Financial Analysis Research Foundation, 1977), p. 30.

44. Lowe, *Benjamin Graham on Value Investing*, p. 223.

45. E-mail interview with Professor Richard Roll, August 8, 2011.

46. Lawrence Cunningham and Warren Buffett, *The Essays of Warren Buffett: Lessons for Corporate America* (New York: Cunningham Group, 1998), p. 208.

47. Joseph Calandro Jr., *Applied Value Investing: The Practical Application of Benjamin Graham and Warren Buffett's Valuation Principles to Acquisitions, Catastrophe Pricing, and Business Execution* (New York: McGraw-Hill, 2009).

48. Mark Hirschey, "Warren Buffett Q&A: May 6, 2005," *Motley Fool*, July 12, 2005.

INDEX